The Miraculous and the
Writing of Crusade Narrative

Crusading in Context

Series Editor
William J. Purkis

The crusading movement was a defining feature of the history of Europe, the Mediterranean and the Near East during the central and later Middle Ages. Ideas and practices associated with it touched the lives of people within and beyond Christendom and the Islamicate world, regardless whether they were ever directly engaged in, witnesses to, or victims of acts of crusading violence themselves.

This series aims to situate the medieval experience of the crusades and crusading societies in the broader social, cultural and intellectual contexts of the Middle Ages as a whole. Chronologically, its scope extends from the eleventh to the sixteenth century, and contributions from a range of disciplines are encouraged. Monographs and edited collections are both welcome; critical editions and translations of medieval texts will also be considered.

Proposals and queries should be sent in the first instance to the series editor or to Boydell and Brewer, at the addresses below.

Dr William J. Purkis, School of History and Cultures, University of Birmingham, Edgbaston, Birmingham, B15 2TT
w.j.purkis@bham.ac.uk

Boydell and Brewer Ltd, PO Box 9, Woodbridge, Suffolk, IP12 3DF
editorial@boydell.co.uk

Previously Published

Eyewitness and Crusade Narrative: Perception and Narration in Accounts of the Second, Third and Fourth Crusades, Marcus Bull

Baldric of Bourgueil: "History of the Jerusalemites": A Translation of the Historia Ierosolimitana, translated by Susan B. Edgington, introduction by Steven J. Biddlecombe

The Miraculous and the Writing of Crusade Narrative

Beth C. Spacey

THE BOYDELL PRESS

First published 2020
The Boydell Press, Woodbridge

ISBN 978 1 78327 518 2

The Boydell Press is an imprint of Boydell & Brewer Ltd
PO Box 9, Woodbridge, Suffolk IP12 3DF, UK
and of Boydell & Brewer Inc.
668 Mt Hope Avenue, Rochester, NY 14620–2731, USA
website: www.boydellandbrewer.com

A CIP catalogue record for this book is available
from the British Library

The publisher has no responsibility for the continued existence or accuracy of URLs for
external or third-party internet websites referred to in this book, and does not guarantee that
any content on such websites is, or will remain, accurate or appropriate

This publication is printed on acid-free paper

Printed and bound in Great Britain by TJ International Ltd, Padstow, Cornwall

For Mum and Dad

Contents

Acknowledgements

I am fortunate in having amassed many debts of gratitude over the duration of this project. The greatest of these is undoubtedly owed to my former PhD supervisor, William Purkis, whom I thank for his generosity and support, and blame for introducing me to the history of the crusades in my first year of undergraduate study. His knowledge, guidance and encouragement have been instrumental in this book's journey to realisation. I am also grateful to Marcus Bull and Simon Yarrow for their insights and advice over the years and for their continued support.

For their generous counsel, stimulating discussion and other kindnesses over the past few years, I would like to thank Steven Biddlecombe, Laura Cleaver, Susan Edgington, Martin Hall, Katie Hodges-Kluck, Elizabeth Lapina, Sjoerd Levelt, Katy Mortimer, Amanda Myers, Léan Ní Chléirigh, Helen Nicholson, Simon Parsons, Joanna Phillips, Jay Rubenstein, Thomas Smith, Stephen Spencer and Carol Sweetenham. I am especially grateful to Andrew Buck and Megan Cassidy-Welch for reading drafts of sections of this book and making such detailed and helpful recommendations for its improvement. Thanks also to the many undergraduate and graduate students at the University of Birmingham, Trinity College Dublin and the University of Queensland who have discussed medieval miracles and crusades sources with me over the years.

I also wish to express my gratitude to the Arts and Humanities Research Council, whose generous financial support from 2012 to 2015 made the research for this book possible. Further, I would like to thank Caroline Palmer, Marianne Wilson, Elizabeth McDonald and Emily Champion at Boydell for their guidance as I prepared this book for publication, and to the anonymous reader for providing such valuable recommendations. My thanks also to staff at the libraries of the University of Birmingham, the University of Queensland, Trinity College Dublin, Senate House, the Morgan Library and the British Library.

Finally, to my family and friends (both human and animal) for their love, support and understanding. I am especially grateful to my partner Fred, for supporting me throughout the entire process, even when I moved to the other side of the planet. Also, to my cats Poppy and Merlin, for their only occasionally disruptive supervision of the writing process. Finally, to my wonderful parents, for believing in me and giving so selflessly in order that I might pursue this opportunity, I dedicate this book.

Abbreviations

AA	Albert of Aachen, *Historia Ierosolimitana*, ed. and trans. S.B. Edgington (Oxford, 2007).
BB	Baldric of Bourgueil, *The Historia Ierosolimitana of Baldric of Bourgueil*, ed. S. Biddlecombe (Woodbridge, 2014).
CCCM	*Corpus Christianorum Continuatio Mediaevalis* (Turnhout, 1966–).
CCSL	*Corpus Christianorum Series Latina* (Turnhout, 1953–).
Chronica 2	Roger of Howden, *Chronica: Magistri Rogeri de Houedene*, ed. W. Stubbs (Rolls Series, 51.2; London, 1869).
Chronica 3	Roger of Howden, *Chronica: Magistri Rogeri de Houedene*, ed. W. Stubbs (Rolls Series, 51.3; London, 1870).
DeL	*De expugnatione Lyxbonensi: The Conquest of Lisbon*, ed. and trans. C.W. David, rev. J.P. Phillips (New York, NY, 2001).
EA	Ekkehard of Aura, 'Hierosolymita', *RHC Oc.*, 5, pp. 1–40.
FC	Fulcher of Chartres, *Fulcheri Carnotensis Historia Hierosolymitana, 1095–1127*, ed. H. Hagenmeyer (Heidelberg, 1913).
GF	*Gesta Francorum et aliorum Hierosolimitanorum*, ed. and trans. R. Hill with R.A.B. Mynors (Edinburgh, 1962).
GN	Guibert of Nogent, *Dei gesta per Francos*, ed. R.B.C. Huygens, (CCCM, 127A; Turnhout, 2002).
GP	Gunther of Pairis, *Hystoria Constantinopolitana: Untersuchung und Kritische Ausgabe*, ed. P. Orth (Hildesheim and Zürich, 1994).
*GR*1	Roger of Howden, *Gesta Regis Henrici Secundi Benedicti Abbatis, The Chronicle of the Reigns of Henry II, and Richard I, A.D. 1169–1192; known commonly under the name of Benedict of Peterborough*, ed. W. Stubbs (Rolls Series, 49.1; London, 1867).
*GR*2	Roger of Howden, *Gesta Regis Henrici Secundi Benedicti Abbatis, The Chronicle of the Reigns of Henry II, and Richard I, A.D. 1169–1192; known commonly under the name of Benedict of Peterborough*, ed. W. Stubbs (Rolls Series 49.2; London, 1867).

HB	Helmold of Bosau, *Slavenchronik*, ed. B. Schmeidler (MGH SSRG, 32; Hanover, 1937).
HeFI	'Historia de expeditione Friderici Imperatoris', in *Quellen zur Geschichte des Kreuzzuges Kaiser Friedrichs I.*, ed. A. Chroust (MGH SSRG Nova Series, 5; Berlin, 1928), pp. 1–115.
HP	'Historia Peregrinorum', in *Quellen zur Geschichte des Kreuzzuges Kaiser Friedrichs I.*, ed. A. Chroust (MGH SSRG Nova Series, 5; Berlin, 1928), pp. 116–72.
*IP*1	*Das Itinerarium Peregrinorum: Eine Zeitgenössische Englische Chronik zum Dritten Kreuzzug in Ursprünglicher Gestatt*, ed. H.E. Mayer (Stuttgart, 1962).
*IP*2	*Itinerarium Peregrinorum et Gesta Regis Ricardi*, ed. W. Stubbs, *Chronicles and Memorials of the Reign of Richard I* (Rolls Series, 38.1; London, 1864).
Itinerarium Kambriae	Gerald of Wales, *Giraldi Cambrensis opera, Vol. VI: Itinerarium Kambriae et Descriptio Kambriae*, ed. J.F. Dimock (Rolls Series, 21.6; London, 1868).
MGH	Monumenta Germaniae Historica.
MGH SS	*Monumenta Germaniae Historica, Scriptores in Folio et Quarto*, ed. G.H. Pertz et al. (Hanover, Weimar, Stuttgart and Cologne, 1826–).
MGH SSRG	*Monumenta Germaniae Historica, Scriptores rerum Germanicarum is usum scholarum separatim editi* (Hanover and Berlin, 1971–).
NPNF	*Nicene and Post-Nicene Fathers of the Christian Church, Volume IV – St Augustine: The Writings Against the Manichaeans and Against the Donatists*, ed. P. Schaff (Grand Rapids, MI, 1979).
OD	Odo of Deuil, *De profectione Ludovici VII in Orientem*, ed. and trans. V.G. Berry (New York, NY, 1948).
OFC	Otto of Freising, *Chronica sive historia duabus civitatibus*, ed. W. Lammers and trans. A. Schmidt (Berlin, 1960).
OFGF	Otto of Freising, *Ottonis et Rahewini Gesta Frederici I. imperatoris*, ed. G. Waitz (MGH SSRG, 46; Hannover, 1912).
OV	Orderic Vitalis, *The Ecclesiastical History of Orderic Vitalis*, ed. and trans. M. Chibnall, 6 vols (Oxford, 1969–80).

PL	*Patrologiae cursus completes, series Latina*, ed. J.-P. Migne, 221 vols (Paris, 1844–64).
PT	Peter Tudebode, *Historia de Hierosolymitano itinere*, ed. J.H. Hill and L.L. Hill (Paris, 1977).
RA	Raymond of Aguilers, *Le 'Liber' de Raymond d'Aguilers*, ed. J.H Hill and L.L. Hill (Paris, 1969).
RC	Ralph of Caen, *Radulphi Cadomensis Tancredus*, ed. and trans. E. D'Angelo (CCCM, 231; Turnhout, 2011).
RHC	*Recueil des historiens des croisades*, ed. Académie des Inscriptions et Belles-Lettres (Paris, 1841–1906).
RHC Oc.	*RHC Historiens Occidentaux*, 5 vols (Paris, 1844–95).
RM	Robert the Monk, *The Historia Iherosolimitana of Robert the Monk*, ed. M.G. Bull and D. Kempf (Woodbridge, 2013).
WT	William of Tyre, *Chronicon*, ed. R.B.C. Huygens (CCCM, 63 and 63A; Turnhout, 1986).

Timeline of Key Events and Sources

While it is often difficult to precisely date the composition of texts, and debates on the dating of certain sources continue, this timeline situates indicative dates of important texts alongside key events to offer a quickly navigable chronology.

1063 June	Battle of Cerami
1085 May	Alfonso VI of León-Castile conquers Toledo
1095 27 November	Pope Urban II proclaims the First Crusade at the Council of Clermont
1096 November–1097 May	Crusader armies in Constantinople
1097 1 July	Battle of Dorylaeum
1097 20 October–1098 3 June	Siege of Antioch
1098 14 June	Discovery of the Holy Lance at Antioch
1098 28 June	Battle of Antioch
1099 15 July	Crusader conquest of Jerusalem
1099 12 August	Battle of Ascalon
c. 1099–*c.* 1100	*Gesta Francorum et aliorum Hierosolimitanorum* completed by anonymous author
c. 1101–*c.* 1110	Peter Tudebode compiles the *Historia de Hierosolymitano itinere*
c. 1101	Raymond of Aguilers completes the *Historia Francorum qui ceperunt Iherusalem*
c. 1101–*c.* 1127	Fulcher of Chartres writes the *Historia Hierosolymitana*
c. 1102	Albert of Aachen begins work on the first six books of the *Historia Ierosolimitana*
c. 1105	Baldric of Bourgueil writes first version of *Historia Ierosolimitana*
1107–1108	Guibert of Nogent writes *Dei gesta per Francos*
c. 1110	Robert the Monk completes the *Historia Iherosolimitana*
1113–1117	Ekkehard of Aura compiles the *Hierosolimita*

1115 September	Battle of Tall Danith
1118	Ralph of Caen completes the *Tancredus*
c. 1135	Orderic Vitalis compiles his narrative of the First Crusade for the *Historia Ecclesiastica*
1143–1147	Otto of Freising writes the *Historia duabus civitatibus*
1144 24 December	Zengi conquers Edessa
1145 1 December	Pope Eugenius III proclaims the Second Crusade in the bull *Quantum praedecessores*
1146–1147	Bernard of Clairvaux preaches the Second Crusade
1147 23 May	Fleet of crusaders depart from Dover to the Holy Land (via Lisbon)
1147 June	Armies of Louis VII of France and Conrad III of Germany depart for Holy Land
1147 July–September	Wendish Crusade
1147 24 October	Crusaders and forces of Afonso I of Portugal capture Lisbon
1147 September–October	Armies of Louis and Conrad at Constantinople
1147 October	Defeat of Conrad's army in Asia Minor
Late 1147	Raol writes the *De expugnatione Lyxbonensi*
1148	Odo of Deuil writes the *De profectione Ludovici VII in Orientem*
1148 23–28 July	Failed siege of Damascus by remaining crusaders
1156–1159	John of Salisbury writes the *Policraticus*
1157–1158	Otto of Freising writes the *Gesta Frederici*
c. 1167–1171	Helmold of Bosau writes the *Chronica Slavorum*
1170–1184	William of Tyre writes the *Historia Ierosolymitana*
1172	Duke Henry the Lion's Jerusalem pilgrimage
1187 1 May	Battle of the Spring of Cresson
1187 4 July	Battle of Hattin

1187–1224	Ralph of Coggeshall writes the *Chronicon Anglicanum*
1187 2 October	Saladin conquers Jerusalem
1187 29 October	Pope Gregory VIII proclaims the Third Crusade in the bull *Audita tremendi*
1188	Gerald of Wales accompanies Archbishop Baldwin of Canterbury on preaching tour of Wales
1188–1189	Gerald of Wales writes the *Expugnatio Hibernica*
1189 11 May	Frederick Barbarossa departs on crusade
1189 6 July	Death of Henry II of England
1190–1208	Saxo Grammaticus writes the *Gesta Danorum*
1190–1217	Gerald of Wales writes the *De Principis Instructione*
1190 10 June	Frederick dies in Göksu River in Asia Minor
1190 July	Richard I of England and Philip II of France depart on crusade
1191	Gerald of Wales completes the *Itinerarium Kambriae*
1191 12 July	Acre surrendered to Richard and Philip
1191 3 August	Philip returns to France
1191 7 September	Battle of Arsuf
c. 1192	Roger of Howden finishes the *Gesta Regis Henrici Secundi* and begins work on the *Chronica*
1192 2 September	Treaty of Jaffa agreed between Richard and Saladin
1192 9 October	Richard departs for Europe
c. 1193	Richard of Devizes writes the *Chronicon*
1198 August	Innocent III proclaims the Fourth Crusade
1199 November	Fourth Crusade preached at Ecry-sur-Aisne
c. 1200	*Historia de expeditione Friderici Imperatoris* and *Historia Peregrinorum* compiled
1201 March–April	Negotiations between French envoys and Venetians
1202 October	Fourth Crusade departs from Venice to Zara

1202 24 November	Zara surrenders to the crusaders
1203 June	Fourth Crusade arrives at Constantinople
1203 5–18 July	First siege of Constantinople
1204 12–15 April	Crusaders conquer and sack Constantinople
1204 9 May	Baldwin of Flanders elected first Latin Emperor of Constantinople
c. 1205	Robert of Clari writes the *La Conquête de Constantinople*
1205	Gunther of Pairis completes the *Hystoria Constantinopolitana*
1205 June–1207 September	The Anonymous of Soissons writes the *De terra Iherosolimitana*
1208	Geoffrey of Villehardouin begins writing the *De la Conquête de Constantinople*
1209	*Gesta episcoporum Halberstadensium* written by unknown author
1210–1214	Gervase of Tilbury writes the *Otia imperialia*
c. 1216–1220	Richard de Templo compiles the *Itinerarium Peregrinorum*
1219–1223	Caesarius of Heisterbach writes the *Dialogus miraculorum*
1227–1251	Alberic of Trois-Fontaines writes the *Chronica*

Introduction

Behold, the journey for Jerusalem has been begun by God.[1]

Almost forty years had passed since the Council of Clermont of November 1095 when, in *c.* 1135, Orderic Vitalis thus attributed to divine inspiration the origins of the events known to posterity as the First Crusade. Such a claim was not an innovation of Orderic's. Rather, the Norman monk, writing from the monastery of Saint-Evroult where he spent most of his life, was contributing to an already established tradition. An explosion of historical and literary endeavour had occurred in western Europe in the wake of the crusader conquest of Fatimid-held Jerusalem on 15 July 1099, and many of the authors and compilers of these works, including sources for Orderic's own later reimagining, had looked back from that conquest to find a starting point of suitable proportions for the retelling of such momentous events. Many, like Orderic, found it in Pope Urban II's now famous sermon at Clermont and were therefore able to offer a cohesive narrative of an act of God, heralded through his messenger the pope and enacted by those who subsequently took the cross. When viewed in this way, the First Crusade of 1096–9 was a miracle. As Jonathan Riley-Smith has demonstrated, many Latin Christian contemporaries believed that these crusade participants, confessed, penitent and cleansed by the ordeal of the expedition, had acted as conduits for the divine power that had delivered the earthly Jerusalem into the hands of its rightful custodians.[2] At the heart of these conceptualisations of the First Crusade

---

[1] OV, vol. 5, p. 4: 'En Ierosolimitanum iter diuinitus initur.' For Orderic's view of sacred history, see C. Watkins, *History and the Supernatural in Medieval England* (Cambridge, 2007), pp. 25–7. On Orderic and his work more generally, see especially M. Chibnall, *The World of Orderic Vitalis: Norman Monks and Norman Knights* (Woodbridge, 1984); D. Roach, 'Orderic Vitalis and the First Crusade', *Journal of Medieval History*, 42.2 (2016), 177–201; and C.C. Rozier, D. Roach, G.E.M. Gasper and E. van Houts, eds., *Orderic Vitalis: Life, Works and Interpretations* (Woodbridge, 2016).

[2] See J. Riley-Smith, *The First Crusade and the Idea of Crusading*, 2nd edn (London, 2009), esp. pp. 91–152. On contemporaneous responses to the First Crusade, see also M.G. Bull, *Knightly Piety and the Lay Response to the First Crusade. The Limousin and Gascony, c. 970–c. 1130* (Oxford, 1993); and W.J. Purkis, *Crusading Spirituality in the Holy Land and Iberia, c. 1095–c. 1187* (Woodbridge, 2008), esp. pp. 12–58. On responses which situated the First Crusade in relation to ideas of the Apocalypse and End Times, see J. Rubenstein, *Armies of Heaven: The First Crusade and the Quest*

were the divine auspices under which it was believed to have occurred, and the resulting spiritual merit from which participants were thought to benefit. Crusades, like miracles, were contingent on divine agency.

When it came to composing narratives of the First Crusade, conveying its significance was, generally speaking, of greater concern than creating a strictly accurate record of its constituent events. Consequently, and as Elizabeth Lapina has shown through the examination of key imagery, the demonstration of God's involvement in this new type of salvific warfare and, in association with this, the importance of the crusade as part of sacred history, are themes to which these sources regularly return, often with recourse to the miraculous.[3] However, while Lapina focused on the motif of the miraculous intervention of celestial knights at the battle of Antioch in June 1098 in her study, this book situates that episode among the many other miraculous motifs contained in the Latin Christian sources of not only the First Crusade, but of subsequent crusades. Consequently, it makes the case that the miraculous and its related themes offered the medieval authors of crusade narrative a far more versatile tool than has previously been appreciated.[4]

The idea underpinning the prevalence of the miraculous in First Crusade narratives was that the victorious expedition, as an act of God, was itself miraculous, and that this could be conveyed through the inclusion of miraculous episodes. However, as it will be argued, this idea became problematic when it came to narrating subsequent, less successful crusades. The Holy Land expedition of the Second Crusade (1147–9), called in response to the loss of Christian-held Edessa to Zengid forces in December 1144, could boast of no climactic victory comparable to that of 15 July 1099.[5] Indeed, it was rationalised that repeated failures and setbacks both on crusade and in the Latin East, culminating in the loss of Jerusalem in October 1187 to the sultan of Egypt and Syria, Salah al-Din

---

for Apocalypse (New York, NY, 2011), and *Nebuchadnezzar's Dream: The Crusades, Apocalyptic Prophecy, and the End of History* (Oxford, 2019), pp. 1–63.

[3] See E. Lapina, *Warfare and the Miraculous in the Chronicles of the First Crusade* (University Park, PA, 2015).

[4] On the miraculous in medieval Latin Christian thought, see especially B. Ward, *Miracles and the Medieval Mind: Theory, Record and Event, 1000–1215* (London, 1987); J. Le Goff, 'The Marvelous in the Medieval West', in *The Medieval Imagination*, trans. A. Goldhammer (London, 1988), pp. 27–44; S.F. Kruger, *Dreaming in the Middle Ages* (Cambridge, 1992); C.W. Bynum, 'Wonder', *The American Historical Review*, 102.1 (1997), 1–26; and M.E. Goodich, *Miracles and Wonders: The Development of the Concept of Miracle, 1150–1350* (Aldershot, 2007).

[5] For an overview of the Second Crusade and its sources, see especially G. Constable, 'The Second Crusade as Seen by Contemporaries', *Traditio*, 9 (1953), 213–79 (a more recent version of this article can now be found in G. Constable, *Crusaders and Crusading in the Twelfth Century: Collected Studies* (Aldershot, 2008), pp. 229–300); and J.P. Phillips, *The Second Crusade: Extending the Frontiers of Christendom* (London, 2007).

(1137–93), or Saladin, represented a withdrawal of divine favour in response to the lust, pride and greed of the Latins. William of Tyre (*c.* 1130–*c.* 86), writing in the Latin kingdom of Jerusalem between 1170 and 1184, explained the failure of the Second Crusade thus:

> For they started on the way as if contrary to the will of an angry God, and, in punishment for the sins of man, they accomplished nothing pleasing to Him on that entire pilgrimage. Nay, they even rendered worse the situation of those to whom they intended to bring succour.[6]

The remainder of William's account of the affairs of the Latin East continues in a tone judiciously described by Peter Edbury and John Rowe as 'gloom-laden'.[7] When viewed in hindsight, William's pessimism was not ill-founded; Jerusalem was surrendered to Saladin's forces only a year after William's death. However, it was not the news of the city's loss which ignited the desire for a new crusade in western Europe. Rather, it was in response to news of Saladin's earlier victory at Hattin on 4 July 1187, where Ayyubid forces captured the king of Jerusalem and the relic of the True Cross, that Pope Gregory VIII issued his call to crusade, *Audita tremendi*.[8] The news of the loss of Jerusalem three months later would not reach the papal curia until the end of November.[9] While the resulting expeditions, now known collectively as the Third Crusade (1189–92), could claim the participation of kings and several strategic victories, they did not recapture Jerusalem nor decisively defeat Saladin.[10] The textual response to

---

[6] WT, p. 741: 'Nam tanquam invita divinitate et eis irata iter assumpserunt: in tota illa profectione nichil deo placitum, peccatis nostris exigentibus, operati sunt, sed nostrum, quibus opem se laturos arbitrabantur, statum in deteriorem mutaverunt conditionem'; English translation is from E.A. Babcock and A.C. Krey, ed. and trans., *A History of Deeds Done Beyond the Sea*, vol. 2 (New York, NY, 1943), p. 165. On punishments for sins as part of William's causal framework, see T.M.S. Lehtonen, 'By the Help of God, Because of Our Sins, and by Chance. William of Tyre Explains the Crusades', in *Medieval History Writing and Crusading Ideology*, ed. T.M.S. Lehtonen and K.V. Jensen (Helsinki, 2005), pp. 71–84.

[7] P.W. Edbury and J.G. Rowe, *William of Tyre: Historian of the Latin East* (Cambridge, 1988), p. 173.

[8] Gregory VIII, 'Audita tremendi', *PL*, 202, cols. 1539–42. On *Audita tremendi*, see especially P. Cole, *The Preaching of the Crusades to the Holy Land, 1095–1270* (Cambridge, MA, 1991), pp. 63–79.

[9] P.W. Edbury, 'Celestine III, the Crusade and the Latin East', in *Pope Celestine III (1192–1198): Diplomat and Pastor*, ed. J. Doran and D.J. Smith (Farnham, 2008), p. 129.

[10] Useful overviews of the Third Crusade can be found in H.E. Mayer, *The Crusades*, trans. J. Gillingham, 2nd edn (Oxford, 1988), pp. 137–51; J. Riley-Smith, *The Crusades: A History*, 3rd edn (London, 2014), pp. 163–72; T. Asbridge, *The Crusades: The War for the Holy Land* (London, 2012), pp. 367–516; J.P. Phillips, *The Crusades,*

the Second and Third Crusades was lukewarm in comparison to that prompted by the First, and yet we continue to find miraculous anecdotes integrated into those sources, albeit – and as this book will demonstrate – divorced from an overarching theme of crusade as miracle.

The picture changes yet again when we turn to the miraculous content of many narratives of the Fourth Crusade (1202–4). In a letter addressed to the crusade participant Boniface of Montferrat from between *c.* 15 August and 15 September 1205, and in a moment of what would prove to be short-lived optimism, Pope Innocent III (*c.* 1160–1216) reflected on how the events now known as the Fourth Crusade had 'marvellously conquered by God's strength alone' not the erstwhile holdings of the polities of Outremer, but the Byzantine capital Constantinople.[11] Various Latin and Old French narratives of that expedition, including accounts of the translation of Constantinopolitan relics to western Europe in the aftermath of 1204, contain efforts to justify the crusade's controversial outcome as God's will, many using miraculous themes in support of this.[12] Yet, while the premise behind the employment of the miraculous – demonstrating divine investment in the events narrated – remained largely the same, this was employed in the service of subtly different narrative agendas.

This book provides the first dedicated, far-reaching study of the miraculous as it features in crusade narratives written or compiled between *c.* 1099–*c.* 1250 and concerning the crusades of 1096 to 1204, a period that witnessed the birth, frustration and transformation of the early crusading movement. In taking a pluralist approach to the crusades, it examines sources from this period which relate not only to crusades to the eastern Mediterranean, but also to Iberia and, albeit to a lesser extent, the Baltic Sea region.[13] It will be demonstrated how

---

1095–1204, 2nd edn (London, 2014), pp. 166–81. For a critical perspective on Richard I's role in the Third Crusade, see M. Markowski, 'Richard Lionheart: Bad King, Bad Crusader?', *Journal of Medieval History*, 23.4 (1997), 351–65.

[11] *Die Register Innocenz' III, 8. Band, 8. Pontifikatsjahr, 1205–1206, Texte und Indices*, ed. O. Hageneder, A. Sommerlechner, H. Weigl, C. Egger and R. Murauer (Wien, 2001), 8.134 (133), p. 246: 'Qua sola Dei virtute mirabiliter triumphata.' On anxieties expressed later in Innocent's pontificate concerning the authenticity of miracles, see B. Bolton, 'Signs, Wonders, Miracles: Supporting the Faith in Medieval Rome', in *Signs, Wonders, Miracles: Representations of Divine Power in the Life of the Church*, ed. K. Cooper and J. Gregory (Studies in Church History, 41; Woodbridge, 2005), pp. 157–78.

[12] For an overview of the events of the Fourth Crusade, see especially D.E. Queller and T. Madden, *The Fourth Crusade: The Conquest of Constantinople*, 2nd edn (Philadelphia, PA, 1997); and J.P. Phillips, *The Fourth Crusade and the Sack of Constantinople* (London, 2004). For a detailed consideration of the nineteenth-century literature on the Fourth Crusade, see D.E. Queller and S.J. Stratton, 'A Century of Controversy on the Fourth Crusade', *Studies in Medieval and Renaissance History*, 6 (1969), 233–77.

[13] For useful overviews of the 'pluralism' debate, see N. Housley, *Contesting the*

the form and function of the miraculous, as a narrative 'ingredient' shaped by prevailing ideas informed by foundational late antique and early medieval authorities, can be seen to change in response to the challenges of narrating the crusades of this period. It will also ask why the rhetorical potential of the miraculous made it such a common, if not integral, aspect of so much of the historical writing about the crusades of this period, and consider what was so particular about crusading that its narration should include such frequent recourse to the miraculous.

The miraculous themes contained in the Latin narrative histories of the crusades and informing the present study can be loosely and necessarily imperfectly arranged into the following pairings: miracles and marvels, visions and dreams, and signs and augury. It becomes apparent once we begin to scrutinise these categories that only some of these phenomena can be considered truly miraculous, as per the definitions in circulation in Latin Christian intellectual circles in the period under consideration and discussed in more detail throughout this book. Consequently, reference to 'the miraculous of crusade narrative' in the general sense, as appears in this introduction, denotes all of the abovementioned groupings holistically, including both the truly miraculous or revelatory and their more mundane or theologically illicit counterparts. It is a reference to both the vision of the Virgin Mary and the prognostication derived from the alignment of the cosmos, the restoration of a person's sight and the unusual redness of the moon.

Most of the sources examined in this book appear to have been intended as histories or records of deeds (*res gestae*), though chronicles, annals, verse and prose epic, as well as accounts of relic translations, are also drawn upon. It is worth noting that while many of these works shade between genres, comprising various characteristics and highlighting the anachronisms of modern notions of genre for understanding the medieval, they all nonetheless constitute narrative.[14] Therefore, this book analyses a range of texts which narrate – or tell stories

---

Crusades (Oxford, 2006), pp. 1–23; and J.T. Roche, 'The Second Crusade: Main Debates and New Horizons', in *The Second Crusade: Holy War on the Periphery of Latin Christentom*, ed. J.T. Roche and J. Møller Jensen (Turnhout, 2015), pp. 1–32. On Iberian enterprises as crusades, see especially J.F. O'Callaghan, *Reconquest and Crusade in Medieval* Spain (Philadelphia, PA, 2003); Purkis, *Crusading Spirituality*, pp. 120–78; and P.J. O'Banion, 'What has Iberia to do with Jerusalem? Crusade and the Spanish Route to the Holy Land in the Twelfth Century', *Journal of Medieval History*, 34 (2008), 383–95. On Baltic enterprises as crusades, see especially E. Christiansen, *The Northern Crusades*, revised edn (London, 1997); and A.L. Bysted, C.S. Jensen, K.V. Jensen and J.H. Lind, *Jerusalem in the North: Denmark and the Baltic Crusades, 1100–1552* (Turnhout, 2012).

[14] Keith Busby has highlighted the perils inherent in attempting to impose rigid categorisation upon what represented more fluid genre definitions in the Middle Ages. See K. Busby, 'Narrative Genres', in *The Cambridge Companion to Medieval French Literature*, ed. S. Gaunt and S. Kay (Cambridge, 2008), pp. 139–52.

about – crusades with recourse to varying styles. In some instances, a source's entire narrative arc is dedicated to the story of a crusade, while in others a crusade might comprise only one part of a much greater narrative whole.

Stories of miracles in crusade narratives often have more in common with the miraculous contained in annals, chronicles and what we might call histories, than with those of hagiography, except perhaps in certain accounts of the Fourth Crusade. It is unusual to find a relic or saint acting as a conduit of divine potency in crusade narrative, for example; divine intervention is often direct. Related to this is the frequent absence of a geographical or communal anchor. As accounts of a 'military monastery on the move', crusade narratives travel through the spheres of influence of particular shrines or sites.[15] The narrative focus is itinerant and consequently precludes prolonged engagement with the landscapes, including the sacred landscapes, through which they travel. Further, the miracles considered in this book were not intended for use in canonisation proceedings or – again with the exception of certain accounts of the Fourth Crusade – in the support of a particular shrine.[16]

Recent decades have witnessed the growing acceptance of the study of the medieval miraculous; it is no longer the superfluity of an 'Age of Faith', to be dutifully excised in favour of more sober historical pursuits. The work of Pierre-André Sigal, Benedicta Ward and Jacques Le Goff, among others, has been instrumental in demonstrating the value of the miraculous as a legitimate field of inquiry.[17] Building on their findings, numerous important studies have since focused on varying aspects of miracles, wonders, visions, dreams and signs in a Latin Christian context, unearthing perceptions and examining the intellectual authorities that informed them.[18] Despite this, the rich corpus represented by the miraculous of crusade narrative has, with some important

---

[15] Riley-Smith, *The First Crusade*, p. 2.

[16] Although beyond the temporal reach of this book, an important exception to this rule is Joinville's *Vie de Saint Louis*. See C. Smith, *Crusading in the Age of Joinville* (Aldershot, 2006); and M.C. Gaposchkin, *The Making of Saint Louis: Kingship, Sanctity, and Crusading in the Later Middle Ages* (London, 2008).

[17] P.-A. Sigal, *L'homme et le miracle dans la France médiévale: XIe–XIIe siècles* (Paris, 1985); Ward, *Miracles*; Le Goff, *The Medieval Imagination*.

[18] See especially Kruger, *Dreaming*; Bynum, 'Wonder'; S. Yarrow, *Saints and their Communities: Miracle Stories in Twelfth-Century England* (Oxford, 2006); G.W. Adams, *Visions in Late Medieval England: Lay Spirituality and Sacred Glimpses of the Hidden Worlds of Faith* (Leiden, 2007); Goodich, *Miracles and Wonders*; R. Bartlett, *The Natural and the Supernatural in the Middle Ages* (Cambridge, 2008); R. Koopmans, *Wonderful to Relate: Miracle Stories and Miracle Collecting in High Medieval England* (Philadelphia, PA, 2011); M.M. Mesley and L.E. Wilson, eds., *Contextualising Miracles in the Christian West, 1100–1500* (Oxford, 2014); and J. Keskiaho, *Dreams and Visions in the Early Middle Ages: The Reception and Use of Patristic Ideas, 400–900* (Cambridge, 2015).

exceptions, been largely overlooked by scholars of both the medieval miraculous and of the crusades. Until recently, two miraculous episodes received the most scholarly attention, and both are derived from sources for the First Crusade: first, regarding Peter Bartholomew, his visions, and the *inventio* of the Holy Lance of Antioch; and second, concerning the appearance of celestial knights during the battle of Antioch.

The work of Colin Morris and John France in identifying the political implications of Peter's visions, with recourse to the content of the visions themselves, represents a marked sea change from Steven Runciman's description of those events as 'strange' and 'baffling' in an article from 1950.[19] Studies of the sources for the mysterious knights at Antioch, most notably by Lapina, Nicholas Morton and Carol Sweetenham, have offered valuable insights into their complex textuality by identifying the role of scriptural allusions in their representations, and the significance of that miracle as part of many sources' narrative agendas.[20] Moving beyond the First Crusade, David Perry's important examination of the *translatio* narratives pertaining to the Fourth Crusade has shown how those texts employ miracles as devices that work to legitimise the redistribution of Constantinopolitan relics seized during, or shortly after, the crusader sack of the city in 1204.[21] Unlike these existing studies, however, a wider net has been cast in the preparation of the present study, which is not limited to the investigation of a single motif, episode, or crusade.[22] By viewing the miraculous across texts

---

[19] C. Morris, 'Policy and Visions: The Case of the Holy Lance at Antioch', in *War and Government in the Middle Ages. Essays in honour of J.O. Prestwich*, ed. J. Gillingham and J.C. Holt (Woodbridge, 1984), pp. 33–45; and J. France, 'Two Types of Vision on the First Crusade: Stephen of Valence and Peter Bartholomew', *Crusades*, 5 (2006), 1–20. Cf. S. Runciman, 'The Holy Lance Found at Antioch', *Analecta Bollandiana*, 68 (1950), 197.

[20] N. Morton, 'The Defence of the Holy Land and the Memory of the Maccabees', *Journal of Medieval History*, 36 (2010), 293; E. Lapina, 'The Maccabees and the Battle of Antioch', in *Dying for the Faith, Killing for the Faith: Old-Testament Faith-Warriors (1 and 2 Maccabees) in Historical Perspectives*, ed. G. Signori (Leiden, 2012), pp. 147–59, and *Warfare and the Miraculous*; C. Sweetenham, 'When the Saints Go Marching In: The Memory of the Miraculous in the Sources for the First Crusade' (forthcoming in *Crusades Subsidia*). See also B.C. Spacey, 'The Celestial Knight: Evoking the First Crusade in Odo of Deuil's *De Profectione Ludovici VII in Orientem* and in the Anonymous *Historia de Expeditione Friderici Imperatoris*', *Essays in Medieval Studies*, 31 (2015), 65–82.

[21] D. Perry, *Sacred Plunder: Venice and the Aftermath of the Fourth Crusade* (University Park, PA, 2015).

[22] Further important exceptions to the observation that the miraculous of crusade narratives has been largely overlooked, all of which are concerned with the First Crusade, include B. Hamilton, '"God Wills It": Signs of Divine Approval in the Crusade Movement', in *Signs, Wonders, Miracles*, pp. 88–98; C. Kostick, 'The Afterlife of Adhémar of Le Puy', in *The Church, the Afterlife and the Fate of the Soul*, ed. P.

and time, this book offers a broad-ranging analysis of the narrative responses to the nascence, frustration and transformation of the early crusading movement.

My findings owe much to important studies by Monika Otter and Carl Watkins, which foreground the complex textuality of medieval Latin Christian historical narrative.[23] Otter and Watkins, both focusing on historical writing produced in England in the central Middle Ages, examine notions of fictionality and the supernatural respectively. Watkins also demonstrates how the works of early Christian authorities, such as St Augustine of Hippo, informed the application of the miraculous in English historical writing of the central Middle Ages.[24] By analysing the use of intellectual authorities on the miraculous in crusade narrative, I argue that the crusades, and medieval understandings of the crusades, posed distinct challenges for the medieval authors who sought to narrate them, and that crusade narrative offers a revealing laboratory in which to examine how miraculous themes were put to work in the service of different narrative agendas.

Recently, scholars have turned their attention to crusade narratives as texts. Marcus Bull has revealed the complex implications of so-called 'eyewitnessing' in crusade narrative.[25] In a similar vein, Stephen Spencer has examined the use of emotional rhetoric in crusade narrative, while an edited collection by Lapina and Morton has brought together a selection of essays analysing the use of the Bible in crusade texts.[26] The present study aims to contribute to such understandings of the textuality of crusade narrative by exploring the changeable role that the miraculous might play in them.

Clarke and T. Claydon (Studies in Church History, 45; Woodbridge, 2009), pp. 120–9; Rubenstein, *Armies of Heaven* and 'Miracles and the Crusading Mind: Monastic Meditations on Jerusalem's Conquest', in *Prayer and Thought in Monastic Tradition, Essays in Honour of Benedicta Ward*, ed. S. Bhattacharji, R. Williams and D. Mattos (London, 2014), pp. 197–210; and S. John, 'Historical Truth and the Miraculous Past: The Use of Oral Evidence in Twelfth-Century Latin Historical Writing on the First Crusade', *The English Historical Review*, 130.543 (2015), 263–301.

[23] M. Otter, *Inventiones: Fiction and Referentiality in Twelfth-Century English Historical Writing* (Chapel Hill, NC, 1996); and Watkins, *History and the Supernatural*.

[24] Watkins, *History and the Supernatural*, esp. pp. 23–67.

[25] M.G. Bull, *Eyewitness and Crusade Narrative: Perception and Narration in Accounts of the Second, Third and Fourth Crusades* (Woodbridge, 2018). For an important collection of essays on the medieval historiography of the crusades, see M.G. Bull and D. Kempf, eds., *Writing the Early Crusades: Text, Transmission and Memory* (Woodbridge, 2014).

[26] S.J. Spencer, 'The Emotional Rhetoric of Crusader Spirituality in the Narratives of the First Crusade', *Nottingham Medieval Studies* 58 (2014), 57–86, 'Piety, Brotherhood and Power: The Role and Significance of Emotions in Albert of Aachen's *Historia Ierosolimitana*', *Literature Compass*, 13.6 (2016), 423–43, and '"Like a Raging Lion": Richard the Lionheart's Anger during the Third Crusade in Medieval and Modern Historiography', *The English Historical Review* 132.556 (2017), 495–532; E. Lapina and N. Morton, eds., *The Uses of the Bible in Crusader Sources* (Leiden, 2017).

Certain approaches derived from the field of narratology have proved useful for better accessing the role of the miraculous as an element of historical narrative. The most important influence for the present book concerns approaches to the historical author, and to the authors both delivering and conjured by the narrative itself: the implied author (the author that one can infer from the content of the narrative) and the narrator (the agent, or 'voice', delivering the narrative).[27] As both the narrator and implied author represent textual effects constructed by the historical author, it is important not to over-biographise the historical author, or speculate about his (all of the sources discussed in this book were written by men, so far as we can tell) 'real life' circumstances, using the evidence he provides. This book does not claim to access the 'reality' of contemporaneous attitudes towards the miraculous. This is not a study of crusader belief in the miraculous, or the beliefs of any given historical author. Indeed, the conclusions of this book only reach out towards contemporaneous perceptions of the miraculous insofar as it is able to detect anticipated audience responses within narratives, or to what Gabrielle Spiegel has called the 'social logic' of a text.[28] For example, if we discount for a moment the commonplace for including proofs of reliability in texts such as these, one might argue that an anecdote supported by numerous claims to authenticity is indicative of an anticipation that the audience may receive said anecdote sceptically.[29] Yet, even if we accept the potential to identify anticipated audience responses, it should be noted that we are still accessing an expectation that is not necessarily that of the historical author, but rather an expectation that the author was capable of conceptualising and including in his narrative.

In addition, it should be remembered that the audiences of these works were neither intellectually inert, homogenous, nor insular, and that we cannot, therefore, access the reality of audience response to a given narrative. Consequently, this book is chiefly concerned with narratives produced, so far as we are able to tell, by ecclesiastically educated men: an admittedly narrow yet inescapable lens to which examinations of the 'constructedness' of historical narratives of the crusades from this period are ultimately limited.

In focusing on the miraculous as a narrative ingredient, I intend neither to resurrect the spectre of the 'Age of Faith', nor to undermine the capacity for (or

---

[27] For a useful introduction to the narrator, see H.P. Abbott, *The Cambridge Introduction to Narrative*, 2nd edn (Cambridge, 2008), pp. 68–77. On the implied author, and for the first coinage of the term, see W.C. Booth, *The Rhetoric of Fiction,* 2nd edn (Chicago, 1983), pp. 67–86. For a consideration of the value of these approaches in relation to the study of medieval crusade histories, see Bull, 'Narratological Readings of Crusade Texts', in *The Crusader World*, ed. A.J. Boas (Abingdon, 2016), pp. 646–60, and *Eyewitness and Crusade Narrative*, pp. 52–7.

[28] G. Spiegel, 'History, Historicism, and the Social Logic of the Text', in *The Past as Text* (Baltimore, 1997), pp. 3–28.

[29] See Watkins, *History and the Supernatural*, pp. 16–18, 38–44.

indeed the complexities of) medieval belief in miracles. The 'truth' of whether a certain historical author really believed in a miracle portrayed as genuine in his history – should such a thing even be provable – is largely irrelevant to the present study. It matters, rather, that these texts could conceivably play host to both genuine, and indeed, dubious or false, miracles. Such an approach allows for the contradictory, processual and self-reflexive aspects of medieval Latin Christian belief and scepticism only insofar as they are of importance to the role played by the miraculous in historical writing.[30]

While a degree of blurring and overlap is unavoidable, the six chapters of this book are arranged into three parts governed by the abovementioned theoretical dichotomies (miracles and marvels, visions and dreams, and signs and augury). This is done for four main reasons: first, in order to draw attention to the potential for these narratives to engage with sophisticated terminological and conceptual nuance; second, because these varying groupings often differ from one another not only in form but, crucially, in function; third, that the developmental trajectories and intertextual evocations particular to each type of phenomenon might be conveyed more clearly; and finally, that a large amount of material might be rendered more easily navigable for the reader.

Part I examines the form and function of miracles and marvels in the sources for the period in question. Chapter 1 looks first to the contemporaneous learned definitions of the miraculous, and identifies how these can be seen to inform the representation of such phenomena in crusade narrative. In doing this, it will be demonstrated how these texts can be seen to speak to broader contemporaneous trends in how the miraculous, and, crucially, its relationship to Creation, might be conceptualised. Having established divine agency's place at the heart of what was considered truly miraculous, Chapter 1 moves on to demonstrate how authors tapped into this aspect of the miraculous in their work, honing it in support of their narrative agendas. It will do this by focusing on the use of miracles in representations of crusade preaching and battlefield intervention. Chapter 2 proceeds to examine miracles and marvels in narrative histories of failed or otherwise controversial crusades. This chapter will show that the absence of a

---

[30] Steven Justice has proposed an approach to medieval belief which recognises it as an active process embracing, even requiring, cognitive problematisation and confrontation. See S. Justice, 'Did the Middle Ages Believe in Their Miracles?', *Representations* 103.1 (2008), 10. On medieval scepticism and doubt, see especially J. Van Engen, 'The Christian Middle Ages as an Historiographical Problem', *The American Historical Review*, 91.3 (1986), 519–52; S. Reynolds, 'Social Mentalities and the Case of Medieval Scepticism', *Transactions of the Royal Historical Society*, Sixth Series, 1 (1991), 21–41; J. Arnold, *Belief and Unbelief in Medieval Europe* (London, 2005) and 'The Materiality of Unbelief in Late Medieval England', in *The Unorthodox Imagination in Late Medieval Britain*, ed. S. Page (Manchester, 2010), pp. 65–95; and K. Brewer, *Wonder and Scepticism in the Middle Ages* (Abingdon, 2016).

narrative of victory, like that of the First Crusade, did not preclude the inclusion of stories of the miraculous, and that accounts of these phenomena continued to perform important functions in many of these narratives.

Part II examines the role of visions and their everyday cousins, dreams. Chapter 3 begins by arguing that certain crusade narratives reveal a sophisticated level of engagement with intellectual authorities on the relationship between visions and dreams, and that a greater sensitivity to a text's use of discrete terminology can offer fresh insights into their narrative agendas. By focusing on two visionaries discussed in narrative histories of the First Crusade, this chapter will demonstrate the various ways in which these works navigate the uncertainties surrounding the representation of these mysterious phenomena.

That there was much at stake in getting the audience on side when it came to narrating visions becomes clear in Chapter 4. This chapter shows how visions were used in support of the perceived legitimacy of crusading ventures, both in terms of divine approbation of and involvement in that expedition, and of the reality of the spiritual rewards received by those who took part in it. Further aspects examined in this chapter include how visions could help prove the authenticity of a relic, or add layers of implication to critical perspectives.

Part III turns to the final means by which God might communicate with humankind, signs, and to the related 'ways of knowing' deemed superstitious by the medieval Latin Church, identified here as augury. In fact, in addition to what might be considered more 'traditional' signs, we also find reference to astronomy, astrology, horoscopy, divination from animal remains, and Sibylline and Joachimite prophecy in Latin crusade histories. Chapter 5 outlines contemporaneous attitudes towards certain of these practices and the authorities underpinning them, before situating examples from crusade narrative in relation to this broader narrative. It will be argued that crusade narratives navigate the often blurry line between licit and illicit methods of prognostication in order to employ these themes in their rhetorical strategies, for example, by incorporating the discussion of superstitious practices into practices into constructions of perceived religious Others. Finally, Chapter 6 concentrates on how signs could function as indicators of the divine disposition, for good or ill. Through the examination of key case studies, it will show how prognostications might be incorporated into narratives in order to highlight the perceived significance or urgency of a given event or issue, or as evidence that an occurrence was divinely willed or predestined and, by extension, legitimate.

Any important intra-thematic patterns or conclusions are addressed in the Conclusion, which takes a chronological view, by crusade, across all of the book's core themes. Finally, a brief source overview is provided as an appendix, in order that the content of this book might be more easily navigable for those unfamiliar with the corpus of Latin histories pertaining to the crusading expeditions to the Eastern Mediterranean, Iberian Peninsula and Baltic region of 1096 to 1204.

By approaching the miraculous in this way, this book aims to reposition miracles and related phenomena as the significant narrative tools that they represented to many Latin Christian authors of crusade narrative. In other words, the miraculous should be credited as having offered authors a particular means of communicating the divine agency thought to be at the heart of crusade. Orderic Vitalis supports his abovementioned attribution of the First Crusade to divine origins, for example, with a description of the miraculous intervention of Sts George, Demetrius and Mercurius at Antioch in 1098.[31] As we shall see, however, the narrativisation of crusading activity was not always so straightforward, and the malleability of the miraculous, and its ability to function in subtly different ways, helps us to explain the continued role of the miraculous even in accounts of crusades wherein the role of divine agency might be questioned. Thinking about the miracles of crusade narrative informs our understanding of these texts in other ways, too. By examining the application of intellectual authorities concerning the miraculous, we gain a window onto the priorities and preoccupations of our authors, and are reminded of the intellectual embeddedness of crusade narrative; that these texts were written not in a vacuum, but by individuals who were able to bring much broader intellectual discourses to bear on their narratives. In short, we stand to gain a richer understanding of how Latin Christian contemporaries conceptualised crusading if we recognise the place of the miraculous in its narrativisation. Miracles helped authors to construct compelling narratives about crusades, and this book sets out to examine how.

---

[31] OV, vol. 5, pp. 112–14.

PART I

Miracles and Marvels

1

Divine Agency

Crusade as Miracle

In the prologue to his narrative history of the First Crusade, Guibert of Nogent argues that the events of that venture should be viewed as inspired and accomplished by God's will, and God's will alone. Even his act of writing the crusade's history, he adds, was the will of God. The idea that the First Crusade was God's achievement, enacted through the Franks, even extends to the work's title: *Dei gesta per Francos* (*The Deeds of God through the Franks*). In these times, Guibert states, God worked miracles greater than any He had previously performed. According to Robert the Monk, another Benedictine monk who, like Guibert, was writing a history of the First Crusade in the first decade of the twelfth century, the 1099 crusader conquest of Jerusalem was God's third most significant miracle, after the Creation and Christ's Crucifixion.[1] In around 1200, the author/compiler of the *Historia Peregrinorum*, likely a Cistercian monk at the Swabian monastery of Salem (Salmansweiler), noted that Frederick Barbarossa's involvement in the Third Crusade was a miracle of divine, not human, power. Around five years later another German Cistercian monk, Gunther of Pairis, stated in his *Hystoria Constantinopolitana*, an account of the Fourth Crusade's capture of Constantinople, that however impious the crusaders' actions might appear, no one should doubt that their achievement was God's will.[2] Importantly, the idea that crusading, as salvific armed pilgrimage, was an act of God in which the participants were earthly instruments, can be found throughout various medieval narratives of crusading activity. Indeed, the emphasis that authors like Guibert and Robert placed on the divine agency at the heart of crusading reflects transforming attitudes towards warfare in a Latin Christian context. While the belief that violence could be divinely sanctioned was far from novel, however, the penitential form of warfare that the First Crusade represented *was*. Moreover, as the works of authors like Gunther and the anonymous composer of the *Historia Peregrinorum* reveal, the importance of emphasising God's involvement in subsequent crusading endeavours did not necessarily diminish over time.

It is this idea of divine agency that this chapter is primarily concerned with, in particular the role which miracles played in demonstrating God's involvement

---

[1] GN, pp. 79–81; RM, p. 4. On the First Crusade as miraculous in the works of Baldric, Guibert and Robert, see especially Riley-Smith, *The First Crusade*, pp. 135–52.

[2] *HP*, pp. 116–7; GP, p. 107.

in crusading efforts. As we will see, according to many twelfth-century Latin Christian understandings, it was God's intervention which elevated the miraculous from the everyday workings of Creation. It was by this logic that Guibert could argue for the First Crusade's status as a miracle: it was, in and of itself, a divine intervention. Not only this, but it was an intervention scattered with its own constituent miracles, each contributing to a scaffold of proofs for God's involvement in the events narrated. In other words, a crusade could be portrayed as a temporally protracted, spatially itinerant miracle, punctuated with transient expressions of divine intervention that serve to bolster the status of the whole. Thus, while Elizabeth Lapina has shown that miracles were a means by which an author might demonstrate 'the exceptional nature of the crusading enterprise', this chapter will show that miracles were not limited to indicating the significance of crusade.[3] Rather, it will argue that the miraculous could also be harnessed as part of different justificatory agendas, such as demonstrating the sanctity of a particular individual or group. In addition, this chapter will show how discussion of miraculous themes might be used to manipulate the audience's perception of the author, as well as act as an intertextual cue designed to evoke existing crusade narrative and encourage an audience to draw comparisons across traditions, for example through the use of a recognisable motif. Before moving on to examine the functions of stories of the miraculous, however, it is instructive to consider the ideas and authorities which can be seen to have informed their application in narratives of crusading expeditions.

Miraculously, Rather Than Marvellously

On 15 July 1099, the forces of the First Crusade stormed the walls of the city of Jerusalem. According to William of Tyre, who was writing his *Historia* of the Latin states of Outremer from within the kingdom of Jerusalem in the second half of the twelfth century, several manifestations of God's agency were witnessed in the city on that day. These manifestations, William specifies, occurred 'miraculously, rather than marvellously' ('miraculose magis quam mirabiliter').[4] In his narrative of the First Crusade, which occupies eight of the *Historia*'s twenty-three books, the expedition is portrayed as a triumphal, if lamentably unparalleled, episode for Latin Christendom, one in which the conquest of Jerusalem was the climax. The concentration of miraculous episodes at this point in the text is indicative of this.[5] By specifying that the expressions of divine mercy at Jerusalem were miraculous (the result of God's intervention in the natural processes instilled

---

[3] Lapina, *Warfare and the Miraculous*, p. 3.
[4] WT, p. 415.
[5] B.C. Spacey, 'Refocusing the First Crusade: Authorial Self-Fashioning and the

at Creation), rather than marvellous (the result of natural processes instilled at Creation, yet inspiring wonder because of their rarity or unexplained nature), the *Historia* points to the perceived inferiority of the latter, more mundane cause, while also calling on the association between the miraculous and divine agency. Strikingly, the *Historia* is not the only crusade source to voice this sentiment. In the initial recension of the Third Crusade history called the *Itinerarium Peregrinorum et Gesta Regis Ricardi*, also known as *IP1*, several notable stories surrounding the 1191 siege of Acre are introduced as being 'no less miraculous than marvellous' ('non minus miraculosi quam mirandi').[6] While it is unclear whether these instances represent examples of the use of a popular, late twelfth-century phrase, its logic nonetheless requires an understanding of the miraculous as superior to the marvellous on the grounds of divine implication.

The abovementioned distinction between the miraculous and marvellous was a very twelfth-century one, in that it tapped into contemporaneous discourses surrounding the desacralisation of nature. The terms *miracula* and *mirabilia* – miracles and marvels – stem etymologically from the same root, *mira*, which is indicative of the sense of wonder inspired by such instances.[7] Until around the twelfth century, these terms appear to have been used interchangeably, and in relation to less clearly defined concepts. Before Thomas Aquinas' (d. 1274) authoritative thirteenth-century clarification of the relationship between the miraculous and the marvellous, Latin Christians who sought to reflect on this issue were largely reliant on the work of St Augustine. In his *De utilitate credendi* (written *c.* 391–2), Augustine describes a miracle as 'that which is difficult or unusual above the hope or power of those who wonder'.[8] By this broad definition, a miracle was identifiable by its transcendence of comprehension and the sense of wonder that it inspired. It was above (*supra*), rather than against (*contra*), God's creation.[9] Augustine clarifies in his later *Contra Faustum Manichaeum* (written 397–9) that wherever he uses *contra naturam* he in fact meant contrary to human experience of the course of nature, or as Bernhard Bron abbreviates, 'against what we know as nature':[10]

    Miraculous in William of Tyre's *Historia Ierosolymitana*', *Journal of Religious History, Literature and Culture*, 5.2 (2019), 51–66.

6   *IP1*, p. 337.

7   On Wonder, see Bynum, 'Wonder'; and Brewer, *Wonder and Scepticism*.

8   Augustine of Hippo, 'De utilitate credendi ad Honoratum Liber Unus', *PL*, 42, 16.34, col. 90: 'Miraculum voco, quidquid arduum aut insolitum supra spem vel facultatem mirantis apparet.'

9   The idea that being *contra naturam* was distinctly negative can be found in both the Old and New Testaments. See Judges 19.24, and Romans 1.26, 2.24.

10 B. Bron, *Das Wunder: Das theologische Wunderverständnis im Horizont des neuzeitlichen Natur- und Geschichtsbegriffs* (Göttingen, 1975), p. 14: 'gegen die uns bekannte Natur.' See also, Bynum, 'Wonder', 8.

> But God, the Author and Creator of all natures, does nothing contrary to nature... For we give the name nature to the usual common course of nature; and whatever God does contrary to this, we call mighty deeds or marvels.[11]

Notably, Augustine appears to use *miracula* and *mirabilia* interchangeably here, instead focusing on the significance of their status as challenges to humankind's typical experience of Creation. The implication of this sentiment is that all miracles and marvels were natural (and, crucially, that all of nature was God's creation); they were simply the drawing out of the hidden potentialities, the *seminales rationes*, instilled in all matter by God.

The Augustinian, sacramental worldview left relatively little room for the 'scientific' study of nature and causation, an impetus that, as Marie-Dominique Chenu has shown, was growing among certain Latin Christian intellectual circles in the twelfth century. This 'search for the causes of things', undertaken by individuals such as Adelard of Bath (d. 1152) and William of Conches (d. *c.* 1154), was buoyed by a growing interest in natural philosophy driven by growing access to Greek and Arabic intellectual traditions in the schools of Europe.[12] Those who continued to cleave to the Augustinian cosmology in the early decades of the twelfth century – often members of the Benedictine and Cistercian orders – feared that the potential reach of the miraculous would shrink as a result.[13] Such fears were not ill-founded. As explication became more acceptable and available, a reduced emphasis on the miraculous nature of Creation as a whole did emerge. The conclusion that an event was miraculous became less satisfactory. Rather, events that exceeded understanding and inspired wonder could be explicable through the application of reasoning or advances in natural philosophy, while the miraculous became a restricted class for which divine instrumentality was the only explanation. The most intellectually dominant pre-fifteenth-century formulation of this latter issue regarding the nature of the miraculous can be found in Thomas Aquinas' *De potentia* (written 1259–68). At around the same time, Albertus Magnus (d. 1280) more precisely situated marvels in relation to this

---

[11] Augustine of Hippo, 'Contra Faustum Manichaeum Libri XXXIII', *PL,* 42, 26.3, cols. 480–1: 'Deus autem creator et conditor omnium naturarum, nihil contra naturam facit... Hanc enim etiam appellamus naturam, cognitum nobis cursum solitumque naturae, contra quem Deus cum aliquid facit, magnalia vel mirabilia nominantur.' English translation is adapted from Augustine of Hippo, *NPNF,* 26.3, pp. 321–2.

[12] M.-D. Chenu, *Nature, Man and Society in the Twelfth Century: Essays on New Theological Perspectives in the Latin Medieval West*, ed. and trans. J. Taylor and L.K. Little (London, 1997), pp. 11–14. See also Ward, *Miracles*, pp. 3–9; L. Daston and K. Park, *Wonders and the Order of Nature, 1150–1750* (New York, 1998), pp. 109–20; and Watkins, *History and the Supernatural*, pp. 23–67.

[13] An example of this sort of criticism can be found in a letter of William of St Thierry to Bernard of Clairvaux, in which he condemns the work of William of Conches. See *De erroribus Guillelmi de Conchis, PL,* 180, cols. 339–40. See also Ward, *Miracles*, p. 7.

definition of the miraculous. Marvels were extraordinary phenomena that, unlike miracles, could be explained.[14]

While being careful not to impose a linear progression towards the articulations of Thomas Aquinas and Albertus Magnus upon the preceding centuries, it is important to bear in mind that the ideas and authorities which informed the narratives considered in this book are the products of the climate of concentrated intellectual negotiation and problematisation of the miraculous from which these works would arise. Indeed, such was the distinction between miracles and marvels by the closing decades of the twelfth century that William of Tyre and the author of *IP*1 were able to make the abovementioned observations about the nature of events at Jerusalem and Acre.

It is possible to see the plasticity of Augustine's theory of the miraculous in the face of scholastic approaches to nature in the works of Gerald of Wales. Gerald had been schooled in Paris, Gloucester and Lincoln, where he would likely have been exposed to the study of natural philosophy and of 'New Platonisms'.[15] As Robert Bartlett and Carl Watkins have discussed, Gerald's works often echo the Augustinian position that nothing occurs beyond the natural capacities instilled at the Creation; the daily rising and setting of the sun was deserving of wonder, but the solar eclipse, born of that same natural impetus, stimulated wonder because of its rarity.[16] Frequently, however, when it came to discussing individual phenomena, Gerald would move beyond such a sacralised worldview, one which discouraged exploration, to investigate patterns and causation. In Gerald's works, then, we often find a discordance between his reverence for the Augustinian worldview and his desire to explore naturalising explanations, which led him to distinguish between miracles and marvels in a way reminiscent of Albertus Magnus' definition.

Gerald's near-contemporary, Gervase of Tilbury, received similar schooling. His *Otia imperialia* (written 1210–14) reveals a similar approach to wondrous phenomena:

---

[14] See Goodich, *Miracles and Wonders*, pp. 19–21. Aquinas dedicated the sixth of the ten 'questions' discussed in his *Quaestiones disputatae de potentia Dei* to miracles and explores various facets of the miraculous in relation to the natural in detail. See Thomas Aquinas, *De potentia* in *Quaestiones disputatae*, 2, ed. P. Bazzi, M. Calcaterra, T.S. Centi, E. Odetto and P.M. Pession (Turin, 1965), quaestio 6; and Albertus Magnus, *Summa theologiae, vol. II,* ed. A. Borgnet (Opera Omnia 32; Paris, 1895), 8.30–2, pp. 319–60.

[15] On twelfth-century Neo-Platonisms, see especially W. Wetherbee, *Platonism and Poetry in the Twelfth Century: The Literary Influence of the School of Chartres* (Princeton, NJ, 1972); P. Dronke, ed., *A History of Twelfth-Century Western Philosophy* (Cambridge, 1988); and Chenu, *Nature, Man and Society*, pp. 49–98.

[16] Bartlett, *Gerald of Wales: A Voice of the Middle Ages* (Stroud, 2006), p. 99; Watkins, *History and the Supernatural*, pp. 27–33.

From these causes arise two things, miracles and marvels (*miracula et mirabilia*), though they both result in wonderment. Now we generally call those things miracles which, being preternatural, we ascribe to divine power, as when a virgin gives birth, when Lazarus is raised from the dead, or when diseased limbs are made whole again; while we call those things marvels which are beyond our comprehension, even though they are natural: in fact the inability to explain why a thing is so constitutes a marvel.[17]

According to Gervase, both miracles and marvels appeared to be beyond the usual capacity of things: miracles went beyond the natural as a result of divine intervention, while wonders simply appeared to do so because they could not be explained (an ability contingent on an individual's own level of learning). Thus, narratives like those of Gerald and Gervase reveal dynamic engagement with early Christian authorities on miracles that simultaneously tap into the changing contemporaneous intellectual landscape that would become famously manifest in the work of Thomas Aquinas and Albertus Magnus.

It is striking that so many crusade narratives should have had such significant recourse to the miraculous at a time when naturalising explanations were becoming more fashionable in certain intellectual circles. Certainly, the monastically authored sources for the First Crusade appear to adhere more closely to an Augustinian sacramental worldview, though this may well be a symptom of their concerted efforts to demonstrate the divine agency at the heart of crusade, as we will see. The capacity for naturalising explanations is also particularly noticeable in the case of the First Crusade because it is possible to examine descriptions of the same events across different accounts. For example, Peter Tudebode's description of the battle of Ascalon in August 1099 describes how a vast herd of animals moved in formation alongside the crusader army. This, Peter states, was a 'miracle of God' ('Dei... miraculum').[18] Raymond of Aguilers also describes this phenomenon, attributing it to divine intervention but not explicitly identifying it as a miracle in the same way as Peter. According to Raymond, 'God multiplied his army' ('multiplicavit Deus exercitum suum') in the eyes of the enemy through the presence of these herds.[19] By contrast, however, Albert of Aachen,

---

[17] Gervase of Tilbury, *Otia imperialia, Recreation for an Emperor*, ed. and trans. S.E. Banks and J.W. Binns (Oxford, 2002), p. 559: 'Ex his, duo proueniunt: miracula et mirabilia, cum utrorumque finis sit admiratio. Porro miracula dicimus usitatius que preter naturam diuine uirtuti ascribimus, ut cum uirgo parit, cum dicimus que nostre cognicioni non subiacent, etiam cum sunt naturalia; sed et mirabilia constituit ignorantia reddende rationis quare sic sit.' On Gervase's catalogue of marvels in relation to thirteenth-century understandings of wonder, see Daston and Park, *Wonders and the Order of Nature*, pp. 21–5.

[18] PT, p. 146; cf. *GF*, p. 94, which mentions only that many animals and goods were seized from the area around Ascalon before the battle.

[19] RA, p. 158.

a non-participant who wrote his history of the First Crusade and the Latin East independently from the *Gesta Francorum* tradition (of which Peter Tudebode's account is part), offers a more mundane interpretation. The flocks were simply amazed by the brilliance of the crusaders' armour and fascinated by the great clamour created by the vast army.[20] The three different representations of the same event are indicative of the potential for the coexistence of interpretative extremes. Whether Albert's naturalising version of animal behaviour at Ascalon is derived from the interpretations of the participants who were his sources, or from the application of his own judgement to their accounts, it nonetheless reveals a different narrative rendering of events than that provided by Peter and Raymond, one which aligns itself with the increasing scope allowed to naturalising explanatory frameworks in this period.

Besides such opportunities to compare representations of the same phenomenon, it is also possible to identify instances of narratorial reflection on the contested miraculous status of an event with a natural explanation. An example of this can be found in the *Gesta Danorum* (written 1190–1208) of Saxo Grammaticus, in which miracles and marvels feature with some frequency. In the fourteenth book, incidentally the book which contains the majority of the work's crusade-related content, a heavily-armoured knight named Eskillus is described as being able to flee across dangerous marshland without sinking into the mud. Rather than attribute this to the knight's agility, the passage continues that this feat should be seen as a manifestation of God's grace: 'we should ascribe it to a heavenly miracle rather than to manly courage'.[21] Here, the narrator anticipates naturalising explanations of Eskillus' feat and explicitly challenges them. It is also possible to find narratorial intervention that does the reverse. In turning to consider such instances, this chapter also moves on to examine the first of several functions of the miraculous in crusade narrative.

'Vulgar Fables' and Authorial Self-Fashioning

For the miraculous to successfully convey divine agency in historical narrative, the audience had to be convinced of its genuineness. It was therefore crucial that the narrative foster audience confidence in its implied author. One of the most common ways we can see this is in examples of accompanying statements bolted onto stories of the miraculous establishing the trustworthy nature of the source, usually either through an appeal to the character of the witness or to the author's relationship to that witness. An example of this can be found in the *Chronica* (written 1227–51) of Alberic of Trois-Fontaines, a brother at the

---

[20]   AA, p. 462.
[21]   Saxo Grammaticus, 'Ex Saxonis Gestis Danorum', ed. G. Waitz, *MGH SS*, 29, p. 118.

Cistercian monastery of Trois-Fontaines at Chalôns-sur-Marne in Champagne.[22] The *Chronica* documents the events of the Fourth Crusade and includes an account of posthumous miracles performed by the deceased Baldwin I of Constantinople (formerly Baldwin count of Flanders and Hainaut). According to the *Chronica*, the abandoned body of the murdered crusade leader was seen illuminated in light by a passing Burgundian woman. Once the body was buried, certain 'miracles' (*miracula*) occurred in that place. The means by which the author obtained this information are related in the text; Alberic was told by a Flemish priest, who had happened to stay at the woman's house in Tirnovo whilst returning from Constantinople, where he in turn had been informed about the events. [23] By tracing the provenance of the account, and establishing the story's 'pedigree', Alberic rendered the miracle story more credible in the eyes of his intended audience while simultaneously encouraging confidence in the author, as viewed by the audience.

This technique was not limited to the legitimisation of miracle accounts, but rather could be exercised as a means of encouraging confidence in any form of anecdotal evidence or source.[24] However, the frequency with which it is employed in relation to stories of the miraculous indicates that these sorts of anecdotes were more likely to be received critically by an anticipated audience. This is likely on account of the added weight of the divine implication which came with miracles, alongside the increasingly restricted space occupied by the miraculous in twelfth- and thirteenth-century cosmologies.

The dismissal of allegedly miraculous phenomena by the narrator (who usually, in crusade narratives, is intended to represent the author) also played a role in what might be called authorial self-fashioning, a method which served to enhance the credibility of anecdotes presented positively elsewhere in a narrative. There are several examples of this in the narratives of the First Crusade, usually concerning the 'popular' misidentification of the mundane in order that they might be discredited explicitly. The narratives which offer such ambivalent representations of imprudent interpretation, aside from contributing to the shaping of expectations regarding the appropriate expression of popular crusading enthusiasm, were also presenting these stories in order to conjure a trustworthy authorial persona. In Albert of Aachen's *Historia Ierosolimitana*, a woman and her followers are scorned for believing that a goose – and in another instance a nanny goat – had been inspired by the Holy Spirit to undertake the

---

[22] A.J. Andrea, ed. and trans., *Contemporary Sources for the Fourth Crusade: Revised Edition* (Leiden, 2008), p. 265.

[23] Alberic of Trois-Fontaines, 'Chronica Albrici monachi trium fontium', ed. P. Scheffer-Boichorst, *MGH SS*, 23, p. 885.

[24] On the use of oral evidence in First Crusade narratives, see John, 'Historical Truth and the Miraculous Past'.

pilgrimage for the liberation of the Holy Land. The language is indisputably negative, describing these people as 'foolish' (*stultus*), guilty of 'frenzied levity' (*vesanus levitas*), and privy to 'abominable wickedness' (*scelus detestabilis*).[25] Albert dedicates this entire section to a monologue warning against such things: God forbid that such dull and senseless animals be permitted to visit the tomb of Christ's most holy body. Such beliefs are equated to idolatry.[26] While providing a fascinating insight into how popular enthusiasm for the call to crusade might be represented in historical narrative, this passage also raises questions about why an author might seek to include the story at all. The act of rendering this story in text would presumably perpetuate at least an awareness of the tradition, which indeed it has done.

Guibert of Nogent, whose proclivity towards the ambivalent representation of popular devotion has been identified by Simon Yarrow, also discusses a 'laughable' (*ridiculus*) rumour of a goose that many thought was destined to help redeem Jerusalem.[27] The passage concludes by noting that the episode was incorporated in order to warn against the trivialising nature of the common peoples' 'vulgar fables' ('vulgi fabulis').[28] Ekkehard of Aura's *Hierosolymita* also briefly mentions and critiques the story of the woman and the goose, stating that such 'deceivers' should be 'pointed out', 'searched for everywhere' and be 'forced to do penance'.[29] It would appear, therefore, that these anecdotes were included for the purpose of authorial self-fashioning, and also didacticism; including the anecdote for the purpose of repudiation alongside clear condemnation appears to have been considered more valuable to posterity than omission. Sceptical narrative intervention in the name of authorial self-fashioning can also be found in William of Tyre's *Historia*.[30] A similar sense of responsibility on the part of the author is expressed by Henry of Huntingdon (d. *c.* 1157) in the ninth book of his *Historia Anglorum*, dedicated to stories of the miraculous. In this, he comments that truth itself is God and therefore any acts which oppose truth are also acts against God. Those who are too eager to believe something to be miraculous, either through their own lack of discernment or for financial enrichment, are criticised.[31] According to Henry, therefore, there was an added spiritual dimension to the responsibilities inherent in telling stories about miracles, they were, after all, accounts of God's own interventions in the world.

---

[25] AA, p. 58.
[26] AA, p. 30.
[27] S. Yarrow, 'Miracles, Belief and Christian Materiality: Relic'ing in Twelfth-Century Miracle Narratives', in *Contextualising Miracles in the Christian West, 1100–1500*, ed. M.M. Mesley and L.E. Wilson (Oxford, 2014), pp. 41–62, esp. pp. 42–9.
[28] GN, p. 331.
[29] EA, p. 19.
[30] See Spacey, 'Refocusing the First Crusade', 53–6.
[31] HH, p. 622.

Crusade Origins and Preaching

According to the anonymous *Gesta Francorum*, the southern Italian Norman Bohemond of Taranto took the cross at the siege of Amalfi in 1096 because he had been inspired to do so by the Holy Spirit. Bohemond took his valuable cloak, the *Gesta* continues, and had it cut into crosses to be worn by those of his men who would join him on this new venture.[32] In doing this, Bohemond momentarily took on the role of conduit, through which God was able to inspire the southern Italian Normans to take crusade vows. It is a statement about Bohemond's character that he was a fitting recipient of the Holy Spirit from the crusade's opening stages. Not only does the story of the Holy Spirit's intervention serve to situate Bohemond as the *Gesta*'s key protagonist, it also establishes divine intervention as a central driving principle behind the events narrated.[33] The *Gesta* is by no means the only First Crusade narrative, let alone crusade narrative, to use miracles in order to establish God's involvement from an early stage. Fulcher of Chartres records how, in March 1097, a ship recently departed from Brindisi broke up and foundered near the shore, killing four hundred crusaders. Those who recovered the bodies discovered crosses imprinted in the flesh of some of the dead. This miracle, Fulcher explains, was a sign that those marked with the 'symbol of victory' ('signum victoriosum') had obtained eternal life.[34] The marked bodies of the drowned crusaders were visible proofs of God's investment in the expedition.

It is notable, however, that none of the participant narratives of the First Crusade, of which the *Gesta* and Fulcher's *Historia Hierosolymitana* are both examples, have miracles occurring before the departure of the main crusader contingents in summer 1096. Rather, in these texts the miraculous is associated with those who were, in some cases literally, marked with the sign of the cross. The Benedictine histories of the crusade are markedly different in this regard: the miraculous is integrated earlier in their narratives, before the crusaders departed, often in their prologues and in their accounts of crusade preaching. Indeed, the *Gesta Francorum* is explicitly criticised in Robert the Monk's work for failing to give appropriate attention to the crusade's preaching and subsequent events. Carol Sweetenham has demonstrated how Robert set about rewriting the *Gesta Francorum*'s version of the First Crusade by – among other things – integrating scriptural cues from the very beginning of his narrative

---

[32] *GF*, p. 7.

[33] Simon Parsons has recently raised an important challenge to the idea that the *Gesta Francorum* was a straightforward panegyric of Bohemond. See S.T. Parsons, 'The Valiant Man and the *Villain* in the Tradition of the *Gesta Francorum*', in *Crusading and Masculinities*, ed. N.R. Hodgson, K.J. Lewis and M.M. Mesley (Abingdon, 2019), pp. 36–52.

[34] FC, pp. 169–70. On the stigmata miracles of First Crusade narratives, see W.J. Purkis, 'Stigmata on the First Crusade', in *Signs, Wonders, Miracles*, pp. 99–108.

which would serve to firmly situate the First Crusade within providential history.[35] Undoubtedly, the miraculous was another tool for the anchoring of the crusade within sacred history.

As we have already seen, Guibert of Nogent made it clear in the prologue to his crusade narrative that the events he was about to describe were inspired and accomplished by the will of God alone, and that this was clear from the myriad miracles which occurred at the time of its preaching. The enthusiasm for the expedition was so great, Guibert explained, that those who had vowed to participate sold their possessions at outrageously low prices in order that they might depart sooner. This, Guibert continued, was a miracle in itself.[36]

While papal involvement in the call to crusade is treated cursorily in the *Gesta Francorum*, Urban II receives hagiographical treatment in Guibert's *Dei gesta*, which includes a digression on how the pope's death and subsequent burial in 1099 was marked by miracles and signs.[37] One example concerns a young man who, standing by Urban's tomb, swore on the loss of limb that no sign had been or would ever be given by the merits of the dead pope. The man was struck with paralysis in that very place and died the following day.[38] This retributive miracle, punishing the individual who doubted the association between Urban and manifestations of divine power, signals Urban's sanctity by drawing upon a common hagiographical motif.[39] Baldric of Bourgueil's *Historia* achieves a similar end by representing Urban as a mouthpiece for the divine word. On two occasions, Baldric describes Urban as spreading the 'word of God' ('verbum Dei'), that is, the call to crusade.[40]

The influence of such portrayals of crusade preaching and preachers in miraculous terms can also be identified in accounts of later crusades. Not only were such narratives drawing on the ability of the miraculous to convey divine instrumentality, but they were also able to evoke the precedent of the First Crusade and the memory of Urban as its pious instigator. Along with that conceptual lineage came a claim to comparable significance, particularly in terms of divine

---

[35]   C. Sweetenham, '"*Hoc enim non fuit humanum opus, sed divinum*": Robert the Monk's Use of the Bible in the *Historia Iherosolimitana*', in *The Uses of the Bible in Crusader Sources*, pp. 133–51.

[36]   GN, p. 119.

[37]   Ibid., p. 107.

[38]   Ibid.

[39]   See P.-A. Sigal, 'Un aspect du culte des saints: le chatiment divin aux XIe–XIIIe siècles d'après la littérature hagiographique du Midi de la France', in *La religion populaire en Languedoc du XIIIe siècle à la moitié du XIVe siècle*, ed. E. Privat, (Cahiers de Fanjeaux, 11; Toulouse, 1976), pp. 39–59; and R. Bartlett, *Why Can the Dead Do Such Great Things? Saints and Worshippers from the Martyrs to the Reformation* (Woodstock, 2013), pp. 401–9.

[40]   BB, pp. 6, 11.

support. Thus, as Penny Cole has discussed, Pope Eugenius III opened his crusade bull, *Quantum praedecessores* (December 1145, reissued March 1146), with a summary of Urban's crusade and an appeal to recreate the achievements of that expedition.[41] According to the bull, it was as though Urban had sounded a 'heavenly trumpet' ('tuba coelestis'), and those who answered his call were victorious on account of 'divine aid' ('divino auxilio').[42]

Of the narrative histories of the Second Crusade, Urban's spectre looms especially large in Odo of Deuil's portrayal of Bernard of Clairvaux, contained in his *De profectione*. Bernard was entrusted with the responsibility of preaching the crusade in France, Germany and the Low Countries by his friend and former tutee, the pope himself. On account of this it is often Bernard, and not Eugenius, who appears as the primary initiator of the crusade in the sources. According to *De profectione*, King Louis VII of France had cultivated a desire to take the cross, which he first made public at his Christmas court at Bourges in 1145. The following year, Louis appealed to the pope, who in turn delegated to Bernard the task of blessing Louis' undertaking in person at Vézelay in March 1146. The crowd which gathered to witness Bernard's preaching at Vézelay was, according to Odo, so huge that a platform had to be erected in a field outside of the town, in order that Bernard could be seen above the throng. In terms evocative of Baldric's description of Urban's preaching, Odo describes Bernard as a 'heavenly instrument' ('caeleste organum'), who on that platform communicated the 'word of God' ('divini verbi') to the assembled people.[43] The response, according to the *De profectione*, was suitably enthusiastic, and the crowd's demand for crosses was so great that Bernard's supply soon ran out, so that the abbot was forced, like Bohemond in the *Gesta Francorum*, to tear his own garments to make more. Likewise, many miracles occurred at the time of Bernard's preaching on account of his sanctity. Odo did not go so far as to recount them, however; instead, he argued that it would draw him too far away from the original theme of the work. It appears to be enough for the purposes of his narrative simply to conclude that those miracles demonstrated God's approval of the undertaking. Even without the inclusion of specific miracle stories associated with Bernard's preaching, Odo's use of the motif of the crusade preacher as a heavenly instrument communicating God's word clearly echoes earlier representations of Urban's crusade preaching. Further, it is consistent with his use of other miraculous themes from First Crusade narratives elsewhere in the *De profectione*, as will be discussed in further detail

---

[41] Cole, *The Preaching of the Crusades*, pp. 40–3. For the text of *Quantum praedecessores*, see Otto of Freising, *Gesta Friderici imperatoris*, ed. R. Wilmans, *MGH SS*, 20, pp. 371–2.

[42] 'Quantum praedecessores', in *MGH SS*, 20, p. 371.

[43] OD, pp. 8–10.

below. Odo's detailed recourse to First Crusade narrative can be explained by the likelihood that he had at least one history of that campaign with him during his participation on the Second Crusade. Indeed, as Marcus Bull has shown, Odo's framing of eyewitness knowledge in the *De profectione* also bears striking similarities to that of certain First Crusade narratives.[44] His use of miraculous imagery should be viewed as further evidence of this possibility.[45] As Jay Rubenstein has shown, appeals were made to Louis to replicate the successes of the First Crusade during the decade leading up to the Second Crusade, an aim which Odo has Louis voice in direct speech in the *De profectione*.[46] The projection of miraculous themes associated with the First Crusade onto the narrative of Louis' crusade should therefore be viewed as indicative of a desire, on the part of Odo and among certain of Louis' followers, for the Second Crusade to emulate its predecessor. Louis' crusade ended somewhat ignominiously, however, and I will turn to discuss the implications of this in the next chapter. For now, it is sufficient to recognise that access to certain First Crusade narratives enabled Odo to call upon a range of motifs, including miraculous ones, to use in the narrativisation of Louis' crusade.

Otto of Freising's discussion of the miraculous elements of Bernard of Clairvaux's crusade preaching is even vaguer than Odo's. In his *Gesta Frederici*, Otto describes how King Conrad III of Germany and his own nephew, the future emperor, Frederick Barbarossa, took the cross at Speyer in 1146, and notes that Bernard performed many miracles both publicly and privately.[47] On another occasion, he describes Bernard as renowned for signs and miracles, though again he does not elaborate on this.[48] There are no explicit parallels between Bernard's preaching and that of Urban, and Otto only presents the Second Crusade as divinely sponsored at the preaching stage, highlighting the contrast between Bernard's piety and the sinfulness of the crusaders whose behaviour, he argues, led to the withdrawal of that support.[49] Indeed, Otto's portrayal of the preaching of the Second Crusade in his *Gesta Frederici* represents the miraculous high-point of his lacklustre treatment of that enterprise, which, he admits, he only discusses

---

[44] Bull, *Eyewitness and Crusade Narrative*, pp. 156–92, esp. p. 159.
[45] On the possibility that Odo travelled on the Second Crusade with a copy of a crusade narrative, see J.P. Phillips, 'Odo of Deuil's *De profectione Ludovici VII in Orientem* as a Source for the Second Crusade', in *The Experience of Crusading, 1: Western Approaches*, ed. M. Bull and N. Housley (Cambridge, 2003), pp. 80–95, esp. p. 83, and *The Second Crusade*, p. 185. On Odo viewing the First Crusade as a model for Louis' crusade, see J. Rubenstein, 'Putting History to Use: Three Crusade Chronicles in Context', *Viator* 35 (2004), 131–68.
[46] Rubenstein, 'Putting History to Use'. OD, pp. 130–1.
[47] OFGF, p. 59.
[48] OFGF, p. 54.
[49] OFGF, p. 93.

cursorily on account of its unfavourable outcome.[50] Here, then, the miraculous is localised, and its positive implications begin, and end, with Bernard's preaching.

Significantly, Helmold of Bosau's account of the Second Crusade does include an example of a preaching miracle attributed to Bernard. According to the *Chronica*, Bernard was made famous by the rumours of signs and wonders that had been worked through him.[51] During his description of the diet at Frankfurt on 13 March 1147 (which he appears to conflate with an earlier diet at the same location), it is noted how a certain Count Adolph, desiring to witness proof of Bernard's sanctity, watched closely as a lame and blind boy was presented to the abbot. [52] As if instructed by God of the count's incredulity, Bernard promptly healed the boy.[53] This is followed by a description of Bernard's preaching and the many who were signed with the cross as a result. As with the punitive miracle which Guibert attributes to the bodily remains of Urban, here a miracle is used to undermine Bernard's potential critics. Rather than commit a punitive miracle against Adolph, however, Bernard is divinely instructed to address the count's scepticism through a benevolent miracle, and as a result of this proof, an army of bishops, princes and common people too numerous to count was roused.[54] The significance of the miraculous anecdote is twofold: it emphasises Bernard's sanctity, while helping to explain the enthusiastic response to his crusade preaching.

The abovementioned portrayals of Bernard's preaching of the Second Crusade all draw upon miraculous themes, albeit to differing degrees and to differing effect. It is the case in all three versions that association with miracles emphasises Bernard's saintly reputation, in a way reminiscent of Saints Lives (*vitae*); he is presented as a suitable conduit for God's power. Otto uses Bernard's preaching to hint at the unrealised potential of the Second Crusade. While Helmold does include other accounts of miracles or wondrous phenomena in his narrative of the Second Crusade's Holy Land campaign, as we will see, these are infrequent, and certainly do not convey the crusaders' status as instruments of divine agency in the way that several narratives of the First Crusade, and to an extent Odo's account of the Second, do. In comparison, Odo's account of Bernard's preaching integrates miraculous motifs which evoke Urban's preaching of the First Crusade, thereby simultaneously drawing attention to the divine auspices under which Louis' crusade was launched, and emphasising the character of his king's crusade as emulating the First Crusade. As I argue in the next chapter, Otto and Helmold's more reserved representations are indicative of the challenges that the narration of failed or controversial crusades could pose for medieval historians.

---

[50] OFGF, p. 65.
[51] HB, p. 114.
[52] See F.J. Tschan, trans., *The Chronicle of the Slavs* (New York, NY, 1966), p. 171, n. 2.
[53] HB, p. 114.
[54] HB, p. 115.

None of the Latin narratives of the Third Crusade discuss its preaching in miraculous terms. This is likely the result of several factors: the preaching for that campaign was protracted and frequently unsuccessful; there was no preaching figurehead with a reputation comparable to St Bernard's; and the resulting campaign, despite some key victories, ultimately failed in its objective of recovering Jerusalem. Consequently, the motif of a heavenly instrument spurring the populous to rapid, divinely inspired action would not sit comfortably in the resulting histories. Having issued *Audita tremendi* in 1187, Pope Gregory VIII charged Henry, cardinal bishop of Albano, with the preaching of a crusade.[55] When Henry died in January 1189, the crusade's departure remained far from realisation. King Henry II of England had made crusade vows in 1172 and 1188, and while he himself received criticism from both contemporary chroniclers and Patriarch Heraclius of Jerusalem for his tardiness, and his ultimate failure, in fulfilling his vows, he did organise a preaching tour of Wales.[56] This preaching tour was conducted by Archbishop Baldwin of Canterbury in 1188, and documented by Gerald of Wales, who accompanied him.[57] Gerald's account of Baldwin's preaching tour, the *Itinerarium Kambriae*, is largely comprised of remarkable anecdotes associated with the places they travelled through, from the miraculous to the marvellous or simply notable; thus (and like many of Gerald's extant works) the *Itinerarium Kambriae* shades between what we might recognise as travel literature, history, natural history, miracle collection (*miracula*), ethnography and, on occasion, theology.[58] While Gerald did not go on to produce a narrative of the Third Crusade, as far as we are able to tell, there are instances in the *Itinerarium Kambriae* where miracles occur in relation to Baldwin's crusade preaching, which causes the reader to anticipate an author who still harboured hopes that Henry would act on his crusade vow.

In the eleventh chapter of Book One, Gerald describes some of the miracles associated with Baldwin's preaching tour. It seemed wonderful and 'as if by a miracle' ('quasi pro miraculo') that so many flocked to take the cross when the preaching was in Latin and French, neither of which would have been understood by the majority in the audience. Gerald then describes a miracle associated directly with this crusade preaching. An elderly woman who had been blind for three years sent her son to where the preaching was due to take place so that he might acquire some means of healing her, perhaps through part of the archbishop's

---

[55] On *Audita tremendi* and the preaching of the Third Crusade, see Cole, *The Preaching of the Crusades*, pp. 71–9.

[56] On criticism of Henry for failing to go on crusade, see M. Staunton, *The Historians of Angevin England* (Oxford, 2017), p. 229.

[57] See P.W. Edbury, 'Preaching the Crusade in Wales', in *England and Germany in the High Middle Ages*, ed. A. Haverkamp and H. Volrath (Oxford, 1996), pp. 221–33.

[58] On Gerald as a historian, see Staunton, *The Historians of Angevin England*, pp. 95–107.

garments. This implies that Baldwin had a reputation for association with the miraculous, perhaps in a similar way to St Bernard, though it is just as likely indicative of the regard in which Gerald held the archbishop, and the former's investment in the righteousness of the crusade. However, Gerald continues, the young man was only able to acquire some of the earth on which the preacher had stood. Upon applying the turf to her mouth and eyes the woman had her sight restored to her through the merits of the holy man.[59] The earth appears to function in the same way as a contact relic; it has itself become charged with divine potentiality through contact with Baldwin, who is by extension represented in saint-like terms. As discussed above, thaumaturgy in the context of crusade preaching could be used to demonstrate the sanctity of both the message and the messenger, and thus, like Helmold's St Bernard, the popularity of Baldwin's crusade preaching is portrayed as explicable on account of this.

Over a decade had passed since his first crusade vow when Henry ordered the preaching tour of Wales. However, in the intervening years between the 1188 recruitment campaign and Gerald's estimated completion of the *Itinerarium* in 1191, Henry had died without ever going on crusade. When we view Gerald's discussion of Baldwin's preaching miracles alongside the former's other expressions of reserved optimism and, after Henry's death, frank frustration regarding the king's crusade obligations, we can identify a consistent level of investment in crusading and the maintenance of Latin Christian territory in the East on the part of the Gerald conjured by his corpus of work.[60] Further, the crowds of Welsh people who flocked to take the cross, inspired to do so despite their alleged unfamiliarity with the languages used in the preaching, throw Henry's reticence into sharp relief. As I argue in Chapter 4, the discussion of miraculous crusade preaching was not the only way in which Gerald called upon miraculous themes in order to draw attention to his erstwhile king's failure to go crusade.

The absence of preaching miracles in the Latin narratives of the Third Crusade is rendered even more notable given its relative abundance in narratives of the Fourth Crusade, especially those with a vested interest in demonstrating the legitimacy of relic thefts resulting from the crusader conquest of Constantinople. Certain narratives are explicit in portraying the Fourth Crusade as a miracle divinely sanctioned from the very beginning, and even evoke the preaching of prior crusades. One Fourth Crusade preacher who is portrayed as particularly charismatic is Fulk of Neuilly, whose preaching is described in varying degrees of detail by two Cistercian commentators, Ralph of Coggeshall and, to a lesser extent, Gunther of Pairis. According to Ralph's *Chronicon Anglicanum*, Fulk acted as a mouthpiece for the crusading message:

---

[59] *Itinerarium Kambriae*, p. 83.
[60] Compare, for example his *Expugnatio Hibernica* (written *c.* 1188–9) with his *De principis instructione* (*c.* 1190–1217). I return to this issue in Chapter 4.

God had bestowed his voice upon Fulk, and strengthened the latter's preaching with certain 'emblems of power', namely signs and miracles.[61] The parallels between this representation of Fulk and earlier descriptions of the crusade preaching of Urban and Bernard are clear, and as such we are able to identify that the motif of the miracle-working crusade preacher continued to be of use to the authors of crusade history well into the thirteenth century.

The *Chronicon*'s detailed description of Fulk's preaching continues by noting that the preacher restored sight to the blind, hearing to the deaf and speech to the mute, gave mobility to those unable to walk, and healed many through the 'divine power' of prayer, the sign of the Cross and the imposition of his hand.[62] There were also many signs at that time, though Ralph does not describe these.[63] A further gift which God had granted Fulk was the ability to 'discern spirits', which enabled the preacher to determine when, and – perhaps more importantly, when *not* – to heal an individual, dependent upon whether or not their sins had been redressed by the 'scourge of divine censure'.[64] Perhaps the most striking aspect of the *Chronicon*'s discussion of Fulk is the repeated identification of his preaching as the 'word of God' ('verbum Dei'), a feature of several earlier descriptions of crusade preaching, as we have already seen.[65]

The preaching of Abbot Eustace of St Germer de Flay in England in 1200 and 1201 is also discussed by Ralph.[66] He is described as a 'comrade in preaching' of Fulk and incorrectly introduced as abbot of Flavigny. Eustace, too, is attributed with spreading the 'word of God' ('verbum Dei').[67] A particular aspect of his preaching, Ralph notes, was the reassertion of the strict observance of feast days and of the abstention from manual labour on Sundays and after Saturday Nones. It was reported how 'many astounding miracles' had occurred throughout England, in which those who had ignored Eustace's preaching and partaken in labour were struck by 'divine retribution'.[68] While Coggeshall Abbey is not known to have benefited from relics acquired in the aftermath of the Fourth Crusade, the *Chronicon* does communicate a partisanship which Alfred Andrea has attributed to a Cistercian milieu, while also tracing in detail the translation of a relic of the True Cross from Constantinople to the priory of Saint Andrew at Bromholm.[69] By

---

[61] Ralph of Coggeshall, 'Chronicon Anglicanum', ed. J. Stephenson, in *Rerum Britannicarum Medii Ævi Scriptores,* 66 (London, 1875), p. 81.

[62] Ibid.; cf. Luke 7.22–3.

[63] Ralph of Coggeshall, 'Chronicon Anglicanum', p. 83.

[64] Ibid., p. 82.

[65] Ibid., twice on p. 82, and once on p. 83.

[66] C. Tyerman, *England and the Crusades, 1095–1588* (London, 1996), p. 96.

[67] Ralph of Coggeshall, 'Chronicon Anglicanum', p. 133.

[68] Ibid., p. 134.

[69] Andrea, *Contemporary Sources,* p. 275; Ralph of Coggeshall, 'Chronicon Anglicanum', pp. 201–3. On the Bromholm relic of the True Cross, see F. Wormald, 'The Rood of

stating that the preaching of the Fourth Crusade was the word of God, Ralph was calling upon the precedents established by other crusade narratives, and setting the scene for an account of divinely sanctioned events.

A source which sits apart from other Fourth Crusade histories is the *Devastatio Constantinopolitana*. In the *Devastatio*, the crusade leaders are the villains, who repeatedly cheat and overlook the interests of the lower ranks. As Andrea has identified, the supernatural does not feature in the *Devastatio*.[70] The only instance which might be considered a fleeting reference occurs in the account of Peter Capuano's crusade preaching, which is described as 'marvellous'.[71] It is interesting that this should occur at a point in the narrative before the expedition was corrupted by the crusade leadership, as though the crusade leaders should be considered guilty of debasing something that had the potential to be divine in outcome. While there was no need for the author of the *Devastatio* to use miracles to establish a narrative framework of divine instrumentality, a brief allusion does serve to help the narrative communicate its central agenda: demonstrating the crusade leadership's betrayal of the undertaking and its participants in the name of personal gain.

Divine Aid and Battlefield Intervention

Many of the miraculous episodes described in historical narratives of the crusades occur in relation to military encounters. Martial conflict was an expected component of these armed pilgrimages, and the narration of these occasions offered authors a symbolic microcosm of the greater salvific struggle that crusade participation was supposed to represent. These were the moments when God's instrumentality was at its most critical and at its most easily identifiable. Discussions of divinely inspired victories are not limited to crusade narrative. However, there is an identifiable difference between discussions of divine sponsorship, such as can be found in William of Poitiers' description of William of Normandy's 1066 Hastings campaign, and divine intervention.[72] In many

---

Bromholm', *Journal of the Warburg Institute* 1.1 (1937), 31–45 (which includes as an appendix a Latin edition of Ralph of Coggeshall's discussion of the relic, alongside Roger of Wendover's from his *Flores historiarum*).

[70] Andrea, *Contemporary Sources*, p. 207.

[71] A.J. Andrea, 'The *Devastatio Constantinopolitana*, a Special Perspective on the Fourth Crusade: An Analysis, New Edition, and Translation', *Historical Reflections* 19.1 (1993), 132.

[72] William of Poitiers describes how Duke William received a banner and approval for the Hastings campaign from Pope Alexander II. See William of Poitiers, *The Gesta Guillelmi of William of Poitiers*, ed. and trans. R.H.C. Davis and M. Chibnall (Oxford,

crusade sources, God was involved in a very literal way that was indicative of the divine agency that many contemporaries believed lay at the heart of crusading.

Albert of Aachen describes divine intervention at the battle of Antioch, during which crusader forces sallied out from the city to engage the numerically superior armies of Kerbogha, *atabeg* of Mosul, on 28 June 1098. According to Albert, God rendered the bowstrings of the enemy archers unusable through rainfall.[73] He also includes a story about a knight who was seen to fall from his horse during the battle, but when two enemy soldiers made to attack him, their horses suddenly halted and refused to respond to the spur, giving the knight enough time to mount his horse, thereby saving his life. Those who saw this, Albert concluded, had clearly witnessed the work of the 'finger of God'.[74] Here, fortuitous reversals are presented as evidence of divine instrumentality, and as a clear indicator of who the recipients of divine approbation were. An analogous example can be found in the *Chanson d'Antioche*, where God and St Michael save Raimbaut Creton from drowning in the River Orontes by miraculously removing his hauberk and dragging him to the water's surface.[75]

Battlefield intervention could also indicate the divine sponsorship of the undertaking and the crusaders' status as the instruments of God's will. Military encounters thus provided the conditions for one of the most dramatic types of miracle: intervention at a point of seemingly inevitable defeat or against insuperable odds. These miracles had the benefit of functioning as proof of their own authenticity; how else could such a reversal have occurred if not by the divine hand? An example of this is the crusader victory against a numerically superior Seljuk army at Dorylaeum on 1 July 1097, during which the Turkish forces were eventually routed by the beleaguered Christian forces, pushed back against their own camp, thanks to the arrival of the other half of the crusade army, which had been travelling separately. Indeed, its representation in crusade narratives reveals how divine intervention in battle could be harnessed in the service of different authorial agendas. According to Fulcher of Chartres, at the point at which defeat seemed certain, the papal legate, Adhémar of Le Puy, clothed in white vestments and accompanied by various bishops and priests, prayed to God

---

1998), p. 105. He also makes some allusions to the outcome of the battle being a judgement of God, see William of Poitiers, *The Gesta Guillelmi*, pp. 123, 131.

[73] AA, p. 236: 'Dei etiam auxilio et misericordia nerui arcuum eorum pre pluuia molliti ac defecti nil poterant, quod illis magno fuit impedimento, et fidelibus in triumphi augmento.' Cf. RA, 8, p. 82: 'Non minus hoc idem mirabile equis nostris etiam contigit.' OV, 5, p. 110: 'Hoc nempe a multis probabilibus uiris qui interfuerunt relatum est.' The miraculous rainfall is also described by Baldric of Bourgueil (BB, pp. 79–80) and William of Tyre (WT, p. 333).

[74] AA, p. 314: 'In cuius liberatione manifeste digitum Dei affuisse experti sunt.'

[75] *La Chanson d'Antioche: chanson de geste du dernier quart du XIIe siècle*, ed. and trans. B. Guidot (Champion classiques moyen âge, 33; Paris, 2011), laisse 169, p. 494.

for help against the enemy.[76] This is portrayed as a turning point in the crusaders' fortunes.[77] Consequently, it was on account of divine grace that the crusader forces rallied in the face of defeat, and so complete was this victory – which he described as 'a great miracle of God' – that the Turks fled continuously for days after the initial rout.[78] Raymond of Aguilers' account of the encounter at Dorylaeum, however, attributes the crusader victory to a much more tangible demonstration of divine intervention. Although unseen by him, he admits, some of the participants in the battle reportedly witnessed a 'wonderful miracle' in which two horsemen bearing 'glittering arms' threatened the Turkish forces and rendered them unable to fight.[79]

Yet, the reputation of the battle of Dorylaeum as a site of miraculous intervention on the First Crusade has been dwarfed by that of the battle of Antioch, an encounter that came to be associated with one of the most iconic miracles of the First Crusade. Several accounts of the battle describe how, at a point of crisis when Kerbogha's forces threatened to outflank the already stretched crusader regiments, a celestial army riding white horses and brandishing white standards descended from the nearby mountains to aid the Christians and reverse the fortunes of battle.[80] Initial confusion gave way to the realisation that this was divine aid, with the leaders of the heavenly host being identified as Sts George, Mercurius and Demetrius.[81] This is the version contained in the *Gesta Francorum*,

---

[76] FC, p. 196. Cf. Bartolf of Nangis, *Gesta Francorum Iherusalem Expugnantium*, in *RHC Oc.*, 3, p. 496.

[77] FC, pp. 196–7.

[78] FC, pp. 197–8.

[79] RA, pp. 45–6: 'Fertur quoddam insigne miraculum, sed nos non vidimus quod duo equites armis coruscis et mirabili facie exercitum nostrum precedentes, sic hostibus imminebant ut nullo modo facultatem pugnandi eis concederent. At vero cum Turci referire eos lanceis vellent, insauciabiles eis apparebant.'

[80] I have also discussed the celestial knight motif in Spacey, 'The Celestial Knight'. See also Lapina, *Warfare and the Miraculous*, esp. pp. 37–96; and Sweetenham, 'When the Saints Go Marching In'. On the significance of the celestial intervention at Antioch in relation to concepts of martyrdom, see H.E.J. Cowdrey, 'Martyrdom and the First Crusade', in *Crusade and Settlement: Papers Read at the First Conference of the Society for the Study of the Crusades and the Latin East and Presented to R.C. Smail*, ed. P.W. Edbury (Cardiff, 1985), p. 52.

[81] On the association between crusading and certain warrior saints, see especially R. Cormack and S. Mihalarias, 'A Crusader Painting of St. George: "Maniera greca" or "lingua franca"?', *Burlington Magazine* 126 (1984), 132–41; J.B. MacGregor, 'The Ministry of Gerold d'Avranches: Warrior-Saints and Knightly Piety on the Eve of the First Crusade,' *Journal of Medieval History* 29.3 (2003), 219–37, especially 223, and his 'Negotiating Knightly Piety: The Cult of the Warrior-Saints in the West, ca. 1070–ca. 1200,' *Church History* 73.2 (2004), 317–45; J. Folda, 'Mounted Warrior Saints in Crusader Icons: Images of the Knighthoods of Christ', in *Knighthoods of Christ: Essays on the History of the Crusades and the Knights Templar*, ed. N. Housley

which closes its description of this event with an assertion of veracity; these words should be believed, because many of the men saw it.[82] The *Gesta*'s celestial horsemen became a recurring motif for divine intervention in crusade battles, probably on account of the enthusiasm with which it was adopted and adapted by those who used the *Gesta* as a source for their own histories.[83] As Piotr Grotowski, Lapina and Carol Sweetenham have discussed, however, it is not the earliest example of the motif; white-clad horsemen are described in Revelation (19:11–14), for example, and can be found intervening in battle in various ancient Greek and Roman, and early Christian and Byzantine, traditions.[84]

A version of the motif which displays striking similarities to the *Gesta Francorum* tradition is contained in Geoffrey of Malaterra's account of the 1063 battle of Cerami, Sicily, fought between a Muslim coalition and the forces of Roger I of Sicily. According to Geoffrey, there appeared a knight, riding a white horse and bearing splendid arms and a white banner topped with a cross.[85] While the mysterious knight is not explicitly identified, Geoffrey describes how the southern Italian Norman warriors, upon seeing the knight riding into battle, cried out to God and St George.[86] There has been some discussion over the dating of Geoffrey's account, and whether it represents a precedent for, or derivative of, the *Gesta Francorum*'s version. Most recently, Lapina has concluded that they were likely written concurrently yet, importantly, independently – linked only by their association with the Normans of southern Italy.[87] Specific links between the motif and twelfth-century notions of *Normanitas* were quickly overshadowed, however, by its association with sacralised warfare more generally. As we have seen, the Provençal cleric Raymond of Aguilers describes a similar miracle at

---

(Aldershot, 2007), pp. 87–107; and E. Lapina, 'Demetrius of Thessaloniki: Patron Saint of Crusaders', *Viator* 40.2 (2009), 93–112, and *Warfare and the Miraculous*, pp. 54–74.

[82] *GF*, p. 69; cf. PT, pp. 111–12.

[83] BB, p. 81; GN, p. 240; RM, pp. 76–7; *La Chanson d'Antioche*, laisse 358, p. 921.

[84] Piotr L. Grotowski, *Arms and Armour of the Warrior Saints: Tradition and Innovation in Byzantine Iconography (843–1261)*, trans. R. Brzezinski (Leiden, 2010), pp. 99–100; Lapina, 'Demetrius of Thessaloniki' and *Warfare and the Miraculous*, pp. 37–53; and Sweetenham, 'When the Saints Go Marching In'. See also Spacey, 'The Celestial Knight', 67–9.

[85] Geoffrey of Malaterra, *De Rebus Gestis Rogerii Calabriae et Siciliae Comitis et Roberti Guiscardi Ducis Fratris Eius*, ed. E. Pontieri (Rerum Italicarum Scriptores, 5.1; Bologna, 1928), p. 44.

[86] Ibid.

[87] For a detailed discussion of the relationship between the two versions, see Lapina, *Warfare and the Miraculous*, pp. 75–80. On the dating of Malaterra's work, see also, K.B. Wolf, *Making History: The Normans and Their Historians in Eleventh-Century Italy* (Philadelphia, 1995), p. 146; and N. Webber, *The Evolution of Norman Identity, 911–1154* (Woodbridge, 2005), pp. 56–7.

Dorylaeum, and, as I will now demonstrate, the motif continues to feature in historical narrative throughout the twelfth century.

To return to the pervasiveness of the *Gesta Francorum* tradition of the celestial knight at Antioch, the versions of Baldric and Guibert feature few changes and both carefully note that many witnesses had testified to its truthfulness. Robert the Monk's *Historia*, though, features the name of an additional saint – St Maurice.[88] Significantly, in addition to the inclusion of this motif in several other narratives of the First Crusade, it can also be found in narrative histories of later crusading endeavours.[89] Repeated reference to the motif in the vernacular *chansons de geste*, as examined by Sweetenham, is further testament to its popularity.[90] In particular, two of the three chansons comprising the early thirteenth-century Old French Crusade Cycle (the *Chanson d'Antioche* and the *Chanson de Jérusalem*) have frequent recourse to the motif, with the *Antioche* drawing on the version of Robert the Monk.[91]

Notably, the motif is also visible in narratives of later crusades. Odo of Deuil's *De profectione*, as we have already seen, contains various evocations of imagery associated with the First Crusade. The celestial knight is another example of this. In an account of an encounter between Louis VII's crusading army and a Turkish force near to the Maeander River in Asia Minor in 1147, Odo again draws on familiar imagery and proofs when describing how certain of the crusaders witnessed ahead of them a white-clad knight, who struck the first blows in the ensuing battle but who had been seen neither before nor since. In concluding that the crusaders had been in such dire straits that such an easy victory could only have occurred through God's power, Odo's inclusion of the celestial knight motif should thus be considered as serving both as an indicator of divine agency, but also as an appeal to the story of the First Crusade, in much the same way as his discussion of St Bernard's preaching.[92] This confirms Jay Rubenstein's

---

[88] RM, p. 76. Robert's development of the celestial knight theme, however, is not limited to the introduction of an additional saint. He engages at length with ideas surrounding how this intervention had been interpreted by Muslim eyewitnesses. On the conversation between Bohemond and Pirrus about the celestial knights, see Lapina, *Warfare and the Miraculous*, pp. 27–8; and Rubenstein, 'Miracles and the Crusading Mind', pp. 200–2. Cf. *HeFI*, p. 82.

[89] Henry of Huntingdon, *Historia Anglorum: The History of the English People*, ed. and trans. D. Greenway (Oxford, 1996), p. 438; OV, 5, pp. 112–14, 154–6; William of Malmesbury, *Gesta Regum Anglorum, The History of the English Kings, Vol. 1*, ed. and trans. R.A.B. Mynors (Oxford, 1998), p. 637; WT, pp. 407, 733–4. On the use of the motif in William of Tyre's *Historia*, see Spacey, 'Refocusing the First Crusade', 57–8.

[90] See Sweetenham, 'When the Saints Go Marching In'.

[91] See *La Chanson d'Antioche*, laisses 100, 124, 210, pp. 363, 411, 590; and *La Chanson de Jérusalem*, ed. N. Thorp, *The Old French Crusade Cycle*, vol. 6 (Tuscaloosa, AL, 1992), laisses 26, 173–4, 248, 265, pp. 53, 166–7, 232, 245–6.

[92] OD, pp. 112–13: 'Certe fueruntqui dicerent album quendam militem ante nostros ad

conclusion, discussed above, that the First Crusade represented an important model and exemplar for Louis' crusade, but also indicates the importance of the literary motifs which emerged from that initial venture's narrativisation to the authors of later crusade narrative. Indeed, key evidence presented as part of Rubenstein's argument is a volume of three texts gifted to Louis in 1137 by William Grassegals, who had himself participated in the First Crusade, and urging the French king to follow in the footsteps of his ancestors.[93] Two of the three texts contained in that codex include examples of the motif, namely, the First Crusade history of Raymond of Aguilers and Walter the Chancellor's *Bella Antiochena*, which traces the affairs of the Latin principality of Antioch between 1114 to 1115, and 1119 to 1122.[94] In Walter's account of the battle of Tall Danith in September 1115, the forces of Bursuq of Hamadan mistake Roger of Salerno's men for white-clad knights ('dealbatis militibus').[95] That the motif was thus appropriated for the representation of conflicts concerning the nascent polities of the Latin East hints at contemporaneous attitudes towards the salvific nature of those encounters. While we cannot connect Odo to the collection, an awareness of its existence and purpose as an instructive gift for Louis helps us to contextualise the narrative agendas of Odo's *De profectione*. In other words, it provides further evidence that certain contemporaries viewed the First Crusade as an appropriate model for Louis' crusade.

Odo was not the last author to utilise the motif of the celestial horseman as an indicator of divine favour and associative cue. During a description of a battle against a Turkish force on 14 May 1190, the *Historia de expeditione Friderici Imperatoris* – an account of Frederick Barbarossa's expedition during the Third Crusade believed to have been compiled in around 1200 – records how a pious layman named Ludwig saw a man riding a white horse and wearing a snow-white tunic come to the aid of the crusaders. He believed the mysterious knight was St George, though others said he was an angel of God. Regardless, he struck down an entire Turkish column using only a single lance.[96] The *Historia de expeditione*, a composite text, has frequent recourse to divine aid and intervention in favour

---

transitum fluminis, quem non viderunt prius vel postea, se vidisse et primos ictus in proelio percussisse. In hoc ego nec fallere vellem nec falli; scio tamen quod in tali districto tam facilis et tam celebris victoria, non nisi divine virtute, fuisset.'

[93] Rubenstein, 'Putting History to Use'. For a Latin edition of William's letter, see FC, p. 827. For a discussion of the letter in the context of notions of crusading obligation, see N. Paul, *To Follow in Their Footsteps: The Crusades and Family Memory in the High Middle Ages* (Ithaca, NY, 2012), pp. 47–8.

[94] The third text contained in *Bibliothèque nationale de France*, MS. lat. 14378 is Fulcher of Chartres' *Historia Hierosolymitana*, which does not feature the motif.

[95] Walter the Chancellor, *Galterii Cancellarii, Bella Antiochena*, ed. H. Hagenmeyer (Innsbruck, 1896), p. 74.

[96] *HeFI*, p. 81.

of the emperor's (and, after his death in June 1190, his son Frederick VI, Duke of Swabia's) campaign.[97] For example, 'God's mercy' ('dei clementia') saves the German crusaders from poisoned wine, while an enormous red cross is seen in the sky over Adrianople, indicating good fortune.[98] The celestial knight motif is therefore one of several indicators of divine agency integrated into the narrative. There is also evidence to suggest that narratives of the First Crusade were in circulation in the court of the Emperor Frederick in the late twelfth century. A copy of Robert the Monk's *Historia*, which, as we have seen, contained a version of the celestial knight motif, is known to have been produced between 1187 and 1189 for presentation to the emperor in advance of his crusade expedition.[99] Therefore, and in a similar way to the white knight of Odo's *De profectione*, it is possible that the use of the motif here is indicative of the motif's currency as an indicator of crusading precedent, even at the turn of the thirteenth century. At the very least, it shows that authors continued to draw upon battlefield intervention as a means associating crusading with divine agency.

Chapters 47 to 57 of the *Itinerarium Peregrinorum*, also known as *IP2*, contain a collection of anecdotes associated with the siege of the port city of Acre (August 1189–July 1191), which shade between the miraculous and marvellous in their demonstration of God's support of the siege.[100] The compiler of the *Itinerarium*, commonly identified as Richard de Templo, translated these stories into Latin from the Old French *Estoire de la Guerre Sainte* of the Norman cleric and Third Crusade participant Ambroise, who was likely writing before Richard I's death in 1199.[101] While the stories are introduced as being 'no less miraculous

---

[97] On the complex composition of the *Historia de expeditione*, see G.A. Loud, *The Crusade of Frederick Barbarossa: The History of the Expedition of the Emperor Frederick and Related Texts* (Farnham, 2010), pp. 1–7.

[98] *HeFI*, pp. 55, 62–3.

[99] Kempf and Bull, *The Historia Iherosolimitana*, pp. x, xlii; D. Kempf, 'Towards a Textual Archaeology of the First Crusade', in *Writing the Early Crusades*, pp. 116–26.

[100] For a narrative of the siege of Acre, see Asbridge, *The Crusades*, pp. 428–55.

[101] For a Latin edition and English translation of the *Estoire*, see Ambroise, *The History of the Holy War: Ambroise's Estoire de la Guerre Sainte*, ed. and trans. M. Ailes and M. Barber, 2 vols (Woodbridge, 2003). On the identity of Ambroise, see Ailes and Barber, *The History of the Holy War*, 2, pp. 1–3; For an alternative view, which argues that the identification of Ambroise as Norman should be abandoned, see F. Vielliard, 'Richard Coeur de Lion et son Entourage Normand: Le Témoignage de l'Estoire de la Guerre Sainte', *Bibliothèque de l'École des Chartes* 160.1 (2002), 5–52. On Ambroise's audience, see Ailes and Barber, *The History of the Holy War*, 2, p. 13. On the *Itinerarium* and the *chanson de geste* tradition, see Nicholson, trans., *The Chronicle of the Third Crusade*, pp. 13–4; and Staunton, *The Historians of Angevin England*, pp. 142–9. Certain of these stories can also be found in the *Libellus de exgpugnatione Terrae Sanctae per Saladinum*. See *The Conquest of the Holy Land by Salah al-Din: A Critical Edition of the Libellus de expugnatione Terrae Sanctae per Saladinum*, ed.

than marvellous', as discussed above, they do include content that is, in the words of Helen Nicholson, 'earthy and sometimes rather distasteful to modern readers; they are amusing'.[102] For example, one passage describes how an unarmed knight, having left the crusader camp to relieve himself, was able to defeat an assailant using a stone that lay nearby. Apparently, someone who had witnessed the event told someone else, and thus it became 'notorious in the camp'.[103] It might strike the modern reader as surprising that Richard should have included such anecdotes in the *Itinerarium*, given his intended clerical, scholarly audience (the *Estoire*, in comparison, was likely aimed at a lay audience of knights and their retinues). However, as Michael Staunton has argued, it is important to allow for the sorts of blurring between genres that works like the *Itinerarium* represent, and, in relation to this, for the possibility that educated and ecclesiastical audiences would have been equally entertained and edified by material more typically associated with works aimed at lay audiences, and vice versa.[104] An illustrative reminder of this, which also serves as an interesting point of comparison to the *Itinerarium*, can be found in Ralph of Caen's history of the First Crusade, when the narrative's 'hero', Tancred, locates vital supplies of wood for the construction of siege engines in a cave, which he ventured into in order to answer the call of nature. According to Ralph, this discovery was a type of miracle ('miraculi species est').[105]

Ailes has argued that the corresponding anecdotes of the *Estoire* are not intended as edification. They do, however, in both the *Estoire* and the *Itinerarium*, imply that God would intervene in the affairs of those who deserved it, for good or ill. For example, there are two anecdotes in which Turkish soldiers are the objects of divine, retributive violence through symbolically and physically emasculating wounds to the genitals. In the first, an emir is burnt on the genitals by the Greek fire he had intended to use on Christian siege machines.[106] The second instance involves a Turk who is shot in the groin before he is able to urinate on a cross: 'And thus as he died he perceived the futility of attempting anything against God', the *Itinerarium* concludes.[107] One story concerns how a man survived unscathed after being hit by a missile launched from a stone thrower. The reader is asked: who would not attribute such a thing to divine compassion? Another man was saved from being injured by a crossbow bolt by a piece of parchment inscribed with God's name, which he had had hanging about his neck in the place

and trans. K. Brewer and J.H. Kane (Crusade Texts in Translation; Abingdon, 2019), pp. 230–2.

[102] Nicholson, *The Chronicle of the Third Crusade*, p. 14.

[103] *IP*1, p. 339. English translation is from Nicholson, *The Chronicle of the Third Crusade*, p. 105; Cf. Ambroise, *The History of the Holy War*, 1, lines 3578–619, p. 58.

[104] Staunton, *The Historians of Angevin England*, pp. 142–9.

[105] RC, p. 100.

[106] *IP*1, p. 342; Cf. Ambroise, *The History of the Holy War*, 1, lines 3656–94, p. 59.

[107] *IP*1, p. 343; Cf. Ambroise, *The History of the Holy War*, 1, lines 3695–764, pp. 59–60.

where the bolt had struck. According to the *Itinerarium*, this was a clear example of God's work.[108] These stories reveal how ostensibly 'unconventional' the miraculous of crusade narratives can be. While they may not be accounts of miraculous cures performed via the spiritual potency of a saintly individual, or of celestial knights aiding crusaders in battle, they are still presented as indicators of God's investment in the siege of Acre, and especially in the fortunes of the crusaders connected to Richard I.

Conclusion

To many Latin Christians of the central Middle Ages, divine agency was instrumental in both miracles and crusades. The ideal crusaders, in a way reminiscent of saints, would act as the earthly conduits of God's power, enacting God's will as instruments of salvific warfare. Consequently, the miraculous offered the authors of crusade narrative a potent tool for communicating the divine agency that they believed lay at the heart of those endeavours. This can be seen at its most elaborate in the Benedictine narratives of the First Crusade, which present the crusade as a mobile miracle, the status of which is repeatedly demonstrated through the occurrence of smaller, constituent expressions of divine mercy. Miraculous intervention in crusade preaching and military encounters were particularly effective for highlighting the divine agency underpinning crusade ventures, and these moments continued to feature stories of miracles in accounts of later crusades, where they were able to evoke the First Crusade as well as demonstrate God's intervention. As the next chapter will demonstrate, however, failed or controversial crusades could pose distinct challenges to the rhetorical efficacy of the miraculous.

---

[108] *IP*1, p. 338. Cf. Ambroise, *The History of the Holy War*, 1, lines 3556–77, pp. 57–8.

2

Writing Failure

The Problem with Defeat

When authors such as Robert the Monk wrote of miracles like that of the celestial knights charging into battle against the Turks at Antioch on 28 June 1098, they were integrating evidence of divine agency into their narratives. This was crucially important for authors who sought to emphasise the sacred significance of a crusade and draw attention to God's very literal involvement in that enterprise. As we have seen, texts like Robert's offer a version of the First Crusade in which that campaign, its victories included, represents an itinerant miracle, the status of which was demonstrated through associated, constituent miracles, like that at the battle of Antioch. Victories were further proofs of divine approbation, especially in cases where the conditions were unfavourable, or the odds ostensibly insurmountable. However, authors who sought to record subsequent crusades, the events of which included setbacks, disappointments, defeats and controversies, could not apply the abovementioned narrative logic so easily. Despite this, narratives of later crusades do continue to discuss miraculous themes, and to draw upon manifestations of divine mercy in the support of their narrative agendas. Thus, and as this chapter argues, while the overarching rationale that the crusade was itself a miracle – what we might call the miraculous metanarrative – disintegrates, the constituent miracles that would have supported it remain, and continue to function as indicators of divine agency, approbation or, in some instances, wrath.

The narratives of the 1145–9 crusade to the Levant, also known as the Second Crusade, contain illustrative examples of the miraculous working in this reduced capacity, and even discuss the challenges that failure posed to the logic of crusade. The Second Crusade campaign to Asia Minor and Syria failed in its goal of recapturing Edessa after its loss to Zengi in 1144, and culminated in an ignominious retreat from a failed siege at Damascus in 1148. Unlike the First Crusade, Latin contemporaries did not herald the Second Crusade as a miracle. Far from it.[1] Looking back on that expedition from the Latin kingdom of Jerusalem in the late twelfth century, a typically gloomy William of Tyre commented that the crusaders 'started on the way as if contrary to the will of an angry God, and, in punishment

---

[1] On contemporary responses to the failure of the Second Crusade to the East, see G. Constable, 'The Second Crusade', in *Crusaders and Crusading*, pp. 281–92; and Rubenstein, *Nebuchadnezzar's Dream*, pp. 116–64.

for the sins of man, they accomplished nothing pleasing to Him on that entire pilgrimage. Nay, they even rendered worse the situation of those to whom they intended to bring succour'.[2]

Otto of Freising, half-brother of King Conrad III of Germany and uncle of Frederick Barbarossa, included an account of the Second Crusade in his *Gesta Frederici I Imperatoris*. After this, he advises his audience of the best way to interpret the events described; namely, that the Second Crusade should be viewed in terms of spiritual, rather than temporal, gain. He begins by outlining the origin and form of the criticism to which he is responding:

> Now because some of the little brethren of the Church being offended, marvel and marvelling are offended [Cf. Matthew 18.6, Luke 17.2, Mark 9.42] at the effort of our aforesaid expedition, inasmuch as starting out from so lofty and good a beginning it came to so pitiful a conclusion – not a good one – it seems that they must be answered as follows.[3]

Here, Otto identifies concerns surrounding how an expedition that, as far as its origins and early stages were concerned, bore all the hallmarks of divine sponsorship, could end not only by failing to meet its declared goals, but with resounding defeat. By acknowledging the 'lofty and good' origins of that campaign, Otto offers a narrative in which the crusade begins well, with manifestations of divine approbation occurring in association with Bernard's preaching, as discussed above. Indeed, he remarks that God truly had inspired Bernard's message, but God later withdrew support because of the crusaders' pride, lawlessness and failure to observe the commandments.[4] Crusader sinfulness had undermined Bernard's, and by extension God's, message:

> If we should say that the holy abbot [Bernard of Clairvaux] was inspired by the spirit of God to arouse us; but that we, by reason of our pride and arrogance

---

2   WT, p. 741: 'Nam tanquam invita divinitate et eis irata iter assumpserunt: in tota illa profectione nichil deo placitum, peccatis nostris exigentibus, operati sunt, sed nostrum, quibus opem se laturos arbitrabantur, statum in deteriorem mutaverunt conditionem.' English translation is from Babcock and Krey, *A History of Deeds Done Beyond the Sea*, vol. 2, p. 165. On the association between sinfulness and crusading failure, see especially B. McGinn, 'Iter Sancti Sepulchri: The Piety of the First Crusaders', in *Essays on Medieval Civilization*, ed. B.K. Lackner and K.R. Philip (Austin, TX, 1978), pp. 33–72; and C. Maier, 'Crisis, Liturgy and the Crusade in the Twelfth and Thirteenth Centuries', *The Journal of Ecclesiastical History*, 48 (1997), 628–57.

3   OFGF, p. 91: 'Porro, quia nonnulli ex pusillis aecclesiae fratribus scandalizati mirantur, mirando scandalizantur de pretaxatae nostrae expeditionis labore, quod tam arduo et bono inchoata principio tam humilem et non bonum exitum acceperit, ipsis hoc modo respondendum videtur.' English translation is adapted from C.C. Mierow, trans., *The Deeds of Frederick Barbarossa* (Toronto, ON, 1994), pp. 103–4.

4   OFGF, p. 93.

not observing the salutary commandments, have deservedly suffered loss of property and persons, it would not be at variance with logical processes or with ancient examples.[5]

It was not all bad news, however. According to Otto, much depended on how one defined 'good' (*bonus*), a word that, he argues, should be interpreted in relation to spiritual, and not temporal, gain. It does not really matter that the Second Crusade failed to invest Edessa or maintain the siege of Damascus. Rather, Otto concludes, the Second Crusade could be viewed as 'good' because it was 'useful' (*utilis*):

> Although it [i.e. the Second Crusade] was not good for the enlargement of boundaries or for the advantage of bodies, yet it was good for the salvation of many souls, on condition however, that you interpret the word 'good' not as an endowment of nature but always in the sense of 'useful'.[6]

The Second Crusade was defensible, therefore, if understood as facilitating the entry of many souls into heaven. In other words, Otto moved the goal posts in order that he might present the Second Crusade as a positive episode in his panegyric of Frederick Barbarossa.

However, and as Otto acknowledges in his *Gesta*, the Second Crusade did fail in military terms, and this is attributed to a withdrawal of divine favour. This absence of supportive divine agency, because of the crusaders' sins, undermines the potential for the miraculous. Consequently, while he does discuss some miracles in relation to Bernard's preaching and a punitive miracle which is examined in more detail below, Otto has no recourse to the miraculous in his narrative of the Second Crusade. It follows, therefore, that beyond the above-mentioned attempt to rehabilitate the crusade's image as spiritually 'good', Otto does little to draw upon the crusade as an opportunity to praise the 'hero' of his narrative, Frederick. Indeed, he does draw attention to Frederick as a recipient of divine favour elsewhere in the *Gesta*. For example, in Book One, Frederick avoids violent traitors by entrusting himself to the aid of 'divine grace', which reveals to him a secret passageway through which he then escapes.[7] Notably,

---

[5] Ibid: 'Quamvis, si dicamus sanctum illum abbatem spiritu Dei ad excitandos nos afflatum fuisse, sed nos ob superbiam lasciviamque nostram salubria mandata non observantes merito rerum personarumve dispendium reportasse, non sit a rationibus vel antiquis exemplis dissonum.' English translation is from Mierow, *The Deeds of Frederick Barbarossa*, p. 106.

[6] OFGF, p. 93: 'Etsi non fuit bona pro dilatatione terminorum vel commoditate corporum, bona tamen fuit ad multarum salutem animarum, sic tamen, ut bonum non pro dato naturae, sed pro utili semper accipias.' English translation is from Mierow, *The Deeds of Frederick Barbarossa*, pp. 105–6.

[7] OFGF, p. 33.

Otto's continuator, Rahewin, maintains this theme by recording how Frederick survived an assassination attempt thanks to 'divine mercy'.[8] While Otto was clearly capable of drawing upon the miraculous as a means of associating Frederick with divine agency, the Second Crusade does not appear to have offered a suitable narrative vessel for this technique. Ultimately, the failure of that campaign posed too great a challenge to the principle that the crusaders were instruments of divine will.

Like Otto, Bernard also appears to have sought to disassociate the preaching from the outcome of the crusade. In his *De consideratione*, an *apologia* addressed to Pope Eugenius III, the Cistercian abbot defends his role as preacher of the Second Crusade by emphasising the unknowable nature of God's will: 'How, then, does human rashness dare reprove what it can scarcely understand?'[9] Judgements based on an incomplete knowledge of temporal affairs are similarly harmful, Bernard continues. Having thus undermined potential critics because of their ignorance of the circumstances, Bernard moves on to problematise the ascription of success and failure to events according to incorrect criteria (namely, that a cause should not necessarily be judged by its outcome):

> These few things have been said by way of apology, so that your conscience may have something from me, whereby you can hold yourself and me excused, if not in the eyes of those who judge causes from their results, then at least in your own eyes.[10]

By separating cause from result, both Bernard and Otto disassociate the former's preaching from the outcome of the Second Crusade, thereby allowing room for the identification of the crusade's preaching as divinely sanctioned. This is a notable departure from the Benedictine First Crusade narratives, which use the association between crusade preaching and divine agency to achieve narrative cohesion. In other words, the metanarrative that several histories of the First Crusade established – that a crusade represented a miracle comprised of constituent miraculous events from start to finish – does not exist in narratives like Otto's, where the miraculous implications of a crusade expedition is limited to its constituent elements, such as preaching.

---

[8]   OFGF, p. 283.

[9]   Bernard of Clairvaux, '*De consideratione libri quinque*', PL, 182, 2.1, col. 743: 'Et quomodo tamen humana temeritas audet reprehendere, quod minime comprehendere valet?' English translation is from J. Brundage, ed., *The Crusades: A Documentary Survey* (Milwaukee, WI, 1962), p. 123.

[10] Bernard of Clairvaux, '*De consideratione*', 2.1, cols. 744–5: 'Haec pauca vice apologiae dicta sint, ut ipsa qualiacumque habeat conscientia tua ex me, unde habeat me excusatum, et te pariter, etsi non apud eos qui facta ex eventibus aestimant, certe apud te ipsum.' English translation is from Brundage, *The Crusades*, p. 123.

It is important to note that not all narrative histories of the Second Crusade to the Levant were as unenthusiastic as Otto's. As we have seen, Odo of Deuil couches his portrayal of Louis VII as the worthy recipient of divine assistance within a narrative of the Second Crusade. In the *De profectione*, Odo presents Louis as a divinely supported and well-meaning crusader king thwarted by the machinations of the Byzantine Emperor Manuel I Komnenos.[11] For example, it is described how Louis became lost taking the shore route from Constantinople to Ephesus on the advice of the Greek emperor. Despite managing to find the way, the French army were forced to proceed through difficult terrain unaided by the Greek inhabitants of the area. Odo alludes to divine support of Louis's army during these tribulations by describing how they had managed to cross three rivers which were flooded by heavy rain immediately after their crossing, much to the amazement of the locals.[12] The passage concludes: 'therefore it was considered miraculous that, contrary to the ordinary course of events, the rains and the winter had spared us'.[13] Elsewhere in the *De profectione*, as we have seen, is an example of the celestial knight motif, which simultaneously highlights divine support of the crusade while evoking the success and precedent of the First Crusade. It is striking that Odo's narrative has similar recourse to the miraculous as several accounts of the First Crusade. This is due, in large part, to his familiarity with at least one narrative history of the First Crusade, and his aim of offering a panegyric of Louis as a crusade leader. However, the miraculous imagery that he uses in order to evoke and eulogise functions effectively because the narrative does not acknowledge the failure of the Second Crusade (the author is presented as entirely unaware of it, and as writing the account on the journey) and, as Marcus Bull has shown, rarely anticipates future events.[14] Rather, it closes at Antioch in early 1148, and therefore does not describe the later siege of Damascus in July. Virginia Berry, and more recently, Bull, have argued that the *De profectione* should be dated to the early summer of 1148, after Damascus had been decided on as a target, but before the siege itself.[15] Consequently, there is

---

[11] On Odo of Deuil's portrayal of the Greeks, see Phillips, 'Odo of Deuil's *De profectione*', p. 85; H. Mayr-Harting, 'Odo of Deuil, the Second Crusade, and the Monastery of Saint-Denis', in *The Culture of Christendom: Essays in Medieval History in Memory of Denis L.T. Bethell*, ed. M.A. Meyer (London, 1993), pp. 225–41; J. Harris, *Byzantium and the Crusades*, 2nd edn (London, 2014), pp. 106–9; and Bull, *Eyewitness and Crusade Narrative*, pp. 156–92.

[12] OD, p. 106.

[13] OD, p. 107: 'Unde habebatur pro miraculo contra solitum nobis imbres et heimem pepercisse.'

[14] Bull, *Eyewitness and Crusade Narrative*, p. 161.

[15] See OD, p. xxiii; and Bull, *Eyewitness and Crusade Narrative*, pp. 161–8. For the argument that Odo was writing in early 1150, see Mayr-Harting, 'Odo of Deuil,' pp. 230–1.

no impediment, within the narrative's internal logic, to the presentation of that crusade as divinely supported in a way comparable to the First Crusade.

In Otto's text, the acknowledgement of the crusade's military failure restricts the positive portrayal of that undertaking to its preaching. Conversely, in Odo's *De profectione*, the absence of defeat, whether as a result of genuine ignorance or deliberate omission (it is possible that Odo wrote as though the siege of Damascus had not yet happened), allows the discussion of divine agency to go unchallenged. Thus, the examination of Otto and Odo's narratives of the Second Crusade reveals the impact that the narration of failure can have on the miraculous of crusade narrative; if failure was indicative of the withdrawal of divine favour then the miraculous, as a mechanism for demonstrating divine agency, was rendered redundant and logically jarring. However, not all expressions of divine agency communicated God's approval.

Divine Punishment

The punishment of crusader sinfulness could be indicative of divine agency. Indeed, according to First Crusade narratives, the greatest spiritual hazards for crusaders were the sins of greed, pride and lust.[16] In a well-known example, Fulcher of Chartres describes how the famine endured by the crusaders besieging Antioch (October 1097–June 1098) was God's punishment for their sexual transgressions.[17] However, First Crusade narratives portray the divine punishment of crusaders as a corrective measure nonetheless indicative of divine investment in the venture, which usually concludes with a positive outcome. The prolonged suffering over winter at Antioch cleansed the crusaders of their sins, Fulcher explains, and once the crusaders had demonstrated adequate contrition, God granted the city of Antioch to them.[18] By contrast, an unusual episode in Otto's narrative of the Second Crusade represents an instance of more pronounced punitive intervention that moves beyond the temporary withdrawal of divine favour. Despite being punitive, it is nonetheless indicative of divine agency. Consequently, such phenomena are still able to communicate divine investment in the endeavour without raising questions about why the crusade ultimately failed.

As we have already seen, Otto disentangles Bernard's preaching from the failure of the Second Crusade in his *Gesta*. Instead, he lays the blame squarely at the feet of the crusaders and leaves little doubt that the result of that crusade

---

[16] See for example FC, pp. 166, 222–4; *GF*, p. 58; RA, pp. 54, 73; RM, p. 67.

[17] FC, pp. 222–4. On this episode see also J. Brundage, 'Prostitution, Miscegenation and Sexual Purity in the First Crusade', in *Crusade and Settlement*, pp. 57–65.

[18] FC, pp. 226–31.

was a form of divine punishment: 'the outcome of that expedition, because of our sins, is known to all'.[19] Otto describes how the German army, himself included, set up camp in an ostensibly pleasant valley near Choirobacchoi to the west of Constantinople on 7 September 1147. However, a storm caused the nearby river Melas to flood, inundating the camp.[20] Otto hints at contemporaneous naturalising responses to the disaster by commenting that it was unclear whether the stream had burst its banks because of a sudden flow of water from the nearby sea or from the heavens, denoting divine vengeance from on high.[21] Whatever the explanation, the interpretation was that the disaster represented a divine punishment. Notably, Otto adds that Frederick had camped beyond the floodwater's reach. As Sverre Bagge has argued, this serves to dissociate the *Gesta*'s hero from the implications of the punishment, while simultaneously highlighting the crusade's status as contingent on the divine disposition.[22]

Notably, two Greek narratives, attributed to Niketas Choniates (d. *c.* 1215/6) and John Kinnamos (d. after 1185), also present this episode as divine punishment of the crusaders. Niketas, in a historical narrative spanning the years 1118 to 1207, comments that those who witnessed the event believed it was the wrath of God.[23] John agrees in his own narrative, concluding that it was reasonable to believe that God was angry with the Germans for their ill treatment of the Greeks.[24] These interpretations of the Melas flood reveal parallel utilisations of the miraculous in Greek narrative histories, particularly in John's text, where the divine punishment of the crusaders serves to highlight the righteousness of the narrative's 'hero', Manuel Komnenos, in his handling of the crusader armies.

Helmold of Bosau also discusses the flood of the crusader camp in his *Chronica*, albeit in rather more dramatic terms than Otto. In his discussion of the 'first' (*primus*) army, namely the army led by the German king, Conrad, Helmold describes how 'many portents' indicating disaster were witnessed by participants.[25] The principal of these occurred one night when a thick fog covered the crusader camp. When the fog withdrew, the tents looked sprinkled with blood, as though the cloud had rained blood upon the camp. This portended

---

[19] OFGF, p. 65: 'Verum quia peccatis nostris exigentibus, quem finem predicta expeditio sortita fuerit, omnibus notum est...' English translation is from Mierow, *The Deeds of Frederick Barbarossa*, p. 79.

[20] The flood is also discussed in Phillips, *The Second Crusade*, pp. 172–3.

[21] OFGF, p. 66.

[22] S. Bagge, 'Ideas and Narrative in Otto of Freising's *Gesta Frederici*', *Journal of Medieval History*, 22.4 (1996), 345–77.

[23] Niketas Choniates, *O City of Byzantium*, trans. H.J. Magoulias (Detroit, MI, 1984), p. 38.

[24] John Kinnamos, *The Deeds of John and Manuel Comnenus*, trans. C.M. Brand (New York, NY, 1976), p. 63.

[25] HB, pp. 115–16.

coming misfortune. It soon became clear what that misfortunate was when a great storm caused the river of a peaceful valley to swell and flood, destroying the German camp. This, Helmold concludes ominously, was the first great loss of that expedition. Helmold's final remarks concerning the Levant campaign of the Second Crusade are striking:

> Oh, the judgements of the Most High! So great was the disaster of the army and so inexpressible the misery that those who took part bemoan it with tears to this very day.[26]

Besides the above reference to the 'Most High', however, Helmold offers no other interpretation of the campaign's failure, and makes no mention of crusader sinfulness as an explanation for the flood. Indeed, he does not explain the flood at all.

Thus, Otto's discussion of the 1147 Melas flood represents an unusually interventionist episode of the divine punishment of crusaders which, like his treatment of Bernard discussed above, draws attention to the thwarted nature of the crusade, while offering an opportunity to distance Frederick from the sinfulness responsible.

The narratives of the Third Crusade offer few comparable examples, despite frequent recourse to more abstract explanatory frameworks of divine wrath or approbation. For example, *IP*1, as it sets the scene for its description of the Third Crusade, ascribes the outcome of the battle of Hattin, the loss of the relic of the True Cross, and the 1187 conquest of Jerusalem, to the sins of the Christians.[27] In doing this, *IP*1 echoes the sentiments of Pope Gregory VIII, as conveyed in *Audita tremendi* (1187), who called upon the entirety of Christendom to be mindful of its sins in the wake of those events.[28] However, the events of the Third Crusade allowed authors to attribute some events to divine mercy. For example, elsewhere in *IP*1, the chaste and disciplined conduct of the crusaders at Iconium in May 1190 is rewarded with success thanks to 'divine power'.[29] The composite *Itinerarium Peregrinorum*, which includes a version of *IP*1, continues this theme by attributing Jerusalem's travails to the depravity and wickedness of those Christians who lived in and defended the city.[30] Similarly, the *Historia de Expeditione* attributes Richard I's capture by Duke Leopold V of Austria in December 1192 to divine punishment. According to the *Historia*, the English

---

[26] HB, p. 117: 'O iudicia excelsi! Tanta fuit clades exercitus et miseria inexplicabilis, ut eorum qui interfuerunt adhuc hodie lacrimis deplangatur.' English translation is from Tschan, *The Chronicle of the Slavs*, p. 174.

[27] *IP*1, p. 259.

[28] Gregory VIII, 'Audita tremendi'.

[29] *IP*1, p. 299.

[30] *IP*2, p. 182. See also p. 398.

king deserved everyone's wrath for his vainglorious conduct while on crusade, and his capture was a just judgement of God.[31] Consequently, beyond explaining setbacks and defeat, discussions of divine punishment could also function to apportion blame; in the *Historia*, Richard's imprisonment is proof of God's wrath in response to his conduct while on the Third Crusade. It also serves to establish Richard as the antithesis of the narrative's 'hero', the magnanimous, divinely supported Frederick Barbarossa.

So far, this chapter has argued that the narration of crusades featuring setbacks and defeats forced certain authors to make innovations in their presentation of the miraculous. In particular, Otto's *Gesta* offers a crusade narrative in which the miraculous is reduced to small-scale expressions of divine mercy (or, indeed, wrath) divorced from any sort of broader demonstration of the crusade's sanctity. In the absence of a victorious conclusion, positive expressions of divine agency challenge the narrative's internal logic, and it is likely because of this that the sources for the Second Crusade offer so little in the way of miraculous material. An exception to this observation has been discussed above: the Odo of the *De profectione* appears entirely ignorant of the outcome of Louis' crusade, and as a result, the narrative can function in much the same way as many of the narratives of the First Crusade, placing continued emphasis on positive divine agency. We will now turn to explore another of the ways in which authors might draw upon the miraculous in the narration of controversial, yet ultimately victorious, crusades, namely, as justification.

The Conquest of Lisbon, 1147

On 23 May 1147, Flemish, Rhenish and Anglo-Norman contingents, including crusaders from Scotland, Brittany and Boulogne, embarked at Dartmouth in England with the intention of fulfilling their crusade vows in the East as part of the Second Crusade. Five months later, however, they had instead assisted King Afonso Henriques with the conquest of Lisbon in the nascent kingdom of Portugal. Helmold, looking across the Iberian, Baltic and Eastern campaigns of 1147 around two decades later, identified the conquest of Lisbon as the only real success of those various crusading ventures.[32] Notably, however, Afonso, the industrious first king of an independent Portugal, had not himself acted under a crusade vow. Rather, he had probably been notified in advance of the passing crusader fleet and arranged to have them met at Porto.[33] To Afonso, the crusaders represented much-needed man and sea power to offer temporary support to his

---

[31] *HeFI*, p. 101.
[32] HB, p. 118.
[33] Phillips has suggested that Afonso's conquest of Santarém, a city about forty-six miles

consolidation of the kingdom, carved in part from Andalusi territory to the south. The siege of Lisbon lasted for seventeen weeks, culminating in victory in late October, after which some of the crusaders remained in Lisbon or dispersed. A depleted force continued to the East.

Scholars continue to debate the extent to which the crusader attack on Lisbon was premeditated, with Alan Forey convincingly arguing that there is no conclusive evidence that the crusaders had planned to assist Afonso before they reached the coast of Iberia, where the bishop of Porto met them.[34] Indeed, scholars have been unable to identify crusading activity in Portugal (either as a semi-autonomous country under the overlordship of the kings of León or, from the early 1140s, an independent kingdom) with any confidence until the 1217 campaign against an Almohad port some 100km to the south of Lisbon. Rather, the counts of Portugal had looked on while, elsewhere on the peninsula, namely in Catalonia and Aragon, crusading was employed as early as the 1090s. Consequently, when the crusaders assisted Afonso in the conquest of Lisbon in 1147, they were taking part in what Jonathan Wilson has called a 'reconquistador/ crusader joint venture'.[35]

The longest and richest source for the conquest of Lisbon is the *De expugnatione Lyxbonensi*, conventionally attributed to a certain Raol, as identified by Harold Livermore.[36] The narrative of the *De expugnatione* is presented as part of a letter addressed to Osbert of Bawdsey, a cleric associated with the Glanvills of East Anglia. Notably, the character in the *De expugnatione* who comes closest to being the 'hero' of the narrative is Hervey de Glanvill.[37] Jonathan Phillips

---

north of Lisbon, on 15 March 1147 represented an anticipation of the crusaders' arrival, though this is conjecture. See Phillips, *Second Crusade*, p. 140.

[34] A. Forey, 'The Siege of Lisbon and the Second Crusade', *Portuguese Studies*, 20 (2004), 1–13. On the conquest of Lisbon as a local initiative, see S. Lay, *The Reconquest Kings of Portugal: Political and Cultural Reorientation on the Medieval Frontier* (Basingstoke, 2009), pp. 99–100. For the argument for premeditation, see H. Livermore, 'The "Conquest of Lisbon" and its Author', *Portuguese Studies*, 6 (1991), 8–12; and J.P. Phillips, 'St Bernard of Clairvaux, the Low Countries, and the Lisbon Letter of the Second Crusade', *The Journal of Ecclesiastical History*, 48.3 (1997), 485–97, and *Second Crusade*, pp. 137–44. Most recently, Bull has suggested that the issue will not be resolved without new evidence. See Bull, *Eyewitness and Crusade Narrative*, pp. 132–3.

[35] J. Wilson, 'Enigma of the *De Expugnatione Lyxbonensi*', *Journal of Medieval Iberian Studies*, 9.1 (2017), 113.

[36] Livermore, 'The "Conquest of Lisbon"'. The most recent challenge to this has been put forward by Jonathan Wilson, who has suggested that the surviving witness in fact represents a copy of an earlier composite text. See Wilson, 'Enigma of the De Expugnatione Lyxbonensi'. On the identification of the 'R' of the *De expugnatione*, see also, Bull, *Eyewitness and Crusade Narrative*, pp. 129–31.

[37] On the representation of Hervey de Glanvill in the *De expugnatione*, see Bull, *Eyewitness and Crusade Narrative*, pp. 129, 135–7, 143–4. On the association between

and John France have argued that the *De expugnatione* represents an effort to justify and legitimise the crusader conquest of Lisbon in 1147 in response to contemporaneous discomfort surrounding the diversion of crusading resources intended for the Levant.[38] As is argued in the following, the use of the miraculous in this text supports these conclusions. In the *De expugnatione*, Raol draws upon miraculous themes, often in ways analogous to the authors of First Crusade narratives, to celebrate manifestations of divine agency and emphasise the legitimacy of that campaign. He does this in two ways. First, he establishes the legitimacy of the five-month diversion of crusading manpower and resources by demonstrating both Iberia's significance as part of the greater patrimony of Christ, and God's sponsorship of the Lisbon campaign. Second, he anticipates criticism of the disunity between the army's contingents by placing the blame for this firmly at the feet of the Flemish and Rhenish crusaders, who are portrayed as the recipients of God's wrath.

The miraculous draws attention to the divine sponsorship of the campaign throughout the *De expugnatione*. For example, the crusaders were chastised by God on the night of 29 May – around a week after they had departed from Dartmouth – when, crossing the Bay of Biscay, a storm scattered the ships. However, divine mercy was present with the army throughout the storm. God reprimanded, but did not destroy, the army. The crusaders, despairing at the disaster confronting their pilgrimage, confessed their sins, wept and groaned, and sought atonement in the eyes of God:

> Thus it happened that divine grace passed no one by, and, indeed, that everyone congratulated himself upon receiving the singular privilege of a heavenly favour, to such an extent that it would be tedious to relate in detail the divine miracles which were revealed in visions.[39]

The *De expugnatione* makes it abundantly clear at this early stage of the narrative that the fortune of the crusaders, and the success of their campaign, was dependent upon their maintaining a level of spiritual health commensurate with crusade.

Raol and Hervey, and on the Glanvill family more broadly, see C.W. David, 'The Authorship of the *De Expugnatione Lyxbonensi*', *Speculum*, 7.1 (1932), 50–7.

[38] J.P. Phillips, 'Ideas of Crusade and Holy War in *De expugnatione Lyxbonensi* (*The Conquest of Lisbon*)', in *The Holy Land, Holy Lands and Christian History*, ed. R.N. Swanson (Studies in Church History, 36; Woodbridge, 2000), pp. 123–41; J. France, 'Logistics and the Second Crusade', in *Logistics of Warfare in the Age of the Crusades: Proceedings of a Workshop held at the Centre for Medieval Studies, University of Sydney, 30 September to 4 October 2002*, ed. J. Pryor (Aldershot, 2006), pp. 87–93.

[39] *DeL*, pp. 60–1: 'Idque adeo actum ut dispensatio divina nullum preteriret, imo etiam cęlestis beneficii singulare privilegium se accepisse unusquisque gratularetur, ut longum sit enumerare per singula quantis visionum imaginibus divina miracula patuerint.'

The *De expugnatione* offers an itinerary of notable sights and legends associated with the crusader fleet's route as it navigated the coast of Iberia, many of which, as Bull has discussed, are derived from the *Collectanea rerum mirabilium* of Solinus.[40] Raol also describes evidence of destruction by Muslim forces, including a monastery and a harbour.[41] He later makes the implications of these sights explicit in a sermon attributed to the bishop of Porto:

> What does the coast of Spain offer to your view but a kind of memorial to its desolation and the marks of its ruin? How many cities and churches have you discovered to be in ruins upon it, either through your own observation or through information given you by the inhabitants? To you the mother church, as it were with her arms cut off and her face disfigured, appeals for help; she seeks vengeance at your hands for the blood of her sons.[42]

There are striking resonances between this representation of Christian Iberia and discussions of a beleaguered Jerusalem in certain versions of Pope Urban II's sermon at Clermont in November 1095. For example, according to Robert the Monk, Urban lamented that 'she [i.e. Jerusalem] begs and craves to be free, and prays endlessly for you to come to her aid'.[43] The bishop continues his sermon by arguing that the crusaders should not continue to be seduced by the desire to continue on to Jerusalem, as it is far more valuable to live well and perform God's works on the way to Jerusalem, than simply to have been there.[44] Here, then, through the voice of the bishop of Porto, Raol establishes the legitimacy of this deviation from the planned progress of the expedition by portraying Iberia as an arena for spiritually meritorious warfare, and by drawing equivalences between Jerusalem and Portugal. It is of no value to leave this frontier open to the ravages of the enemy in the pursuit of the Holy Land.

Elsewhere in the *De expugnatione*, as the crusaders approached the mouth of the Tagus River, where they were due to meet with Afonso to discuss their

---

[40] See Bull, *The Miraculous and Crusade Narrative*, pp. 127, 151–4.

[41] *DeL*, pp. 60, 67–8.

[42] *DeL*, pp. 78–9: 'Quid enim litus Hyspanię vestris aliud obtutibus nisi sue desolationis memoriam quandam et ruinę ostendit indicia? Quot in eo urbium et ecclesiarum desolationes visu et indigenarum indiciis didicistis? Ad vos autem mater ecclesia iam quasi truncis brachiis et deformi facie clamat, sanguinem filiorum et vindictam per manus vestras requirit.'

[43] RM, p. 7: 'Querit igitur et optat liberari, et ut ei subveniatis non cessat imprecari.' English translation is from C. Sweetenham, trans., *Robert the Monk's History of the First Crusade, Historia Iherosolimitana* (Crusade Texts in Translation, 11; Aldershot, 2005), p. 81.

[44] *DeL*, p. 78: 'Nulla ergo itineris incepti vos festinationis seducat occasio, quia non Iherosolimis fuisse sed bene interim invixisse laudabile est; non enim ad ut ad finem gloriosum quis perveniat meretur.'

participation in the siege of Lisbon, a sign of God's approval of the proposed diversion is witnessed. According to Raol, great white clouds swept alongside the crusaders, towards a black cloud which hung over the mainland. The opposing clouds collided like battle lines with an enormous impact and proceeding to fight one another. The cloud that had travelled from the direction of the crusaders cleansed the air of impurities as it advanced, leaving behind a clear blue sky, before taking victory and reducing the dark clouds to nothing. In response, Raol records, 'we shouted, "Behold, our cloud has conquered! Behold, God is with us! The power of our enemies is destroyed! They are confounded, for the Lord has put them to flight!"'[45] Thus, Raol leaves his reader in no doubt that the victorious cloud should be interpreted as representative of the crusaders, victorious over its enemies and leaving in its wake a cleansed Christendom. More specifically, it also foreshadowed victory at Lisbon, and served to situate that impending victory within a broader narrative of the purification of Christ's patrimony, and of the divine sponsorship of the crusaders who were doing so.

Once the *De expugnatione* begins describing the siege itself, the implications of the miraculous appear to shift from legitimising the crusader sojourn in Lisbon to singling out the Rhenish and Flemish contingents as the recipients of divine wrath. Indeed, Raol reveals something of a preoccupation with right intention and spiritually meritorious violence, and a concern over disunity and infighting within and between the crusade contingents.[46] From the moment that the crusaders are required to agree terms with Afonso, greed and discord among the different crusade armies becomes apparent. First, the Flemings tried the unity of the crusaders by independently entering into an (albeit flimsy) agreement with Afonso over payment without adequate discussion with the rest of the crusade leaders. Soon after, a group from Southampton and Hastings raised concerns about Afonso's piety: it transpires that they had joined him in an unsuccessful attempt to capture the same city five years previously, and now argued that he was a traitor, and not to be trusted. The protesting group decided instead that they would depart from Lisbon (amounting to about eight ships), sail south, extort money from African merchant vessels, and take advantage of the season's favourable winds by making progress towards Jerusalem. Raol, through a lengthy speech attributed to the leader of the Anglo-Norman contingent Hervey de Glanvill, carefully identifies such a group as a rogue minority who, under threat of excommunication should they abandon the army, quickly recognised the error of their ways. This episode is crucial to Raol's narrative of a legitimate

---

[45] *DeL*, pp. 88–91: '…nobis acclamantibus: "Ecce nubes nosta devicit! Ecce nobiscum Deus! Dispersa est hostium potentia! Confussi sunt, quoniam Dominus dissipavit eos!"'

[46] On the theme of collective unity in the *De expugnatione*, see Bull, *Eyewitness and Crusade Narrative*, pp. 133–47.

campaign, as it challenges both the criticisms about Afonso's character, and desires among the crusaders to abandon the siege and proceed to Jerusalem, revealed by the potential 'desertion'. The right intention, according to Roal, lay with those besieging Lisbon.

Division is not the only evil discussed by Raol. Crusader greed, especially a desire for monetary gain, is presented as a risk that jeopardised the entire campaign, threatening to relegate it from salvific to distinctly secular warfare. In a narrative focused on showing that this truly was a crusade, and not an opportunistic diversion, any evidence of egregious crusader greed that might reach contemporary audiences needed to be addressed, and Raol employs the miraculous as part of this. Following a description of the various contingents' preparations of siege machinery, Raol describes what he identifies as a prodigious event which took place among the Flemings one Sunday during mass. A priest discovered that the blessed bread, distributed among the crusaders on a regular basis and identified by Susanna Throop as the *eulogia*, was 'bloody' (*sanguineus*).[47] Having ordered the loaf to be cleaned, the priest discovered that the bread was permeated with blood. Raol compares the bloodied bread to flesh, which cannot be cut without the presence of blood. He also notes the public nature of this event, describing how the bread itself was divided up into bloody pieces and could be seen for days after the capture of the city:

> And some, interpreting it, said that this fierce and indomitable people [the Flemish], covetous of the goods of others, although at the moment under the guise of a pilgrimage and religion, had not yet put away the thirst for human blood.[48]

This is reminiscent of a bleeding host miracle. From the late eleventh century, such miracles had served as proof of the real presence of Christ in the Eucharist, and as a form of divine punishment.[49] Caroline Walker Bynum has related the increasing popularity of these miracles to the twelfth-century enthusiasm for holy

---

[47] *DeL*, p. 134. See S. Throop, 'Christian Community and the Crusades: Religious and Social Practices in the *De expugnatione Lyxbonensi*', *The Haskins Society Journal*, 24 (2012), 95–126.

[48] *DeL*, pp. 134–5: 'Quidam vero hoc interpretantes aiebant gentem illam ferocem et indomitam, alieni cupidam, licet tunc sub specie peregrinationis et religionis, sitim sanguinis humani nondum deposuisse.'

[49] G.J.C. Snoek, *Medieval Piety from Relics to the Eucharist: A Process of Mutual Interaction* (Leiden, 1995), pp. 315–20; C.W. Bynum, *Christian Materiality: An Essay on Religion in Late Medieval Europe* (New York, NY, 2011), p. 144. Peter Browe collected over one hundred twelfth- and thirteenth-century Eucharist miracles in P. Browe, *Die eucharistischen Wunder des Mittelalters* (Breslau, 1938).

matter and animated materiality.[50] Permanent host transformations (meaning those which remained bloody or flesh-like) were occasionally stored with relics, and the change undergone by the Lisbon host appears to have been similarly enduring; it was visible to the public for 'many days' in a way reminiscent of the treatment of relics.[51] As well as its representation, the function of the Lisbon *eulogia* miracle also appears similar to these later host miracles described by Bynum, which were commonly perceived to have occurred in response to some abuse done against God, often in the form of some ill committed against the Eucharist itself. While the *eulogia* was not consecrated, as the Eucharist was, its mysterious bloodiness is nonetheless interpreted along similar lines, as punishment for the abuse of 'pilgrimage and religion'. We might therefore view this as a quasi-Eucharistic miracle, insofar as it both looks and functions similarly to its more commonly attested miraculous counterpart, despite the theological differences between the blessed and the consecrated bread. By identifying the Flemings as the recipients of God's wrath, as communicated through the bleeding *eulogia*, Raol simultaneously distances the Anglo-Norman contingent of which he was part from aspects of the conquest which received criticism, while demonstrating divine investment in the enterprise and preparing the reader for the behaviour of the Germans and the Flemings during the looting of the city of Lisbon: a theme to which *De expugnatione* frequently returns from this point onwards in the narrative.

Raol later describes the men of Cologne and the Flemings as having 'an innate covetousness of possessing', and explains how they tricked the Anglo-Normans and reneged on an agreement about the distribution of spoils following the city's conquest.[52] In a similar way to the signs in the *De expugnatione* discussed above (the storm and the cloud battle), the bloodied *eulogia* reveals a certain anxiety surrounding the actions of elements of the crusade army and the impact that this behaviour might have on the contemporary reception of their diversion to Lisbon. Indeed, Stephen Lay has argued that this emphasis on the personal motives of the crusaders suggests that warfare against Muslims was not considered meritorious in and of itself, and Raol's use of the miraculous to align the Lisbon campaign more closely with crusading supports this conclusion.[53]

Other miracles in the *De expugnatione* include a description of how the capture of the city's suburbs by a numerically inferior crusader force was achieved by a 'clear miracle' ('evidenti miraculo'). This phrase is repeated when Raol notes

---

[50] See Bynum, *Christian Materiality*, p. 21.
[51] C.W. Bynum, *Wonderful Blood: Theology and Practice in Late Medieval Germany and Beyond* (Philadelphia, 2007), pp. 183–4, and *Christian Materiality*, p. 144; Snoek, *Medieval Piety*, p. 318.
[52] *DeL*, pp. 170–1: 'Colonenses vero et Flandrenses quibus semper habendi innata cupiditas...'
[53] S. Lay, 'Miracles, Martyrs and the Cult of Henry the Crusader in Lisbon', *Portuguese Studies*, 24.1 (2008), 15.

that it was by a 'clear miracle' that no crusader blood was shed in that operation. Finally, the sudden restoration of the city's food stores to an edible state upon its capture is described as a 'miracle of great wonder'. Each of these contributes towards a narrative of a divinely sponsored endeavour, in a way reminiscent of many narratives of the First Crusade. Indeed, the idea that the crusaders at Lisbon were acting as instruments of God's will is reiterated towards the end of the work, when Raol comments that, 'not in our own righteousness have we overthrown the enemy, but through the great compassion of God'.[54]

Raol's *De expugnatione* simultaneously celebrates and legitimises the conquest of Lisbon by framing it as a divinely sponsored undertaking commensurate with crusade. Other participants in the expedition portrayed the campaign in similar ways. For example, the version of the contemporaneous Lisbon Letter, also known as the 'Teutonic Source', attributed to a priest named Duodechin and addressed to Abbot Cuno of Disibodenberg, describes deceased crusaders at Lisbon as 'our martyrs'.[55] It also relates miracles associated with their burial place, where lights could be seen to mysteriously glow at night, and:

> …two dumb men, well known in the entire army, one on the feast of St Gereon and his holy company, the other on the festival of All Saints, received the use of speech in that same place. We do not mention this from our own inspiration, but on the contrary we have the assent of many and truthful witnesses, we saw it with our own eyes and felt it with our own hands.[56]

Another version of the Lisbon Letter, attributed to Arnulf and addressed to Milo, bishop of Thérouanne, also contains a version of this miracle and identified the dead crusaders as martyrs.[57] Stephen Lay has argued that the confident

---

[54] *DeL*, pp. 182–3: 'Non autem in iustificationibus nostris hostes prostravimus, sed in miseratione Dei multa.'

[55] A full Latin edition of Duodechin's letter is available as part of the 'Annales Sancti Disibodi', ed. G.H. Pertz, *MGH SS* 17, pp. 27–8. On the Lisbon Letter, see Phillips, 'St Bernard of Clairvaux'; S.B. Edgington, 'Albert of Aachen, St Bernard and the Second Crusade', in *The Second Crusade: Scope and Consequences*, ed. J.P. Phillips and M. Hoch (Manchester, 2001), pp. 54–70; Constable, 'The Second Crusade', in *Crusaders and Crusading*, pp. 237–9. For a Latin edition of the letter, see S.B. Edgington, 'The Lisbon Letter of the Second Crusade', *Historical Research*, 69 (1996), 336–9; translated in 'Albert of Aachen, St Bernard and the Second Crusade', pp. 61–70.

[56] 'Annales Sancti Disibodi', p. 28: 'Duo praeterea muti in toto exercitu bene cogniti, unus in festo sancti Gereonis et eius sanctae societatis, alius in festivitate omnium sanctorum in eodem loco locutionis usum receperunt. Quod nos de spiritu nostro non proferimus, immo multis et vera cibus asstipulati testibus, oculis nostris vidimus et manibus attrectavimus.' English translation is from Edgington, 'Albert of Aachen, St Bernard and the Second Crusade', p. 67.

[57] 'De Ulixbona Saracensis erepta', ed. M.M-.M-.J. Brial, *Recueil des Historiens des Gaules et de la France*, 14 (Paris, 1877), p. 327.

representation of the conquest of Lisbon as divinely sanctioned in the Lisbon letters contrasts with the more tentative Raol, whom, he argues, revealed a more ambivalent attitude towards that endeavour.[58] However, the frequent use of the miraculous in the *De expugnatione* is not, I believe, indicative of authorial antipathy, should the reality of such a thing ever be accessible through narrative. Rather, any concerns or doubts raised by the text can be more firmly situated with Raol's intended audience, as it is ambivalence from that quarter which can be seen to be anticipated by the narrative agenda.

Raol offers a triumphal narrative in his *De expugnatione*, but one which repeatedly hints at contemporaneous concerns surrounding the legitimacy of the Lisbon campaign. By including frequent discussion of the miraculous, he presents the campaign as divinely sponsored; the crusaders were enacting God's will, in an embattled region of Christendom, with God exercising agency in their support. In its frequent recourse to the miraculous, the *De expugnatione* appears to mirror the techniques of several First Crusade narratives, though it is unclear whether he had access to specific texts. Unlike those existing narratives however, the *De expugnatione*'s claims to divine agency often address anticipated ambivalences on the part of the intended audience. For example, on one occasion, a punitive miracle serves to single out a group of crusaders as the recipients of divine wrath, in the service of the narrative's concern to highlight the importance of unity and right intention among the crusaders. The *De expugnatione*, therefore, is an example of how the miraculous could serve not only to legitimise, but to prove that a military campaign was, in fact, a crusade.

The *translatio* of Constantinopolitan Relics

A significant proportion of Latin narrative sources for the Fourth Crusade were produced with the intention of recording the means by which relics were acquired from Constantinople and transported to their new devotional sites in the West.[59] The justificatory frameworks employed in many of these narratives often rely on the miraculous to serve as proof of divine approbation. While the theft of relics had been an accepted and licit aspect of Christian devotional practice since Late Antiquity (the very fact of a relic acquiescing to its removal being proof of the approval of the saint in question), the circumstances in which the

---

[58] Lay, 'Miracles, Martyrs and the Cult of Henry', 14–18.
[59] On the translation of Constantinopolitan relics to Europe after the Fourth Crusade, see especially M. Barber, 'The Impact of the Fourth Crusade in the West: The Distribution of Relics after 1204', in *Urbs Capta: The Fourth Crusade and its Consequences*, ed. A.E. Laiou (Paris, 2005), pp. 325–34; Perry, *Sacred Plunder*, pp. 325–32; and A.E. Lester, 'Translation and Appropriation: Greek Relics in the Latin West in the Aftermath of the Fourth Crusade', *Studies in Church History*, 53 (2017), 88–117.

Constantinopolitan relics had been acquired appear to have stimulated particularly rigorous legitimation in narrative renderings of those events.[60] Even at the turn of the thirteenth century, a century which would witness a great diversification of crusading, a significant number of western Europeans would have viewed the use of a crusade force against Christians as a perversion.[61] The papacy's position on the events of 1204 swung between extremes, with Innocent III's initially positive response souring as news of the nature of the sack of the city reached him. In a letter dated 12 July 1205, addressed to the crusade's papal legate Cardinal Peter Capuano, Innocent strongly voiced his disapproval of the crusaders' actions, stating that the Greeks were right to detest them more than dogs. Among the crimes committed by the crusaders, according to Innocent, were the theft of church property, and of particular relevance to this discussion, the carrying away of relics.[62]

The acquisition of relics during the crusader sack of Constantinople was problematic for additional reasons. According to the participant Robert of Clari, the crusade leaders had forbidden the looting of religious property before the final attack on Constantinople, and presumably this included relics.[63] In addition, another participant, Geoffrey of Villehardouin, records that the crusaders swore an oath that any looted material must be handed over for redistribution on pain of excommunication or death.[64] Thus, the relics which did find their way back to the West flaunted not only a basic tenet of the crusading movement until that point, but the commands of the crusade's leadership. Consequently, the narrative justifications for these relics represent a comprehensive defence of their procurement, as well as offering a 'pedigree' for the relics in their new devotional landscapes. Integral to this was the legitimising power of the miraculous, the means through which the divine will might be communicated and made manifest to humankind.

Many of the sources in question emphasise the implicit agreement, or even agency, of the saints in having their relics moved by a certain individual to a certain location. Assumed within this is the suggestion that the erstwhile Greek custodians of those relics were deemed unworthy by the saints themselves,

---

[60] Patrick Geary has identified the relic thefts of 1204 as the apogee of the centuries-old tradition of Italian acquisition of Greek relics. P.J. Geary, *Furta Sacra: Thefts of Relics in the Central Middle Ages*, revised edn (Princeton, NJ, 1990), p. 87.

[61] A.E. Laiou, 'Byzantium and the Crusades in the Twelfth Century: Why Was the Fourth Crusade Late in Coming?', in *Urbs Capta*, pp. 37, 40.

[62] *Die Register Innocenz' III*, 8.127(126), p. 232.

[63] Robert of Clari, *La Conquête de Constantinople*, ed. and trans. P. Noble (Edinburgh, 2005), pp. 84–5.

[64] Ibid.; Geoffrey of Villehardouin, *La conquête de Constantinople*, ed. E. Faral, 2 vols (Paris, 1938), 2, p. 56; Also discussed in A.J. Andrea, trans., *The Capture of Constantinople, The* Hystoria Constantinopolitana *of Gunther of Pairis* (Philadelphia, PA, 1997), p. 16.

justifying the theft. Alberic of Trois-Fontaines, for example, records that the crusader capture of a Greek icon carried into battle by the patriarch at Philia occurred because God had withdrawn his support from the Greeks.[65] Yet this explanatory mechanism rarely seems to have sufficed in isolation, as indicated by repeated appeals to the miraculous, and its capacity as proof of the divine disposition. A miracle might occur at various points during the translation of a relic. For example, a miracle might facilitate the acquisition of a relic or its safe transportation via land and sea despite numerous hazards, or support those who took or were entrusted with it. Similarly, miracles which occur at the relic's new home might communicate the saint's approval of that location. A third way in which the miraculous might bolster a *translatio* narrative is through the emphasis of the crusade's sanctity, thereby highlighting the divine sponsorship of the events which facilitated the relic thefts.

The Anonymous of Soissons' account of the Fourth Crusade features rich examples of miracles communicating the legitimacy of relic thefts, although the stance taken in the *De terra Iherosolimitana* regarding the righteousness of the crusaders' actions at Constantinople is tentative in comparison with the confident assertions of, for example, Gunther of Pairis's *Hystoria Constantinopolitana*.[66] The Anonymous presents the outcome of events as fundamentally predicated upon acts of divine clemency and punishment in response to the actions of the crusaders themselves, which in turn indicates divine investment in the endeavour. It was as a result of 'God's mercy' that the first of the crusaders leapt from the siege engines onto the city walls during the siege of Constantinople.[67] Similarly, it was by the mercy of God that the Greeks surrendered the city and Baldwin of Flanders and Hainaut was crowned emperor. However, the Anonymous only moves beyond such phrases and towards more detailed accounts of the miraculous once the narrative's central protagonist, Nivelon of Chérisy, bishop of Soissons, has transported the Constantinopolitan relics back to Soissons.

The relics in question, presented in two separate lists, were gifted by Nivelon to the cathedral church of the holy martyrs Gervasius and Protasius (the cathedral at Soissons), the Benedictine nunnery at Notre-Dame de Soissons,

---

[65] Alberic of Trois-Fontaines, 'Chronica Albrici', p. 883.

[66] Alfred Andrea and Paul Rachlin have argued that *De terra Iherosolimitana* represents both a *translatio* and a theodical reflection on the conquest of Constantinople. See A.J. Andrea and P.I. Rachlin, 'Holy War, Holy Relics, Holy Theft: The Anonymous of Soisson's *De terra Iherosolimitana*: An Analysis, Edition, and Translation', *Historical Reflections*, 18.1 (1992), 147–56.

[67] Anonymous of Soissons, 'De terra Iherosolimitana et quomodo ab urbe Constantinopolitana ad hanc ecclesiam allate sunt reliquie', in *Contemporary Sources for the Fourth Crusade: Revised Edition*, ed. and trans. A.J. Andrea (Leiden, 2008), p. 341.

the abbey of Saint John at Laon, and the Cistercian abbey of Longpont.[68] All of these recipient institutions were situated within the diocese of Soissons. At the cathedral, the Anonymous records, the ill and infirm were healed from the day the relics arrived onwards. A specific example is offered, wherein an elderly blind man has his sight restored to him, despite having been unable to see for many years.[69] Thus, the Anonymous of Soissons utilises the miraculous in order to justify Nivelon of Soissons' – and indeed the various churches of Soissons' – acquisition of the relics, by demonstrating the saint's acquiescence in the translation of the relics.

Another anonymous account, the *Gesta Episcoporum Halberstadensium*, achieves the same effect by the same means. Namely, Bishop Conrad's return to Halberstadt with Constantinopolitan relics brings unity, order and plenty to an area fraught with schism and hunger. This is attributed to the 'marvellous judgement of God', namely, that God should allow Conrad to translate the saints' remains to Halberstadt.[70]

A third example, the *Historia translationum reliquiarum S. Mamantis*, while focusing more on demonstrating the authenticity of the relic in question, as we shall see in Chapter 4, also employs the miraculous to demonstrate the relic's efficacy in its new home which, by extension, justified the actions of the translator Walon of Dampierre. On the journey from Constantinople, the ship carrying the relic and its custodian is miraculously spared from a storm.[71] Once at Langres, the relic is credited with miraculously extinguishing a fire in the village and punishing a priest for his concubinage by withering his right hand (which is then miraculously cured following the demonstration of adequate contrition and penance).[72]

Many of these texts, commissioned in the wake of the Fourth Crusade and comprising elements redolent of historical and hagiographical *translatio* narratives, were intended to record a relic's authenticity and provenance, and underscore the saints' acquiescence in the translation of their relics following the crusader sack of Constantinople. In texts like the *De terra Iherosolimitana*, the demonstration of the crusade's divine sponsorship is a key aspect of this. Thus, miracles represented an important tool for the authors not only of *translatio* narrative, but of *translatio* narratives which record the translation of relics acquired as a result of problematic circumstances such as those presented by the

---

[68] Ibid, pp. 341–3.

[69] Ibid, p. 342.

[70] 'Gesta episcoporum Halberstadensium', ed. L. Weiland, *MGH SS*, 23, p. 120.

[71] Anonymous of Langres, 'Historia translationum reliquiarum S. Mamantis', in *Exuviae sacrae Constantinopolitanae*, vol. 1, ed. P. Riant (Geneva, 1877–88, reprinted Paris, 2004), pp. 31–2.

[72] Ibid, pp. 32–3.

Fourth Crusade. As we shall see, vision and prophecy are also common ingredients in narrative justifications of the Fourth Crusade and its outcomes.

Conclusion

The miraculous does not disappear from the narrative histories of failed or controversial crusades. While, after the successes of the First Crusade, the miraculous could no longer represent such an easily communicable narrative scaffold, a miracle comprised of miracles, it did remain an important aspect of many crusade histories. Miracles, phenomena which by their very nature are indicative of divine agency, were used in the representation of individuals, like Bernard of Clairvaux and Louis VII, despite the failure or problematic nature of the crusades with which they are associated. Rather, when an author sought to argue for an expedition's legitimacy, as with the 1147 conquest of Lisbon or the 1204 conquest of Constantinople, the miraculous represented a significant ingredient in the author's rhetorical repertoire. What better way to prove that an expedition was indeed divinely sanctioned – an idea so central to the nature of crusading – than by associating it with the miraculous? Finally, the examination of the miraculous in representations of less successful crusading ventures has revealed the increased scope for punitive divine agency: the interventionist punishment of crusaders by miraculous means, which represented a step beyond the general attribution of failure and setbacks to crusaders' sins. Between the closing years of the eleventh century and the opening decades of the thirteenth, the challenges facing those who chose to write historical narrative about crusades changed, and the form and function of the miraculous changed to meet these.

PART II

Visions and Dreams

3

The Mockery of Dreams

Visions, Dreams and the Spaces in Between

Visions temporarily flung back the curtain of mundanity that shrouded the human senses and allowed the visionary to perceive the usually imperceptible, including the saints and Christ himself. Unlike other, everyday experiences of the sacred in Latin Christendom, such as the elevation of the Eucharist during Mass, visionary experiences and their interpretation were free from the intermediary and regulatory influence of the Church. They offered unmediated access to the divine. Consequently, visionaries had the potential to garner significant popular influence. In much the same way as the ascetic holy man of the late antique Byzantine Empire, the visionary Latin Christian of the Middle Ages derived power from this proximity.[1] The Latin Church of medieval Europe jealously guarded its monopoly on access to, and interpretation of, the divine, and recognised the importance of being able to distinguish the truly revelatory from the falsified or misconstrued. This was a particular concern for the Latin Church because of the ubiquity of the vision's typically mundane, yet experientially analogous, cousin: the dream.[2] Dreams, phenomena also believed to offer an opportunity to perceive the sacred or uncanny, shared many characteristics with visions. Further, most people would have been able to recollect something of their sleeping sensory experiences on a daily basis regardless of status or learning. The problem with the resulting blurring between the two phenomena lay in the potential for the mundane to be credited with revelatory significance.

In addition to the problematic ubiquity of dreams was the idea that dreams were themselves capable of being deceptive or of demonic forces wielding them deliberately on account of their ability to mimic the revelatory. Thus, Chapter 34 of Ecclesiasticus notes how 'dreams lift up fools', and have 'deceived many', explicitly identifying dreams (*somnia*) as an untrustworthy category of experience.[3] It was not sufficient to conclude, however, that all dreams were insignificant or deceptive, and that all one needed to do to ascertain authenticity was to determine whether the individual had been asleep at the time of the experience.

[1] P. Brown, 'The Rise and Function of the Holy Man in Late Antiquity', *The Journal of Roman Studies*, 61 (1971), 80–101.
[2] J.-C. Schmitt, *Ghosts in the Middle Ages: The Living and the Dead in Medieval Society*, trans. T.L. Fagan (London, 1998), p. 42.
[3] Ecclesiasticus 34.7.

This is because there was undeniable scriptural precedent indicating that dreams could themselves be revelatory.[4] In Chapter 12 of the Book of Numbers the Lord told Moses, Aaron and Miriam: 'if there be among you a prophet of the Lord, I will appear to him in a vision, or I will speak to him in a dream'.[5] The message here is clear: it was perfectly possible for God to communicate with humans via both dreams *and* visions. Thus, the conceptual blurring between visions and dreams as vehicles for revelatory experience was such that a medieval text might reasonably refer to a dream involving supernatural elements as a vision, and a vision occurring during sleep as a dream.[6]

The relationship between these experiential categories does not appear to have sat comfortably with certain medieval authors, or at least among their anticipated audiences. Odo of Cluny (d. 942), a Cluniac abbot who wrote a *vita* of Gerald of Aurillac in the tenth century, argued that 'the visions of dreams are not always vain. And if faith is to be put in sleep, it seems that this vision agrees in its result with future events'.[7] Odo's defence of dreams as potentially revelatory, pending the proof offered by an eventual outcome, suggests an anticipation of sceptical contemporaneous views. This nod to the problematic nature of dreams taps into an already longstanding discourse on the relationship between the mundane, demonic and revelatory dream, one that extended back to the pre-Christian, classical and Hellenistic past of the Greek and Roman philosophers. Aristotle, Plato, Cicero and Lucretius all theorised on these issues.[8] In the early third century CE, Tertullian produced a coherent Christian treatise on dreams in the form of Chapters 45–49 of his *De anima*.[9] He posited three categories of dream: demonically inspired, prophetic and circumstantial. Thus, while the potential for revelatory dreams was recognised, he situated this alongside other, distinctly non-divine, causations. Efforts were also made to address the disquiet caused by apparent similarities between visions and dreams. Isidore of Seville, writing in the early seventh century, emphasised that, while both perfectly valid forms of

---

[4]   C.M. Carty, 'The Role of Medieval Dream Images in Authenticating Ecclesiastical Construction', *Zeitschrift für Kunstheschichte*, 62 (1999), 45–90. For a list of Old Testament dreams, see Le Goff, *The Medieval Imagination*, pp. 229–31.

[5]   Numbers 12.6.

[6]   Adams, *Visions in Late Medieval England*, p. 176.

[7]   Odo of Cluny, 'De Vita Sancti Geraldi Auriliacensis Comitis', *PL*, 133, col. 643: 'Siquidem somniurum visiones non semper sunt inanes. Et si somno fides adhibenda est, videtur haec visio rerum effectui convenire futurarum.' English translation adapted from G. Sitwell, trans., *St. Odo of Cluny: Being the Life of St. Odo of Cluny by John of Salerno and the Life of St. Gerald of Aurillac by St. Odo* (London, 1958), p. 95.

[8]   Kruger, *Dreaming*, p. 18.

[9]   On Tertullian and the theology of dreams, see Le Goff, *The Medieval Imagination*, pp. 207–10.

prophecy, visions and dreams were discrete phenomena.[10] As Odo's tenth-century defence of revelatory dreams indicates, however, dreams continued to represent a problematic, potentially inferior, category of experience.

One of the most influential theoretical reconciliations of visions and dreams to circulate in medieval Europe, especially from the twelfth century onwards, was Macrobius Ambrosius Theodosius' *Commentarii in Somnium Scipionis*, written in around 430 CE.[11] Numerous medieval texts, including certain crusade narratives discussed below, echo the *Commentarii*'s ideas surrounding dreams and visions, so it is worthwhile to establish the key aspects of these here.[12] The *Commentarii* featured a detailed dream schema derived from the work of several authorities, particularly Artemidorus (second century CE). It identifies visions and dreams as experiences within a complex schema of dream types ranging from the utterly mundane to the truly revelatory, with visions situated above dreams.[13] Macrobius proposed a schema of five dream types, which are (from the mundane to the revelatory): the nightmare (*insomnium*), apparition (*visum*), enigmatic dream (*somnium*), prophetic vision (*visio*) and oracular vision (*oraculum*).[14] He attaches 'no prophetic significance' to nightmares and apparitions; they represent the mundane end of the spectrum. Nightmares, Macrobius writes, are often caused by excessive eating or drinking or by anxiety or distress. Apparitions, by contrast, are an affliction of the state between sleeping and waking. For example, Macrobius suggests, *ephialtes* would fall into this category (a waking nightmare-like state in which subjects feel a weight upon their chest, later interpreted as demonic, and more recently as sleep paralysis).[15] Neither of these two experiences is identified as being of revelatory significance, though the *visum* reaches out fractionally towards the higher types on account of its existence beyond individual psychological process, into the realms of (albeit delusory) reality.[16]

[10] Isidore of Seville, *Isidori Hispalensis Episcopi Etymologiarum sive Originum Libri XX*, ed. W.M. Lindsay (Oxford, 1911), 7.8, lines 33–4.

[11] A. Cameron, 'The Date and Identity of Macrobius', *The Journal of Roman Studies*, 56.1–2 (1966), 25–38.

[12] W.H. Stahl, trans., *Commentary on the Dreams of Scipio* (New York, NY, 1990), pp. 87–8, n. 1. The most recent English translation of Artemidorus's *Oneirocritica* is R.J. White, trans., *The Interpretation of Dreams: Oneirocritica*, 2nd edn (Park Ridge, NJ, 1990). For an edition of the Greek see Artemidorus Daldianus, *Artemidori Daldiani Onirocriticon Libri V*, ed. R.A. Pack (Leipzig, 1963).

[13] Kruger, *Dreaming*, p. 35.

[14] Macrobius Ambrosius Theodosius, *Macrobius, Vol. II. Commentarii in Somnium Scipionis*, ed. J. Willis (Leipzig, 1970), pp. 8–10.

[15] Ibid., p. 10. See M. van der Lugt, 'The *Incubus* in Scholastic Debate: Medicine, Theology and Popular Belief', in *Religion and Medicine in the Middle Ages*, ed. P. Biller and J. Ziegler (York, 2001), pp. 175–200, esp. pp. 186–91.

[16] Kruger, *Dreaming*, p. 22.

These categories mirror those phenomena that Tertuillian would attribute to circumstantial or demonic causes.

At the centre of the Macrobian dream schema, connecting rather than separating the realms of the mundane and the revelatory, is the enigmatic dream, or *somnium*.[17] This is a dream that presents truth in a concealed or ambiguous manner; interpretation is required to arrive at its meaning. While this type of experience may yield a truth eventually, after its couching fiction is subjected to proper elucidation, it cannot communicate meaning as clearly or directly as the higher dream types. Above the *somnium* is the prophetic *visio*, in which an image of everyday events reveals a truth that the dreamer could not have otherwise known. The vision proves to be revelatory when those events transpire. It is this logic, that a revelation is authenticated when events occur as prophesied, that Odo describes in his *vita*. Above the prophetic vision, and described as the highest form of dream by Macrobius, is the oracular vision. These impart knowledge upon the dreamer through a figure of authority, such as a holy individual, saint, or divinity. Because of its delivery, the truth of the *oraculum* is self-evidently divine in origin.[18] While the term *oraculum* rarely appears in medieval sources, and its meaning often appears to collapse into that of *visio*, discussions that situate visions above dreams in their proximity to the revelatory do reflect the influence of hierarchical understandings like Macrobius'.

While Macrobius' schema did not receive widespread attention in western Europe until the twelfth century, Augustine of Hippo's various treatises on the subject were of perennial influence.[19] Augustine's consideration of visions represents an effort to provide a thoroughly Christian epistemology, which moves beyond the classification of dream types towards an analysis of the mechanisms, physical or otherwise, of sight.[20] In his *De Genesi ad litteram*, Augustine describes a threefold typology of vision: corporeal, spiritual and intellectual.[21] The first of these, corporeal sight, refers to the ability to behold something with one's own bodily senses, namely the eyes. If this first means of perception was the most mundane, then intellectual vision, at the opposite end of the spectrum, represented the highest. This intuitive form of sight enables one to perceive a concept and denotes the means by which one might contemplate God. Spiritual sight, which sits between these two poles in Augustine's schema, denotes how one might perceive the semblances of things within one's own mind. This spiritual

---

[17] Macrobius, *Commentarii in Somnium Scipionis*, p. 10.

[18] Ibid.

[19] The twelfth century appears to have been the apogee of the popularity of Macrobius' dream schema. See A.M. Peden, 'Macrobius and Medieval Dream Literature', *Medium Aevum*, 54 (1985), 59–73.

[20] Kruger, *Dreaming*, p. 36; Peden, 'Macrobius', p. 59.

[21] See Keskiaho, *Dreams and Visions*, pp. 137–50.

sight appears most closely aligned to the processes inherent in dream vision. The highest type, intellectual perception, was essentially nonvisual but enabled an individual to interpret the other two types accurately. Augustine elaborates:

> When we read this one commandment, *You shall love your neighbor as yourself,* we experience three kinds of vision: one through the eyes, by which we see the letters; a second through the spirit, by which we think of our neighbor even when he is absent; and a third through an intuition of the mind, by which we see and understand love itself.[22]

In seeking to elucidate his stance regarding intellectual sight, he continues:

> But in the case of love, is it seen in one manner when present, in the form in which it exists [i.e. physical sight], and in another manner when absent, in an image resembling it [i.e. spiritual sight]? Certainly not. But in proportion to the clarity of our intellectual vision, love itself is seen by one more clearly, by another less so. If, however, we think of some corporeal image, it is not love that we behold.[23]

Consequently, Augustine subsumes both mundane and revelatory dreams within the 'middleness' of spiritual vision, and by doing so emphasises their ambiguity. Intellectual vision moves that which is spiritually perceived to the status of the reliable or prophetic.[24] The efficacy of this highest form of vision is dependent upon the level of personal enlightenment.

Spiritual vision, as defined by Augustine, emphasises the mental environment of these experiences, and the nature of spiritually perceived objects as images or apparitions in the semblance of known forms. This was part of Augustine's broader contention that the dead could in no way appear to the living in bodily form.[25] When an individual saw a dead person in a vision or dream, they saw

---

[22] Augustine of Hippo, *De Genesi ad Litteram, Libri Duodecim*, ed. and trans. P. Agaësse and A. Solignac, 7th series (Oeuvres de Saint Augustin, 49; Brussels, 1972), pp. 346–8: 'Ecce in hoc uno praecepto cum legitur: diliges proximum tuum tamquam te ipsum, tria uisionem generas occurrunt: unum per oculos, quibus ipsae litterae uidentur, alterum per spiritum hominis, quo proximus et absens cogitatur, tertium per contuitum mentis, quo ipsa dilectio intellecta conspicitur.' English translation is from Augustine of Hippo, *The Literal Meaning of Genesis, Volume II, Books 7–12*, trans. J.H. Taylor (New York, NY, 1982), p. 185.

[23] Augustine of Hippo, *De Genesi ad Litteram*, pp. 350–2: 'Dilectio autem numquid aliter uidetur praesens in specie, qua est, et aliter absens in aliqua imagine sui simili? Non utique. Sed quantum mente cerni potest, ab alio magis, ab alio minus ipsa cernitur; si autem aliquid corporalis imaginis cogitatur, non ipsa cernitur'. English translation is from Augustine of Hippo, *The Literal Meaning of Genesis*, p. 186.

[24] Kruger, *Dreaming*, pp. 35–43.

[25] Schmitt, *Ghosts*, pp. 17–27.

a mere image: an apparition. The dead individual was not physically present. Saints represented a perplexing exception to this rule, and Augustine appears to have been undecided whether saints appeared of their own volition or through the proxy of angels, concluding only that such instances were miraculous.[26]

The pervasiveness of ideas like those of Macrobius and Augustine in medieval Latin Christian thought cannot be quantified with any precision. Nonetheless, we can see that such authorities could, and did, inform some of the discourse on dreams and visions from the central Middle Ages. This influence is at its clearest in texts which explicitly discuss those ideas, such as John of Salisbury's *Policraticus* (written 1156–9) and Caesarius of Heisterbach's *Dialogus miraculorum* (1219–23). The *Policraticus* provides several illuminating examples of how an author and philosopher educated in the schools of Paris and Chartres in the twelfth century might apply theoretical authorities on visions and dreams. In his lengthy consideration of the authenticity of dreams, John has clear recourse to Macrobius' *Commentarii*. However, the influence of Augustine's vision typology is also visible. John writes, in words evocative of Macrobius', that there are manifold types, causes, forms and meanings of dreams.[27] He reproduces the Macrobian hierarchy, concluding that the *visio* and the *oraculum* present a visible truth, while the intermediate *somnium* is the most common, its truth shrouded as if by a curtain. John is careful to point out, however, that his description of the methods of interpreting dreams should not be misconstrued as approval of that practice. Whosoever, he continues, involves themselves in the 'deception of dreams' is not awake to God's law. He concludes that those who so enjoy divine favour to the extent that they are capable of interpreting allegorical dreams should join the biblical Daniel and Joseph in attributing that ability to God.[28] The idea that the accurate interpretation of such experiences is dependent upon divine favour parallels Augustine's argument that intellectual vision, required for the interpretation of that which is spiritually perceived, is dependent upon enlightenment. While John therefore employs both Macrobian and Augustinian theories of dreams and visions, he subordinates the Macrobian emphasis on the individual's inherent ability to divine in sleep to the Augustinian dependency upon knowledge of God.

The Cistercian monk Caesarius of Heisterbach (d. *c.* 1240) was also influenced by the Macrobian dream schema and Augustinian vision typologies.[29] In Book

---

[26] Augustine of Hippo, 'De cura pro mortuis gerenda ad Paulinum', *PL*, 40, 16.19–20, cols. 606–7. See also Keskiaho, *Dreams and Visions*, pp. 77–81.

[27] John of Salisbury, *Policraticus I–IV*, ed. K.S.B. Keats-Rohan (CCCM, 118; Turnhout, 1993), p. 94. On John of Salisbury and his *Policraticus*, see especially C.J. Nederman, ed. and trans., *John of Salisbury: Policraticus, Of the Frivolities of Courtiers and the Footprints of Philosophers* (Cambridge, 1990), pp. xv–xxvi.

[28] John of Salisbury, *Policraticus*, pp. 99–104.

[29] On Caesarius' *Dialogus miraculorum*, see especially V. Smirnova, M.A. Polo de

Eight of the *Dialogus miraculorum*, and in an echo of Macrobius, Caesarius writes that dreams can be caused by such mundane factors as excessive indulgence, and such revelatory influences as the divine. Caesarius also discusses Augustine's threefold schema of vision types.[30] For Caesarius, echoing Augustine's intellectual vision, contemplation of God was the key to revelatory vision.[31] Thus the *Policraticus* and the *Dialogus miraculorum* reveal recourse, on the part of both the secular and monastic clergy, to Platonic and Patristic authorities on visions and dreams in the central Middle Ages. Indeed, and as will now be demonstrated, crusade narratives also offer examples of the application of these ideas.

Dream Theory in Crusade Narrative

Crusade narratives discuss visions and dreams in numerous different ways, revealing that the people by, about, and for whom these texts were written had access to a multiplicity of ways of thinking about these phenomena. Certain crusade narratives can even be seen to engage with vision and dream theory. They were, after all, products of the same intellectual landscape as the works of, for example, John of Salisbury and Caesarius of Heisterbach. Further, crusade narratives represent rich sources for examining discussions of visions and dreams because many of their authors intended these texts as histories of divinely orchestrated events. Therefore, discussions of divine communications in the form of visions and revelatory dreams are relatively common. It is important to note, however, that even authors who appear to have read authorities like Macrobius and Augustine were not passively rehearsing those theories in their work; they interpreted and applied these schemata and hierarchies in various ways, and often in service of their narrative agendas.[32]

While Colin Morris has identified that the terminology used in crusade narratives to discuss visions and dreams is often imprecise and interchangeable, there is evidence to suggest that this observation requires nuance.[33] It is clear

---

Beaulieu and J. Berlioz, eds., *The Art of Cistercian Persuasion in the Middle Ages and Beyond: Caesarius of Heisterbach's Dialogue on Miracles and Its Reception* (Leiden, 2015). On Caesarius' work in relation to the crusades, see W.J. Purkis, 'Crusading and Crusade Memory in Caesarius of Heisterbach's *Dialogus miraculorum*', *Journal of Medieval History*, 39 (2013), 100–27, and 'Memories of the Preaching for the Fifth Crusade in Caesarius of Heisterbach's *Dialogus miraculorum*', *Journal of Medieval History*, 40.3 (2014), 329–45.

[30] Caesarius of Heisterbach, *Caesarii Heisterbacensis monachi ordinis Cisterciensis Dialogus miraculorum*, ed. J. Strange, vol. 2 (Cologne and Bonn, 1851), pp. 80–3.

[31] Caesarius of Heisterbach, *Dialogus miraculorum*, vol. 2, pp. 83–4.

[32] See Keskiaho, *Dreams and Visions*.

[33] Morris, 'Policy and Visions', p. 39, n. 21.

that at least some authors were capable of sophisticated engagement with Macrobian and Augustinian theory, and that this is reflected in their use of specific terminology. It does not necessarily follow that the authors of crusade narrative interpreted authorities 'correctly', or more accurately, as the authors of those authorities had intended, or that their own representations were consistent throughout. Nevertheless, it remains beneficial to be aware of the potential for the authors of crusade narrative to have engaged with theoretical discourses on dreams and visions, and to have utilised the associated terminology with nuanced conceptual differentiations in mind. Such an awareness allows us to access aspects of the lexical texture of a representation of a dream or vision that would otherwise go unnoticed.

Gunther of Pairis (d. *c.* 1210), a Cistercian monk who wrote an account of the Fourth Crusade centred on his patron Abbot Martin of Pairis, demonstrates an understanding of Macrobius' schema, and appears at pains to make his erudition on this and other matters obvious to his audience. He does this by interrupting his narrative to offer elaborations on various themes, interspersing his *Hystoria Constantinopolitana* not only with allusions to scripture and to the literary works of such classical authorities as Homer, Virgil and Ovid, but also with references to the philosophical works of Augustine and Orosius.[34] That Gunther chose to engage with dream theory as one of the ways in which he might, in Francis Swietek's words, 'parade his erudition', suggests that the intricacies of such schemata would have been known well enough in intellectual circles to serve as an indicator of learning.[35] To make his acquaintance with Macrobius' work explicit, Gunther includes a defence of visions experienced during sleep, much like Odo, in one of his many verse interludes, where he writes:

> Many an image comes to us in the course of the night,
> At the time when we take in dreams with full intensity,
> Some are fantasies, called in Greek *fantasmata*;
> If a dream betokens reality of indisputable events to any extent,
> It is usually accorded one of two names: vision or prophetic dream.
> I believe the vision that, I have often read, was seen by the king
> Was such an image of the city's promised splendour.[36]

---

[34] F.R. Swietek, 'Gunther of Pairis and the *Hystoria Constantinopolitana*', *Speculum*, 53.1 (1978), 62–78. Andrea has also argued that, in emphasising his familiarity with classical works, Gunther sought to rival the *Historia Peregrinorum*, the Third Crusade narrative attributed to a monk from Salem, another of the monasteries which, like Pairis, was a daughter house of Lucelle. See Andrea, *The Capture of Constantinople*, p. 35.

[35] Swietek, 'Gunther of Pairis', p. 64.

[36] GP, p. 149: 'Plurima noctivago nobis occurrit ymago,/ Tempore, dum plenis haurimus sompnia venis./ Quedam sunt ficte, Grecis fantasmata dicte./ Si qua notat verum vel

Gunther's evocation of Macrobius is somewhat confused, but nonetheless identifiable. He appears, perhaps on account of his familiarity with classical material, to depart from Macrobius' suggestion that a *visum* was delusory, and favours the antique Roman usage, whereby *visum* was the most commonly used term for any visionary experience. Indeed, at least one of the authors he cites, Virgil, uses *visum* in the latter way.[37] An alternative explanation is that Gunther momentarily sacrificed the accuracy of his retelling of Macrobian dream theory in favour of alliterative flair. This seems likely, given that elsewhere in the narrative, Gunther consistently uses the schematically higher *visio* when discussing visions.

This section of the *Hystoria* constitutes a theoretical preamble to a much longer demonstration of the revelatory potential of dreams, an issue of some importance to Gunther's narrative agenda, as we shall see. The vision of the king that Gunther introduces in the abovementioned verse is in fact a vision allegedly experienced by Constantine the Great, and also known as the 'Loathly Lady' story, in which Constantine sees an old woman in a dream who is later revealed to be a beautiful maiden representing, so Pope Sylvester I later explains, the city of Constantinople. Gunther includes a version of that vision, likely drawn from Aldhelm of Malmesbury's *De virginitate*, in which he calls Constantine's experience a *visio* on no fewer than four occasions.[38] Gunther uses this story to support his argument that experiences that appear insignificant and fleeting, like dreams, could in fact be indicative of great things, and challenge the belief that what one sees while 'sleeping' (*dormiens*) is entirely illusory and devoid of truth.[39] This is a particularly important issue for Gunther given that the *Hystoria* employs vision accounts as part of its broader defence of Abbot Martin's involvement in the Fourth Crusade, and that the efficacy of these visions depends upon an audience's belief in their revelatory status, as the following chapter argues in further detail. In addition to his discussion of dream hierarchies and Constantine's vision, Gunther adds scriptural precedent to his defence of dream visions. He offers the example of the Old Testament Joseph's dream in which his

---

certa negocia rerum,/ Voce solet duplici visum seu visione dici./ Talem premisse speciei credo fuisse/ Effigiem, regi quam visam sepe relegi.' English translation is from Andrea, *The Capture of Constantinople*, pp. 100–1.

[37] See A. Galloway, 'Visions and Visionaries', in *The Oxford Handbook of Medieval Literature in English*, ed. G. Walker and E. Treharne (Oxford, 2010), pp. 257–60.

[38] Gunther refers to the experience as a *visio* four times during the account of the vision itself. GP, pp. 150–1.

[39] GP, pp. 148–9. Cf. Aldhelm of Malmesbury, *Prosa de Virginitate cum Glosa Latina atque Anglosaxonica*, ed. S. Gwara (CCSL, 124A; Turnhout, 2001), pp. 297–321. Another version of this vision can be found in an anonymous *Vita Beati Silvestri*, see Swietek, 'Gunther of Pairis', p. 66, n. 133. See J. Stevenson, 'Constantine, St Aldhelm and the Loathly Lady', in *Constantine: History, Historiography and Legend*, ed. S.N.C. Lieu and D. Montserrat (London, 2002), pp. 189–206.

parents and brothers are represented by the sun, moon and stars as an example of how the great can symbolise the trivial, and Daniel's dream of the kings as beasts for how the lesser might be indicative of the greater.[40] It is striking that Gunther, like John of Salisbury, uses Daniel and Joseph as his key scriptural exemplars of those who might interpret allegorical dreams, given that John's emphasis was on the deceptive qualities of dreams, while Gunther sought to underscore their revelatory potential. Thus, Gunther's *Hystoria Constantinopolitana* reveals the plasticity of dream theory as it is applied in crusade narrative.

Certainly, such clear allusions to theoretical authorities are rare in crusade narratives. Evidence of influence is more common. For example, the author of the *De expugnatione Lyxbonensi*, commonly known as Raol, drew upon various intellectual authorities – including Augustine – as part of his justification of the Lisbon expedition of 1147.[41] During an account of a sermon attributed to the author himself, it is noted that, 'if the eternal light which is seen through the inner eye appears not to the eyes of sinners, it could not be perceived by the minds of the defiled.'[42] This reflects an understanding of the efficacy of spiritual vision as dependent on the individual's piety, as per Augustinian vision theory. Gerald of Wales reveals a similar conceptualisation of spiritual vision in his account of Baldwin of Canterbury's 1188 preaching tour of Wales, the *Itinerarium Kambriae*. He relates a story about a lord whom God had struck blind as punishment for his spending a night in a church with his hunting dogs. He was later conveyed to Jerusalem in order that his 'inner sight' – or more literally 'lamp' – ('interior ... lucerna') should not suffer a similar fate.[43] These brief allusions to inner, non-corporeal vision, the efficacy of which is sensitive to spiritual wellbeing, in other words, the link between an individual's piety and the ability to perceive and interpret dreams and visions, echo Augustine's proposed spiritual and intellectual vision types. This logic, that sanctity facilitates the seeing of visions, is the same as that which allows the experiencing of visions to function as proof, for example in hagiography, of an individual's piety.

While the above discussion has focused on specific terminology associated with visions and dreams, and the echoes of theoretical treatises concerning dreams in historical narrative, it is worth noting that it was possible for the authors of crusade narratives to avoid this lexis and its associated theory altogether. Most of the explicit references to visions in association with the Third Crusade are contained in the *Gesta Regis* and *Chronica* of Roger of Howden. In these, Roger presents visions in literal and formulaic ways. For example, in

---

[40] Genesis 37.9 and Daniel 7.1–28; GP, p. 148.
[41] Phillips, 'Ideas of Crusade and Holy War', pp. 130–3.
[42] *DeL*, pp. 150–1: 'Si enim non appareret oculis peccatorum lumen eternum quod per oculos interiores videtur, mentibus inquinatis videri non posset.'
[43] *Itinerarium Kambriae*, pp. 16–17.

a vision of St Thomas of Canterbury, the saint 'appeared' (*apparere*), and then 'slipped away' from before the witnesses' eyes.[44] Similarly, the Virgin Mary 'appeared' and was later 'torn from their eyes'.[45] This latter passage is from Roger's later *Chronica*; a reworking of his *Gesta Regis*, in which the Virgin's departure takes a slightly different form. In his earlier work, Roger describes how Mary 'ascended into the heavens', whereupon she was 'hidden from their eyes' by bright clouds.[46] The revised version removed the problem of precisely *how* the Virgin disappeared, she simply did. Such examples reveal the difficulties inherent in any attempt to generalise about the visions and dreams of crusade narrative, particularly when it comes to the terminology used. Despite this, and as will now be demonstrated through the analysis of two particular case studies, it is important to at least allow for the possibility that authors were selective in their use of terminology pertaining to visions and dreams. This is because such an approach has the potential to reveal something of the challenges inherent in the narration of revelatory experiences.

Visions and the Holy Lance of Antioch

Of the numerous vision accounts contained in crusades sources, none has received as much attention – either from medieval commentators or modern scholars – as the visions associated with the discovery of the relic of the Holy Lance of Antioch in 1098 by participants of the First Crusade. The numerous narratives which discuss these visions, supposedly experienced by Peter Bartholomew and Stephen of Valence, present a rich corpus of material for assessing how visions and dreams are represented in crusade texts, and for exploring how and why these representations altered over time.

Peter Bartholomew

On 3 June 1098, after a protracted siege, the forces of the First Crusade entered the city of Antioch. They would soon become the besieged themselves. Despite the crusaders' entry into the city, the citadel remained in Muslim hands, and a relief force led by Kerbogha, *atabeg* of Mosul, arrived outside the city walls on 5 June. Thus, beset from both within and without and suffering from an acute shortage of food and supplies, crusader desertions escalated. Amid these travails, on 10 June, a Provençal peasant named Peter Bartholomew sought out the papal legate Adhémar of Le Puy and the Provençal leader Count Raymond of Toulouse in order to inform them of a series of visions he had experienced at intervals since

---

[44] *Chronica* 3, p. 43.
[45] *Chronica* 3, pp. 119–20.
[46] *GR2*, p. 177.

late December 1097. In these visions, Peter explained, St Andrew the apostle had revealed to him the location of the lance used by Longinus to pierce Christ's side at the Crucifixion. The subsequent discovery of the Lance in the basilica of St Peter in Antioch on 14 June ostensibly proved the legitimacy of Peter's claims, and two weeks later the crusader victory against Kerbogha outside the walls of the city reinforced belief in the relic's authenticity. Raymond of Aguilers, the Provençal cleric and chronicler of the crusade, had carried the relic into battle on 28 June in order that it might serve, in the words of John France, as 'a tangible manifestation of God's favour to the crusader army'.[47] Yet such proofs were considered insufficient to many of those present on the expedition, and Peter's continued politicisation of his ongoing visions resulted in his undergoing an ordeal by fire at Arqah on 8 April 1099. The ambiguity surrounding the cause of his death several days later, either as a direct result of his burns or on account of wounds inflicted upon him by an overzealous crowd, enabled Peter's critics and supporters to continue in their opposing stances.

The visions allegedly witnessed by Peter Bartholomew, and the various narrative representations of these events, have received considerable scholarly attention. Key among these is a study by Morris, in which he demonstrates how the crusaders themselves harnessed the influence of Peter Bartholomew in order to mould policy.[48] Integral to this line of reasoning is the potential influence of the medieval visionary, a theme that France engages with in detail in his examination of Peter's 'highly political' revelations.[49] It is precisely this potentiality for political influence, discussed earlier in this chapter, which underpins contemporaneous anxieties regarding legitimacy and proof. The significance that contemporaries might attach to dreams and visions, and by extension to a dreamer or visionary, meant that there was much at stake in correctly sifting the truly revelatory from the mundane or falsified.

The *Gesta Francorum*'s narrative of Peter Bartholomew's visions contains one of the few usages of *visum* as a noun in the corpus of crusade narratives of this period. It describes how St Andrew appeared to Peter to advise him of the location of the lance. At first, Peter was reluctant to tell the other pilgrims what the saint had revealed to him because he believed that he had seen an 'apparition'

---

[47] France, 'Two Types of Vision', p. 11. Recent scholarship has challenged the previously prevailing view that the discovery of the Holy Lance, and the subsequent zeal that this inspired, were directly responsible for the crusader sally from the city. See especially T. Asbridge, 'The Holy Lance of Antioch: Power, Devotion and Memory on the First Crusade', *Reading Medieval Studies*, 33 (2007), 3–36. On the contemporary significance of the Holy Lance, and for a consideration of its portrayal after the twelfth century, see Sweetenham, 'When the Saints Go Marching In'.

[48] Morris, 'Policy and Visions'.

[49] France, 'Two Types of Vision', p. 9.

(*visum*).[50] Implicit in Peter's fear of recounting the story are his suspicions that he had seen something deceptive, a figment of his imagination. Consequently, the use of *visum* here is in line with the Macrobian definition of *visum*: it has no revelatory significance. In the account of Peter Tudebode, thought to be derived from the *Gesta Francorum* or a work very similar to it, the sentence in which Peter Bartholomew feared that he had witnessed a *visum* is transposed verbatim. Notably, in the *Chanson d'Antioche*, Peter initially fears that he has seen a 'ghost' (*fantosme*), which implies the same sort of illusory quality.[51]

However, as we have seen, the *Gesta Francorum* also represents the base text for three more detailed and theologically erudite monastic prose narratives. All three of these derivative Benedictine narratives replace *visum* with the motif of the deceptive dream. In his *Historia Ierosolimitana*, Baldric of Bourgueil writes that Peter feared that the crusaders would not believe him because the vision came to him in the 'manner of a dream'.[52] The couching of the vision within a dream subverts its potential revelatory significance and draws upon the longstanding idea that dreams were problematic vessels for revelations. Peter is no longer concerned that he has seen an apparition, or *visum*, but that it had merely been a dream. It could be argued that Baldric's inclination towards the poetic, which is often manifested in artful alliteration and assonance in his work, renders this alteration insignificant. However, both Guibert of Nogent and Robert the Monk also erase *visum* from their versions. In Guibert's *Dei gesta* Peter Bartholomew initially considers his experience to have been nothing more than the 'mockery of dreams' ('ludibriis somniorum') which so commonly afflicts everyone.[53] Here the *Dei gesta* engages with the concept of the delusory dream as a fiction. Guibert represents Peter as fearful of pursuing the truth couched within this apparent dream. According to Robert the Monk, and in a moment of alliterative artistry, Peter Bartholomew withheld the details of his experiences because he feared that 'he had seen the vision in vain'.[54] Peter makes this statement in direct speech at a later narrative moment, using the more confident *visio* in order to reflect the later conviction that led Peter to confide in certain of the crusade leaders and was ultimately reinforced by the successful *inventio* of the relic.

Visum fell victim to the editorial rigour of all three Benedictine authors, who opted for terminology with a more established Christian pedigree. It is also possible that this decision was influenced by an awareness of the inherent mundanity of an 'apparition' (*visum*), as per Macrobiam dream theory, in comparison to the

---

[50] *GF*, p. 59.

[51] *La Chanson d'Antioche*, laisse 291, p. 770.

[52] BB, p. 70.

[53] GN, p. 221. English translation is from Levine, *The Deeds of God through the Franks*, p. 101.

[54] RM p. 68: '…existimans me vanam visione vidisse'.

revelatory potential of the 'dream' (*somnium*). By using *somnium*, their narratives convey the same illusory quality without the implication of complete mundanity. Thus, the portrayal of Peter as afraid that he had experienced a *somnium* provides grounds for his hesitation (namely, fear of pursuing the interpretation of his dream), while leaving conceptual room for the experience to have divine signif-icance. Why seek interpretation for something that was self-evidently mundane, as a *visum* was? While we ultimately cannot know the motivations behind these editorial decisions, the case of Peter Bartholomew's visions nonetheless reveals how ambivalence surrounding the legitimacy of different types of visionary experience and their associated terminology – whether on the part of the author or his anticipated audience – shaped the construction of these accounts.

We can also detect the influence of Augustinian vision theory in portrayals of Peter Bartholomew's visions, and especially in the proofs used to support their interpretations of these events. Proof is seen to function at several levels, and efforts to enhance the verisimilitude of vision accounts can reveal much about what an author expected an audience to find convincing. These assurances were often so formulaic that the employment of stock motifs surrounding verisimil-itude could themselves function as proofs. For example, and in an echo of the Augustinian theory that the efficacy of spiritual perception was contingent on spiritual wellbeing, the moral character of the visionary appears to have had considerable bearing upon the probability that experiences would be accepted as revelatory. For example, Albert of Aachen describes how a priest who had experi-enced a vision of St Ambrose was renowned for his good reputation and excellent behaviour, presumably to encourage belief in his story.[55]

The case of Peter Bartholomew throws the importance placed on character into sharp relief. The contemporary debate surrounding the legitimacy of his visions as reflected in the narrative sources often revolves around his alleged character. Ralph of Caen, in his explicitly negative portrayal of Peter, most clearly reveals the belief that the likelihood of divine visitation was dependent upon spiritual merit. He framed his objections to Peter as direct speech, which he in turn attributed to Bohemond. Peter's vision of St Andrew, Ralph wrote, was a 'fine fabrication': Bohemond had heard that Peter frequented taverns, ran through markets, and was a 'friend of nonsense'.[56] Therefore, aside from the simple fact that such a person might be untrustworthy, the idea that St Andrew should have appeared to such a man was unthinkable. Thus, Bohemond sarcastically exclaims that: 'The apostle chose a worthy person to unfold the secret of the heavens to!'[57] Ralph's description of Bohemond's derision appears to represent more than mere literary art when cross-referenced against a comment by Raymond of Aguilers,

---

[55] AA, p. 306.
[56] RC, p. 87.
[57] RC, p. 87: 'Honestam elegit sanctus apostolus personam, cui celi panderet archanum!'

in which he notes how Bohemond and his men mocked the Provençals for their loyalty to Peter and the Holy Lance after the seizure of Ma'arrat an-Numan.[58]

Thus, Ralph's portrayal of Peter reads like a prolonged attempt at character assassination, and it is clear from this that character (and more specifically, piety) represented an important factor in the way that visionaries were perceived, and represented, at the turn of the twelfth century. Beyond this, learning and social standing also appear to have contributed to believability. In his consideration of the interpretation of dreams in his *Policraticus*, John of Salisbury advises that 'careful attention is to be given to the condition of the actors, to the facts, and to the circumstances, for as Nestor says, with regard to the public interest credence should be given to a king's dream'.[59] In this, he is drawing upon Macrobius's discussion of why Scipio was the rightful recipient of a dream about the future of Rome and Carthage, in which Macrobius also refers to Nestor's speech in *The Iliad*.[60] The reasoning here is that credibility should be given to dreams in instances where the standing of the recipient is appropriate to the truth which it communicates. Various First Crusade narratives echo this logic. For example, Raymond of Aguilers, the most enthusiastic supporter of Peter Bartholomew, commented that Peter had feared to reveal his visions to Raymond of Saint-Gilles and Bishop Adhémar because of his poor situation.[61] Further, Raymond notes that when he had tried to tell people of a later vision in which Peter saw the crucified Christ, some could not understand why God would have a conversation with someone as poor and illiterate as Peter.[62] In these instances, it is intellect and social standing which have a bearing on the perceived legitimacy of the vision-ary's claims. By point of comparison, France attributes the general acceptance of Stephen of Valence's vision, discussed in detail below, to Stephen's status as a cleric. Thus, it was Peter's similarities to the ascetic holy man that made his power appear potentially volatile.[63]

Albert of Aachen's – and later William of Tyre's – narratives reflect the importance attributed to the legitimising effect of social position: both portray

---

58   RA, p. 98.
59   John of Salisbury, *Policraticus*, p. 95: 'In his uero omnibus qualitas personarum, rerum et temporum diligentissime obseruatur, Vt enim ait Nestor: de statu publico regis credatur somnio aut eius qui magistratum gerit uel re quidem uel rei uicina praedesti-natione.' English translation is from J.P. Pike, *Frivolities of Courtiers and Footprints of Philosophers, Being a Translation of the First, Second, and Third Books and Selections from the Seventh and Eighth Books of the* Policraticus *of John of Salisbury* (London, 1938), p. 77.
60   Macrobius, *Commentarii in Somnium Scipionis*, pp. 11–12; Cf. Homer, *The Iliad*, trans. M. Hammond (London, 1987), p. 21.
61   RA, p. 70.
62   RA, p. 116.
63   France, 'Two Types of Vision', pp. 1–20.

Peter as a cleric.[64] This representation of Peter by Albert could represent a deliberate elevation of status, or reflect oral testimony used by Albert. However, William of Tyre was not wholly reliant upon Albert for his information about the First Crusade and undoubtedly had access to material describing Peter as a poor peasant. For example, William drew upon Raymond of Aguilers' crusade narrative, which is adamant in its portrayal of Peter as a peasant.[65] Adopting Albert's portrayal of Peter, however, elevated the visionary's social standing. While William's discussion of the lance itself is noncommittal at best, Thomas Asbridge has argued that Peter's elevated status validates Adhémar – a 'hero' of William's narrative – in his support of the relic.[66]

A further proof employed by Raymond in his representation of Peter relies on the fact of the latter's lack of schooling. Raymond describes how he and the bishop of Orange questioned Peter on his knowledge of liturgy. Given that many of Peter's visions resulted in his being given strict liturgical instructions to relay to the crusade leadership, a demonstrable lack of familiarity with that liturgy on Peter's part would prove the divine origin of that information and, by extension, of his visions in general. In other words, it would mean that revelatory vision was the only explanation for his sudden knowledge of the liturgy. Should Peter reveal to Raymond that he had indeed possessed a knowledge of the liturgy then the logic of this proof would collapse. However, Peter answered in the negative, only being able to recall the *Pater Noster, Credo in Deum, Magnificat, Gloria in excelsis Deo* and *Benedictus Dominus Deus Israel.*[67]

Aside from the use of terminology indicative of revelatory significance and motifs emphasising the piety, social standing and learning of Peter Bartholomew, further tools used in the representation of the latter's visions included the evocation of the reluctant visionary motif. Several versions of the story of Peter Bartholomew portray St Andrew as repeatedly pressing Peter to divulge his message to Adhémar and the Provençal count. According to Raymond of Aguilers, the saint miraculously prevented Peter from taking to sea by sending a storm, and inflicted illness upon him that he might finally cease his protestations and seek an audience with the crusade leadership.[68] The initially reluctant visionary motif functioned as proof that the visionary had not fabricated the story while simultaneously constructing the visionary as suitably pious. In this *topos*, recipients attempt to ignore the vision at first, usually because of their humility and disbelief that they would receive such a vision. The visionary is

---

[64] AA, p. 316; WT, pp. 324–5. It is also noteworthy that, in the *Chanson d'Antioche*, Peter is portrayed as a pilgrim. See *La Chanson d'Antioche*, laisse 290, p. 768.

[65] Babcock and Krey, *A History of Deeds Done Beyond the Sea*, 1, p. 29; RA, pp. 56–7.

[66] Asbridge, 'The Holy Lance of Antioch', p. 25.

[67] RA, p. 76.

[68] RA, pp. 71–2.

then revisited (usually by a saint or Christ himself) and urged to act upon the content of the visions, often in a menacing or threatening way. We find other reluctant visionaries in crusade narratives, such as in Fulcher of Chartres' account of Pirrus' betrayal of Antioch, which, he argued, was orchestrated by God. Appeased by the prayers and observances of the army, God appeared to and addressed Pirrus (or Firuz) – identified as a Turk by Fulcher – directly.[69] He kept the vision a secret at first, but God visited him again. Troubled, Pirrus told Yaghi-Siyan, the prince of Antioch at that time, of his visions, but the prince spurned him. Visited by God a third time, Pirrus then contacted the Christian army to plot the betrayal of the city to them.[70] The threefold pattern of repeated visitation and denial, shown here and in Raymond's representation of Peter Bartholomew, is evocative of both the Denial and Restoration of St Peter in the New Testament gospels, and represents another recognisable, and therefore trustworthy, motif.[71] Guibert of Nogent, likely having come across this anecdote in Fulcher's work, flags up how ostensibly inappropriate Pirrus was as a recipient of divine vision. He reassures his audience that we ought not to be surprised at this from he 'who made himself audible to Cain and Hagar, and made an angel visible to an ass'.[72] The fact that Guibert addressed this issue demonstrates that piety and social standing were widely accepted as important factors in the believability of vision accounts. As a Turk, Pirrus was not the typical recipient of divine vision.[73] However, in this instance the positive outcome of this vision for the crusaders – entry into Antioch – rendered the episode explicable and served as another opportunity to demonstrate the divine orchestration of the crusade.

Therefore, the examination of how different narratives go about representing Peter Bartholomew's visions reveals that authors drew upon a range of considerations surrounding the authenticity of such experiences. Whether these represent an author's anticipation of an audience response or are more indicative of the employment of popular motifs, they nonetheless belie contemporaneous discourses surrounding the legitimacy of different types of visionary experience, and of visionaries, that echo the discussions of authorities such as Macrobius and Augustine.

---

[69] FC, pp. 230–1.

[70] FC, pp. 231–2.

[71] Matthew 26.33–5; Mark 14.29–31; Luke 22.33–4; John 13.36–8, 21.

[72] GN, p. 331. English translation is from Levine, *The Deeds of God through the Franks*, p. 156; Cf. William of Malmesbury, *Gesta Regum Anglorum*, p. 636.

[73] While Pirrus is occasionally identified as Armenian (for example in Asbridge, *The Crusades*, p. 72), Guibert and his sources describe him as a Turk. See *GF*, p. 44; FC, p. 231; and GN, p. 200. Alan Murray has argued that he was of Armenian origin but in Turkish service. See A. V. Murray, 'The Enemy Within: Bohemond, Byzantium and the Subversion of the First Crusade', in *Crusading and Pilgrimage in the Norman World*, ed. K. Hurlock and P. Oldfield (Woodbridge, 2015), p. 42.

Stephen of Valence

Raymond of Aguilers records that, on the night after Peter Bartholomew had delivered St Andrew's message to Adhémar and Count Raymond, a priest named Stephen also experienced a vision. Stephen, fearing a Turkish sally from the citadel, fled into the church of the Blessed Mary to confess and sing psalms with a group of companions. Stephen remained awake after the others had fallen asleep, and it was then that a man Raymond described as 'beautiful beyond all beauty' visited him.[74] This is an echo of a description made earlier in Raymond's work of Christ as 'beautiful above the sons of men', used when describing the mysterious figure who appeared alongside St Andrew during Peter Bartholomew's visions. In this earlier example, Raymond quotes directly from Psalm 44.[75] An attentive audience, knowing that Raymond had already revealed that figure to be Christ, would have known who now appeared to Stephen. Stephen, however, only became aware of Christ's identity when he recognised the cross that shone more brilliantly than the sun about the latter's head.[76] As we have seen, France has argued that Stephen's social standing as a cleric made him appear less volatile than Peter, who bore an uncomfortable resemblance to the holy man of Late Antiquity.[77] Indeed, unlike with Peter Bartholomew, the narratives that do discuss Stephen make no effort to defend his character. Despite this, many representations of Stephen's vision, like Raymond's, do still engage with techniques designed to demonstrate authenticity.

A convincing vision account left little room for doubt about the identification of the visitor or visitors. Often the subjects of the vision make themselves known to a bemused visionary, either verbally or through certain visual cues. First Crusade narratives often authenticate Stephen of Valence's vision of Christ by employing the image of the mysteriously appearing cross. The *Gesta Francorum*, whose version also includes St Peter, describes how Stephen saw a 'whole cross' ('integra crux') about Christ's head.[78] Guibert of Nogent elaborates on how the appearance of the cross served to identify Christ: the priest (Guibert does not name Stephen in his version) recognised Christ upon the appearance of a cross in a cloud above his head, 'as is usually done in paintings'.[79] Guibert reiterates this idea through the voice of the priest, who comments that such a symbol is 'specifically' ('specialiter') Christ's.[80] There could be no doubt about the identity of Stephen's visitor. According to Baldric of Bourgueil, Christ asked Stephen if he knew him. It was then that the cross appeared, and Stephen replied: 'If

---

[74] RA, p. 72.
[75] RA, p. 51, n. 1; Cf. Psalm 44.3.
[76] RA, p. 73.
[77] France, 'Two Types of Vision', p. 9.
[78] *GF*, p. 57.
[79] GN, p. 219. On the early medieval use of physical appearance as a means of establishing the truthfulness of a vision, see Keskiaho, *Dreams and Visions*, pp. 35–46.
[80] GN, p. 219.

well, my Lord, I perceive from the sign of the cross imposed about your head, I understand you to be our redeemer and crucified'.[81] Again, the symbol of the Crucifixion serves to identify Christ beyond reasonable doubt. We find an interesting comparison in Raymond of Aguilers' description of Peter Bartholomew's vision of Christ. According to Raymond, when Peter asked the identity of St Andrew's mysterious companion, the saint asked Peter to kiss the man's feet. Peter understood the man to be Christ upon recognition of the marks of crucifixion on his feet, which Raymond vividly describes as being fresh, as though they had recently been bleeding.[82] This is another example of the symbolism of the Crucifixion being the key to the identification of the visitor. Returning to Stephen's vision, several other narratives of the First Crusade use the motif of the appearing cross in their own representations of that encounter.[83] Notable exceptions, however, include the works of Albert of Aachen and Ralph of Caen, neither of which contains any reference to Stephen or his vision.

Once Stephen had identified Christ, Raymond continues, the latter instructs the former to go to Adhémar in order to advise him that the army's current privations were caused by their sins. Should Adhémar follow St Andrew's instructions, then in five days' time Christ's mercy would be with them.[84] The promised mercy transpired to be the discovery of the Holy Lance in the basilica of St Peter. Thus, the accuracy of the prediction proves the revelatory nature of Stephen's vision.

While it has already been demonstrated how the three Benedictine texts – those of Baldric, Guibert and Robert – altered their portrayals of visions at a lexical level by omitting *visum* from their treatments of Peter Bartholomew's visions, scrutiny of the various versions of Stephen of Valence's vision reveals that this sensitivity is also discernible here. In this instance, the representation of the consciousness of the visionary at the time of his experience is at variance. As we have seen, schemata like that of Macrobius aimed to offer a solution to the problems posed by dreams as a potentially revelatory experience. Representations of Stephen's vision of Christ reveal that certain authors of crusade narratives also wrestled with the implications of visions experienced during sleep. Both the *Gesta Francorum* and Peter Tudebode describe Stephen as simply lying prostrate when he experienced his vision; his consciousness, or otherwise, is not mentioned explicitly.[85] Raymond of Aguilers, however, specifies that Stephen was awake.[86] Strikingly, Guibert, Baldric and Robert all alter the consciousness of Stephen in their own versions of the event. Both Guibert and Robert describe Stephen as

---

[81] BB, p. 68: 'Si bene, domini mi, percipio ex signo crucis capiti tuo imposito, crucifixum et redemptorem nostrum te intelligo.'
[82] RA, p. 75.
[83] PT, p. 99; RM, p. 67.
[84] RA, p. 73.
[85] *GF*, p. 57; PT, p. 99.
[86] RA, p. 73.

asleep.[87] Baldric, on the other hand, provides a far more elaborate consideration of Stephen's consciousness at the time of his vision. In direct speech, Stephen proclaims that he had experienced a vision and pre-empts challenge by asserting that he is not mistaken; it was not 'imagination', nor was it 'the trifling of dreams'. Stephen had chosen one night to pray in the church of the Holy Mother of God, that she may intercede in the suffering of the crusader army. He notes that he does not know whether he was awake or 'half lulled to sleep' when he saw Christ, accompanied by the Virgin Mary and St Peter. He beheld all of these truly and not as a 'madman', as had apparently been claimed by others.[88] Thus, despite offering an extended defence of Stephen and his vision, Baldric avoids identifying Stephen's state of consciousness entirely.

Orderic Vitalis, who used Baldric for his own narrative of the First Crusade, also portrays Stephen as half asleep in his own version of the story.[89] Notably, Orderic includes a version of the 'Wild Hunt' or 'Herlequin's Hunt' folktale elsewhere in his *Historia Ecclesiastica* in which he emphasises the consciousness of the visionary.[90] According to Orderic, the witness to this vision, a priest named Walchelin of Bonneval, saw a great procession of ghostly sinners, each suffering the torments appropriate to their roles in life.[91] Here Orderic associates the witness's alertness and consciousness with honesty: that Walchelin was awake when he saw the vision is proof that this was not just an everyday dream.[92] Raymond of Aguilers, who portrayed Stephen as awake, similarly uses the consciousness of a visionary as proof of veracity elsewhere in his narrative; Anselm of Ribemont comments that he was awake and vigilant when he saw his martyred friend Engelrand.[93] It is possible that Guibert and Robert chose to depart from their source materials by specifying that Stephen was asleep to allow for the fact that other people were said to have been present at the time of the vision. Further, by emphasising the internal, mental nature of Stephen's vision, they were framing the experience in terms more closely analogous to Augustine's spiritual and intellectual vision types. Whatever the reason behind these varying representations of Stephen's vision across the corpus of First Crusade narratives, it is clear that authors did attribute significance to the consciousness of the visionary, albeit in contradictory ways. Whether asleep, awake, or somewhere in

---

[87] GN, p. 219; RM, p. 67.

[88] BB, pp. 67–8

[89] OV, vol. 5, pp. 98–100.

[90] On the Hunt see Schmitt, *Ghosts*, pp. 93–121.

[91] OV, vol. 4, pp. 236–51.

[92] Marcus Bull has considered Herlequin's Hunt in relation to understandings of the materiality of visions as derived from Augustine of Hippo's *De cura gerenda pro mortuis*, and the potential for visions to reflect varying understandings of the afterlife. See Bull, *Knightly Piety*, p. 198.

[93] RA, p. 109.

between, the visionary always ran the risk of accusations of falsehood, and these concerns manifest themselves in disparate attempts to prove the veracity of such experiences in narratives.

Indeed, questions surrounding precisely how one witnesses the revelatory appear to have distracted numerous authors of crusade history. In a dialogue between Bohemond of Taranto and Pirrus, who was responsible for the betrayal of the city of Antioch to the crusaders, Robert the Monk raises questions about the celestial army at the battle of Antioch on 28 June 1098.[94] Pirrus asks Bohemond where such an innumerable army might camp, to which the latter replied that it was an army of martyrs come to fight the unbelievers on earth. Pirrus then asked how such an army might come by their white horses, shields and banners. Bohemond, admitting that this question was beyond his own intellect, defers to his chaplain, who explains that, when on earth, the otherwise imperceptible spirits of the righteous take up 'bodies of air' so that they may be visible. It should not be surprising that God, who brought the essence of all things out of nothing, should change matter as he pleases. By suggesting that these celestial knights took on bodies of air, Robert the Monk appears to be acknowledging the Augustinian argument for the non-physicality of visions of the dead.[95] That it is the chaplain who can satisfactorily answer these questions – and not Bohemond – hints at the perceived theoretical sophistication of this response, while also serving to make the answer more authoritative. Robert clearly considered the issue of visionary materiality to be of sufficient importance to merit developed discussion in his text. By including it, he offered his audience a retort to those who may be sceptical of the celestial knight story. Robert was not alone in glossing the story of the celestial army at Antioch. Baldric also engaged with aspects of vision theory while discussing it. He noted that not all those who had been present were able to see the vision; the Lord reveals his secrets to whosoever he may choose. Thus, while some were confused, God showed others their impending triumph.[96] Baldric's confident stance on the selective visibility of the divine may explain why he was content to portray Stephen as unsure whether he was asleep or awake at the time of his vision; if he was awake during the experience it did not necessarily follow that others present would also see the apparition.

It is important to note that sight, whether through bodily, spiritual or intellectual means, was not the only way of perceiving the dead or revelatory. Raymond of Aguilers' description of St Andrew's third visit to Peter Bartholomew is set in Peter's tent, this time while he was in the company of a certain Lord William

---

[94] RM, pp. 51–2.
[95] Bull discusses the paradox this line of thinking introduces, namely how the celestial knights, if they truly were immaterial, were able to look as though they were providing real military aid in the battle. See Bull, *Knightly Piety*, pp. 196–8.
[96] BB, p. 81.

Peter. Raymond notes that although William Peter had not seen the saint, nor his mysterious companion who had also appeared to Peter, he had heard the conversation and could vouch for Peter.[97] This represents an opportunity, on Raymond's part, to add the proof of William Peter's testimony to Peter Bartholomew's claims. It also reveals that Raymond considered it theoretically viable for a vision to be perceptible to other present people by sound alone. A similar logic is revealed in Gerald of Wales's *Itinerarium Kambriae*, in which he describes how 'unclean spirits', presumably demons, were known to have conversed with the inhabitants of a certain area of Pembrokeshire 'not visibly, but sensibly'. In the house of one man named Stephen these spirits would converse with visitors, proclaiming aloud the past misdeeds their victims had formerly hoped to keep to themselves.[98] Thus Raymond is not unusual in representing the otherworldly, divine or otherwise, as visibly imperceptible but audibly discernible.

Descriptions of the visionary experiences of Stephen of Valence reveal similar concerns to those of Peter Bartholomew: namely, that it was important to frame visions and dreams in terms that would encourage an intended audience to find them convincing. One aspect of this was the unequivocal identification of the individual or individuals seen in the vision. An additional issue surrounding the legitimacy of visions appears to have been the consciousness of the visionary, with certain texts revealing a mistrust of visions experienced in sleep akin to that lamented by Odo of Cluny and Gunther of Pairis, discussed above.

Conclusion

We cannot know precisely how similar Raymond of Aguilers' clerical understanding of vision theory was to that of, for example, Baldric's Benedictine one. Even authors who, like Gunther, had engaged with theoretical authorities on dreams offer contradictory discussions of revelatory phenomena and their relationship to the everyday. Despite this, it is clear that certain authors were deliberate in their use of discrete terminology, and that the examination of such examples has the potential to reveal layers of meaning that would otherwise go unnoticed. This, when considered alongside the variety of proofs employed in the representation of dreams and visions in crusade narratives, reveals that the authors of these texts were speaking to broader uncertainties surrounding the ambiguities of visionary experience. It was critical for the authors of crusade narrative to navigate the muddy waters of representing the revelatory, and to encourage their audience, as far as possible, to believe in the revelatory significance of the vision stories they provided. This is because, as the following chapter demonstrates, visions were enormously valuable tools for the narrativisation of crusade history.

[97] RA, p. 71.
[98] *Itinerarium Kambriae*, p. 93.

4

Intercession and Insurance

Revelatory visions and dreams, requiring no human intermediary and circum-
venting the temporal hierarchy of the Latin Church, communicated divine
truths directly to visionaries. Consequently, these experiences, if they were
believed by contemporaries, had the potential to be enormously persuasive. It is
the claim to knowledge of the divine disposition that allows visions to function
rhetorically in narrative as useful mechanisms for coaxing anticipated audience
sympathies in a given direction. In other words, visions could offer proofs of
divine favour, displeasure or instruction, and allow contemporaries a degree of
certainty in issues relating to the condition of the soul after death. It is argued
in this chapter that authors employed visions as part of justificatory narrative
agendas, in the support of events or causes (often crusades themselves), aspects
of doctrine (namely martyrdom), and relics and their translators. It will also be
shown how an author might use visions as part of critical representations of
events or individuals.

Visionary Intercession and Legitimacy

In his *Historia Ierosolimitana*, Albert of Aachen frames the First Crusade as a
response to a revelatory vision experienced by Peter the Hermit.[1] Consequently,
the entire crusade is constructed as a response to a divine commission. Unlike
many of the other narrative histories of the First Crusade, which, as we have
seen, situated its origins with Urban II's preaching at Clermont in 1095, the
figurehead of Albert's narrative is Peter the Hermit.[2] The *Historia* opens with an
account of Peter's pilgrimage to Jerusalem in the years before 1095. One night, as
Peter is praying in the Holy Sepulchre, he experiences a vision of Christ. Christ
instructs Peter to return home in order that he might 'stir the hearts of believers
to the cleansing of the holy places of Jerusalem' by telling them of all the horrors

---

[1] William of Tyre follows Albert in this, see WT, p. 127. The vision is also described in
the *Chanson d'Antioche*, laisse 16, p. 210.

[2] On Peter the Hermit, see especially E.O. Blake and C. Morris, 'A Hermit Goes to
War: Peter and the Origins of the First Crusade', in *Monks, Hermits, and the Ascetic
Tradition*, ed. W.J. Sheils (Studies in Church History, 22; Oxford, 1985), pp. 440–53.
On Peter the Hermit in relation to Guibert of Nogent's *Dei gesta per Francos* and
apocalypticism, see J. Rubenstein, 'How, or How Much, to Reevaluate Peter the
Hermit', in *The Medieval Crusade*, ed. S.J. Ridyard (Woodbridge, 2004), pp. 53–69.

inflicted on the Christians and holy places of the eastern Mediterranean. Albert describes this experience as both a revelation and vision, leaving little doubt as to the divine significance of the event. Peter, having received these directions, visits the patriarch of Jerusalem, who gives him a 'letter of embassy along with the seal of the Holy Cross'.[3] Peter then returns to Europe to rouse the populace to Christ's cause. Thus, a vision provides the mechanism by which Albert offers a narrative of a divinely ordained undertaking.

Elsewhere in his *Historia*, during a description of a moment of crisis for the crusaders, Albert draws upon revelatory vision to explain crusader resolve and, it would seem, to address concerns among his anticipated audience regarding the legitimacy of the crusade. Albert describes how, when the crusaders besieged within Antioch in 1098 were experiencing acute privation, a certain cleric from Lombardy offered them 'great solace' in the form of a story that a priest had related to him before he set out for the Holy Land.[4] Albert encourages confidence in the veracity of the story before he even begins relating it: this priest was renowned for his good reputation and excellent behaviour, and the cleric himself had known that priest since boyhood. In the story, the priest happens upon a pilgrim in a field, who is later revealed to be a thinly disguised St Ambrose. The pilgrim asks the priest about the crusade, which is framed as an expedition that had roused the people of many great kingdoms to seek the sepulchre of Christ and flock to the city of Jerusalem. The priest explains that opinions differed on that journey. Some said that it came from Christ and God, while others said that it was nothing more than the scheming of Frankish leaders and common people. In addition, many believed it would be impossible for the expedition to reach its goal because of reports that the first wave of pilgrims (meaning the expedition led by Peter the Hermit) had met with so many obstacles. The priest concludes that he was still doubtful about the crusade because of these reasons. In response, the pilgrim advises the priest that God had inspired the people to undertake the journey, and that it was not the product of 'shallowness' (*levitas*), as some believed. Further, any who died on that journey as exiles in the name of Christ would undoubtedly be counted among Christ's martyrs in heaven, provided that they had abstained from avarice, theft, adultery and fornication. Having revealed his identity to the priest, St Ambrose assures him that whoever remained on the journey in three years' time would achieve victory in Jerusalem. At this, the saint vanished.

According to Albert, this story convinced its audience not to abandon the siege, but to suffer all things for Christ's sake. While we cannot know whether this passage offers a window onto a 'real' historical moment in which a cleric reassured beleaguered crusaders at Antioch, it nonetheless reveals that

---

[3] AA, p. 6.
[4] AA, pp. 306–8.

contemporaries might consider a vision to be sufficiently convincing, in this case of the expedition's divinity. Albert's intended audience are persuaded of the crusade's sanctity in the same way as the doubtful priest and crusaders of the story. Notably, the significance of the three-year timescale is only recognisable at that point in the narrative if the audience is already aware of the city's capture in July 1099. To the crusaders in Albert's narrative, this would have simply represented a prediction. To Albert's audience, however, the forecasted victory serves as proof of the revelatory significance of the vision.

Like Albert's description of the vision of St Ambrose, other authors also situate visions at moments of crisis in their crusade narrative. As we have already seen, Stephen of Valence experienced his vision after fleeing to the church of the Blessed Mary in Antioch, and Peter Bartholomew's visions increased in urgency from December 1097 until he finally revealed his experiences on 10 June 1098, also in Antioch. The occurrence of visions at moments of crisis speaks to the contemporaneous belief in the role of saints as intercessors for humankind, often in response to the latter's prayers. We find an illustrative later example in Roger of Howden's *Gesta Regis* and *Chronica*. Roger describes how, on 6 May 1190, a ferocious storm dispersed Richard I's fleet shortly after it had left Dartmouth for Lisbon.[5] During Roger's description of that storm, the martyr Thomas, archbishop of Canterbury, appears on three separate occasions to three individuals on board a single ship. Thomas reassures those whom he visits that God had appointed him, along with Edmund the Martyr and Nicholas the Confessor, to be guardians of the fleet. The voyage would be successful if those on board guarded themselves from sin and remained diligent in confession. Having repeated this message three times, Thomas disappears. On one level, this anecdote serves to support the expedition's claim to divine support through saintly intercession. In addition, the choice of saints is significant. Both St Edmund and St Nicholas had a broader association with intercession on behalf of mariners, and so their identification as guardians of the crusader fleet is sensible.[6] In addition, the prominent role given to Thomas of Canterbury has a certain poetic justice given the context of Richard's crusade, which he was undertaking in the shadow of his father Henry II's repeated failure to act upon his own. Notably, one of the reasons why Henry had been convinced to take a crusade vow at Avranches in 1172 was as penance for his involvement in the death of the same Thomas of Canterbury.[7] By identifying Thomas as a guardian of Richard's fleet, Roger encourages his audience to reflect on Richard's diligent fulfilment of his crusading obligation, thrown into sharp relief by his allusion to Henry's tardiness.

---

[5]   *GR*2, p. 117; *Chronica* 3, pp. 42–3:

[6]   See R. Pinner, *The Cult of St Edmund in Medieval East Anglia* (Woodbridge, 2015), pp. 188–92.

[7]   Staunton, *The Historians of Angevin England*, p. 229.

Crusade narratives mirror the increasing popularity of the Virgin Mary as an intercessor that occurred in the eleventh and twelfth centuries.[8] For example, Mary acted as intercessor for Stephen of Valence and the crusaders in numerous First Crusade narratives.[9] In what is perhaps a nod to the various intercessory visions associated with events at Antioch on the First Crusade, Roger of Howden includes a Marian vision during his description of the siege of Acre during his narrative of the Third Crusade.[10] On the night of 8 July 1191, Roger records, many knights and men-at-arms witnessed the Virgin appearing in a heavenly light. She promised the onlookers that the city would be delivered into their hands in four days. The Virgin was then 'torn away' ('avulsa') from before their eyes, and both she and the light disappeared, leaving the crusaders to rejoice at her message. The promise of aid within a certain number of days is evocative of St Andrew's promise to Stephen of Valence that God would aid the crusaders at Antioch in five days. Like the three-year prediction of the vision of St Ambrose in Albert's *Historia*, it also signals the revelatory significance of the experience to an audience that is aware of the accuracy of the prediction.

There is an intriguing example of a Marian miracle in Arnold of Lübeck's *Chronica*, during his description of Duke Henry the Lion's 1172 Jerusalem pilgrimage.[11] The issue of whether or not scholars should view this pilgrimage as a crusade has been a matter of some debate, and Peter Lock has convincingly argued that it should not because of a lack of evidence indicating that contemporaries viewed it as such.[12] While insufficient evidence in its own right, the inclusion of an episode of miraculous maritime intercession does encourage reflection on the implications of divine instrumentality in the narrativisation of that expedition. In the *Chronica*, after departing from Constantinople to continue

---

8   Ward, *Miracles*, pp. 132–65; M.G. Bull, trans., *The Miracles of Our Lady of Rocamadour: Analysis and Translation* (Woodbridge, 1999), pp. 29–30; M. Rubin, *Mother of God: A History of the Virgin Mary* (London, 2009), pp. 130–8. On the origins of the association between the Virgin Mary and the crusades see Riley-Smith, *The First Crusade*, pp. 103–4.

9   BB, pp. 67–8; *GF*, pp. 57–9; GN, pp. 218–20; OV 5, pp. 98–100; PT, pp. 98–100; RA, pp. 72–4; RM, pp. 67–8.

10 *GR*2, p. 177; *Chronica* 3, pp. 119–20.

11 Arnold of Lübeck, *Chronica Slavorum*, ed. J.M. Lappenberg and G.H. Pertz (MGH SSRG, 14; Hanover, 1868), p. 21. On the debate surrounding whether Arnold accompanied Henry on his pilgrimage, see V. Scior, 'Zwischen *terra nostra* und *terra sancta*. Arnold von Lübeck als Geschusshreiber', in *Die Chronik Arnolds von Lübeck: Neue Wege su ihrem Verständnis*, eds. S. Freund and B. Schutte (Oxford, 2008), p. 150.

12 P. Lock, *The Routledge Companion to The Crusades* (London, 2006), p. 151. Riley-Smith discussed Henry's expedition as an example of inter-crusade Jerusalem pilgrimage. See J. Riley-Smith, 'An Army on Pilgrimage', in *Jerusalem the Golden: The Origins and Impact of the First Crusade*, ed. S.B. Edgington and L. García-Guijarro (Turnhout, 2014), p. 113.

towards Jerusalem, a storm threatened the duke's ship. One man, identified as being 'of good conduct' and fast asleep despite the storm, then has a vision of a 'most beautiful virgin', who reassures him that they would come to no harm because someone on the ship had been diligently praying to her and invoking her aid. While it is not explicit, the implication is that the 'virginem pulcherrimam' is, in fact, the Virgin Mary. Arnold notes that some of the pilgrims had later suggested that Abbot Henry of Brunswick had been responsible for these prayers because, in an interesting evocation of Augustine's theory of intellectual vision, 'he who sees in the spirit of God hears little but understands much'.[13] Whoever had been responsible for those prayers, the outcome of those events were sufficient evidence of the vision's revelatory significance: although the storm grew in strength and drove the ship towards a skerry, the rocks parted before them and allowed the ships to proceed unscathed until the storm abated.

While this vision account is insufficient evidence to argue that Arnold was deliberately portraying Henry's pilgrimage to the Holy Land in terms analogous to crusade, it nonetheless presents that expedition as meriting saintly intercession in times of peril. It also serves to create a contrast between Henry's pilgrimage and the later Third Crusade, which Arnold presents in negative terms, with no reference to the miraculous. Rather, he concludes that 'the promised land was not liberated because of our sins'.[14] Elsewhere in the *Chronica*, however, are two accounts of Eucharistic miracles and several visions, so the miraculous was certainly part of Arnold's narrative repertoire.[15] Arnold's Marian vision is an important reminder of the 'situatedness' of the crusading miraculous, including visions, within a much larger historical and hagiographical tradition; all visions indicate divine agency. However, in crusade narrative visions often tap into ideas

---

[13] Arnold of Lübeck, *Chronica Slavorum*, p. 21: 'quia qui in Spiritu Dei videt, pauca quidem audit, sed plura intelligit'. Abbot Henry of Brunswick would later become bishop of Lübeck and founded the monastery at which Arnold would become abbot. While there has been some scholarly debate surrounding whether Arnold was a participant on the 1172 Jerusalem pilgrimage, Graham Loud has recently concluded that he was not, and that his account was likely derived from an account by Abbot Henry. See G. Loud, trans., *The Chronicle of the Slavs by Arnold of Lübeck* (Crusade Texts in Translation; Abingdon, 2019), pp. 21–2. For the argument that Arnold was a participant, see E. Joranson, 'The Palestine Pilgrimage of Henry the Lion', in *Medieval and Historiographical Essays in Honor of James Westfall Thompson*, ed. J.L. Cate and E.N. Anderson (Chicago, IL, 1938), pp. 153–4.

[14] Arnold of Lübeck, *Chronica Slavorum*, p. 147. Arnold also styles Livonia as a 'promised land' (p. 214), and Marek Tamm has shown that this represents part of Arnold's broader belief that the campaigns in that region were analagous with those to the Holy Land. See M. Tamm, 'How to Justify a Crusade? The Conquest of Livonia and New Crusade Rhetoric in the Early Thirteenth Century', *Journal of Medieval History*, 39.4, (2013), 431–55.

[15] Arnold of Lübeck, *Chronica Slavorum*, pp. 33–5, 71–5, 165–9, 283.

surrounding divine sponsorship in ways that are distinct to the challenges of narrating crusade. As we have seen, authors use visions to demonstrate the spiritually salvific nature of an undertaking and, as will now be argued, visions offer a solution to the problems of narrating crusader martyrdom.

Visions and Martyrdom

Spiritual reward was a significant aspect of how Latin Christians conceptualised crusading in the central Middle Ages. Despite this, contemporaneous understandings of what that reward actually looked like appear inconsistent. A particularly urgent question, given the inherently violent nature of armed pilgrimage, was what became of the souls of those who died while on crusade, whether in battle or otherwise.[16] The idea that death in battle against the perceived enemies of Christendom could represent a form of martyrdom gained increasing, if insecure, purchase from the mid-eleventh century onwards.[17] However, the promise of a martyr's crown raised various conceptual difficulties. Strictly speaking, and unlike the precedents of the early Christian martyrs, crusaders often died as the aggressor, and not as the passive and persecuted, offering their necks like lambs to the slaughter (though, as we will see, authors sometimes portrayed them in such terms). There were also questions surrounding the implications of non-violent death on crusade, such as from starvation or disease, the spiritual rewards received by those who conducted themselves in a less than

---

[16] On crusader martyrdom and the First Crusade, see especially J. Flori, 'Mort et martyre des guerriers vers 1100. L'exemple de la première croisade', *Cahiers de civilisation médiévale*, 34 (1991), 121–39; J. Riley-Smith, 'Death on the First Crusade', in *The End of Strife*, ed. D.W. Loades (Edinburgh, 1984), pp. 14–31; Cowdrey, 'Martyrdom and the First Crusade'; C. Morris, 'Martyrs on the Field of Battle Before and During the First Crusade', in *Martyrs and Martyrologies*, ed. D. Wood (Studies in Church History, 30; Oxford, 1993), pp. 93–105; S. Shepkaru, 'To Die for God: Martyrs' Heaven in Hebrew and Latin Crusade Narratives', *Speculum*, 77 (2002), 311–41; and P. Buc, *Holy War, Martyrdom, and Terror: Christianity, Violence and the West, ca. 70 C.E. to the Iraq War* (Philadelphia, PA, 2015), esp. pp. 152–76. For martyrdom and the later crusades, see C. Smith, 'Martyrdom and Crusading in the Thirteenth Century: Remembering the Dead of Louis IX's Crusades', *Al-Masaq*, 15.2 (2003), 189–96; M. Tamminen, 'Who Deserves the Crown of Martyrdom? Martyrs in the Crusade Ideology of Jacques de Vitry (1160/70–1240)', in *On Old Age: Approaching Death in Antiquity and the Middle Ages*, ed. C. Krötzl and K. Mustakallio (Turnhout, 2011), pp. 293–313; and H.J. Nicholson, '"Martyrum collegio sociandus haberet": Depictions of the Military Orders' Martyrs in the Holy Land, 1187–1291', in *Crusading and Warfare in the Middle Ages: Realities and Representations. Essays in Honour of John France*, ed. S. John and N. Morton (Farnham, 2014), pp. 101–18.

[17] Morris, 'Martyrs on the Field of Battle', pp. 93–105 (and 93–4 for notable exceptions to this rule).

pious manner while on crusade, or whether those who died before reaching the Holy Land were to receive their heavenly reward at all. Consequently, we see conceptual fluidities and uncertainties surrounding the martyrdom of crusaders for at least two further centuries.[18]

The idea that crusaders could achieve martyrdom was of benefit to the authors of crusade narratives (and indeed of other materials pertaining to crusading such as sermons) for numerous reasons. In didactic terms, martyrs represented exemplars of appropriate crusader conduct, both in spiritual and militaristic terms. Further, authors who sought to generate enthusiasm for participation in future crusading ventures might emphasise the eternal rewards of martyrdom. In addition, discussions of martyrdom can fit into narrative strategies emphasising the privileged, divinely sanctioned nature of crusades. Thus, while the fact of an author's personal conviction in the idea of crusader martyrdom is ultimately unreachable, we can conclude that it represented a narrative tool which authors expected their audience to find convincing, in the right circumstances.

Numerous Latin crusade narratives support their discussions of crusader martyrdom with visionary proofs, drawing upon the ability of the revelatory to make the invisible, visible. Visions offered a way of proving the fact of martyrdom: martyrs could return posthumously, or even reveal their heavenly home to the living. Colin Morris, in a study examining early ideas of martyrdom in sources for the First Crusade, coined the term 'visionary insurance' for such instances.[19] Accounts of the death of the northern French castellan Anselm II of Ribemont during the siege of Arqah (February–May 1099) offer particularly detailed examples of this.[20] According to both Raymond of Aguilers and Ralph of Caen, Anselm experienced a vision on the night before his death. In Raymond's version, Engelrand of Saint Pol, who had died several months previously at the siege of Ma'arrat an-Numan, visits his erstwhile companion.[21] Engelrand explains his posthumous appearance by reassuring Anselm that whose lives end in the service of Christ will never die.[22] Nor should Anselm wonder at Engelrand's beauty in death, the latter explains, because his new home was itself beautiful. In fact, Engelrand continues, Anselm would be shown to an even more beautiful home tomorrow. Thus, on the following morning, Anselm reported to his priests to request the necessary sacraments in the face of his imminent death. Later that day, according to Raymond, a stone struck Anselm during a melee and

---

[18] See Smith, 'Martyrdom and Crusading in the Thirteenth Century'; and Housley, *Contesting the Crusades*, pp. 41–2.

[19] Morris, 'Martyrs on the Field of Battle', p. 103.

[20] On Anselm of Ribemont, see J. Riley-Smith, *The First Crusaders, 1095–1131* (Cambridge, 1997), pp. 63–5, 74, 122–3, 199, 221.

[21] On Engelrand of Saint Pol, see Riley-Smith, *The First Crusaders*, p. 204.

[22] RA, p. 109.

killed him, and so Anselm departed 'to the place prepared for him by God'.[23] In Ralph's version, Anselm reports his vision to Arnulf of Chocques.[24] Anselm tells Arnulf that he has seen the crusaders martyred on the expedition entering into heaven, and that one of the martyrs (Ralph does not name Engelrand) advised him that he would soon join them. Arnulf then instructs Anselm to confess, receive the Eucharist, and process about the walls of the city. As he is carrying out the latter of these instructions, a falling stone strikes Anselm in the head and kills him. Thus, 'his spirit rose up to its promised blissfulness'.[25] The stories of Anselm's visions and subsequent martyrdom serve both as proofs that those who died on crusade received the spiritual reward of martyrdom, and as exemplars of the proper spiritual diligence required to achieve it. This latter implication mirrors the sentiment displayed in Albert of Aachen's description of the vision of St Ambrose, discussed above, in which the saint comments that those who die on crusade, having abstained from sin, would reside among the martyrs in heaven.[26]

The narrative histories of the First Crusade contain other descriptions of posthumous visitations by martyred crusaders that underscore both the legitimacy of the crusade itself, and the perceived reality of crusader martyrdom. For example, in Fulcher of Chartres's *Historia Hierosolymitana*, a dead crusader appears to his brother during the latter's attempted desertion from the city of Antioch (he is already part way down a rope dangling from the city walls when the vision occurs). The dead crusader reassures his brother that God would be with him, and that those who had already died would continue to fight by his side.[27] There are some similarities between this anecdote and Albert of Aachen's abovementioned story of St Ambrose, which a cleric was supposed to have related to despairing crusaders at Antioch: both describe how visions reassured crusaders in crisis of the sanctity of the undertaking and of the rewards received by those who died during it.

There is evidence in the narrative histories of the Third Crusade to suggest that there was a greater confidence surrounding the discussion of crusader martyrdom from the late twelfth century. Richard of Devizes identified crusaders as martyrs without qualification.[28] The *Historia de expeditione* similarly refers to those who, in their weakened state, had fallen behind only to be beheaded by pursuing Turks, as 'martyrs of Christ', as does Arnold of Lübeck.[29] However, ambivalent discussions of martyrdom and examples of visionary insurance can still be found

---

[23] RA, pp. 108–9: 'Atque sic, ad locum sibi a Deo paratum migravit ad hoc seculo.'
[24] RC, pp. 90–1.
[25] RC, p. 91: 'Spiritus ad beatitudinem ascendit promissam.'
[26] AA, p. 308.
[27] FC, p. 246.
[28] Richard of Devizes, *The Chronicle of Richard of Devizes of the Time of King Richard the First*, ed. and trans. J.T. Appleby (London, 1963), pp. 81, 84.
[29] *HeFI*, pp. 79–80; Arnold of Lübeck, *Chronica Slavorum*, p. 134.

in later crusade narratives, though these are rarely as detailed or elaborate as those we find in First Crusade narratives. For example, the compiler of the *Itinerarium peregrinorum* reveals contemporaneous concerns surrounding non-combative death and martyrdom; precisely the sorts of concerns that the authors of earlier crusade narrative sought to allay through their use of visions. During an account of the winter famine of 1190–1, inserted into Book One, the compiler mused:

> On the basis of the evidence worthy of being recounted it is possible to judge the great extent of the famine, and see that for those who sustained it patiently in the flesh it could be reckoned as a form of martyrdom. But perhaps a murmur of doubt stands in the way of their receiving the grace of merits; for many unworthy deeds were committed under the pressure of necessity.[30]

The tentative suggestion that death by famine might merit martyrdom, alongside concerns about the piety of alleged martyrs, indicates that misgivings surrounding martyrdom persisted. It was, after all, difficult to ascertain whether a person had achieved martyrdom without visionary insurance. This passage represents original material inserted into content derived from Ambroise's *Estoire*.[31] Richard de Templo, the compiler of the *Itinerarium*, is believed to have been present on the Third Crusade, and Helen Nicholson has suggested that Richard compiled the text on the eve of the Fifth Crusade with a view to bolstering recruitment.[32] It is likely, therefore, that the concerns voiced in the abovementioned passage reflect the sorts of doubts that an author expected contemporaries to harbour concerning death on crusade in the late twelfth and early thirteenth centuries. Elsewhere in the *Itinerarium*, during an account of the arrival of reinforcements during the siege of Acre, Richard reassures his audience that those identified as 'martyrs and confessors' truly were martyrs.[33] The identification of crusaders as confessors (*confessores*) is unusual and intriguing; confessors had not been killed for the faith like martyrs had, but had demonstrably lived lives devoted to it. It is possible that again, as with his discussion of the winter famine, Richard is engaging with ideas surrounding piety, right intention and the spiritual merit of endured suffering in comparison with non-combative death. Indeed, Miikka Tamminen has shown how Jacques de Vitry's discussions of the Fifth Crusade also imply that the value of non-combative death on crusade continued to be an issue of debate in this period; despite spilling much ink over the issue elsewhere,

---

[30] *IP2*, p. 130: 'Quae patienter pro carnis conditione sustinentibus non indigne reputatur pro martyrio... nisi forte gratiae meritorum obstiterit murmur pro scrupulo. Quoniam igitur, urgente necessitate, multa nonnunquam comittuntur indigna...' English translation is from Nicholson, *The Chronicle of the Third Crusade*, p. 131.

[31] Nicholson, *The Chronicle of the Third Crusade*, p. 131, n. 281.

[32] Nicholson, '"Martyrum collegio sociandus haberet"', p. 112.

[33] *IP1*, p. 317.

Jacques did not identify those who had succumbed to disease on the banks of the Nile in the winter of 1218–19 as martyrs.[34]

Richard incorporated further discussions of martyrdom into his *Itinerarium*, including considerations of individuals who were members of military orders rather than crusaders. A notable example is *IP*1's account of the death of Jacquelin de Mailly, a Templar knight who was 'not afraid to die for Christ', at the battle of the Spring of Cresson on 1 May 1187.[35] Jacquelin's triumphant soul departs to heaven with the palm of martyrdom, yet the account does not end here. First it describes how Saladin's army, led in this battle by his son al-Afdal, believed that they had defeated St George, because the Templar had been riding a white horse and had borne white arms and armour.[36] Thus, *IP*1 simultaneously ridicules Jacquelin's opponents, while bolstering his reputation through association with the warrior saint. Indeed, the ridicule of Saladin's army continues when the attendant crowd place dust on Jacquelin's body before sprinkling it over their own, in the hope that they would gain courage from contact with the body. They also allegedly removed and kept Jacquelin's genitals so that they might conceive sons of similar quality.[37] When considered in isolation, this episode represents an elaborate portrayal of combative martyrdom which dwells on Jacquelin's military prowess and reflects positively on the military orders. However, when considered alongside other examples from *IP*1, it becomes clear that the anonymous author of that work was also engaging with concerns surrounding martyrdom that sit comfortably alongside Richard's discussions of martyrdom when incorporated into his *Itinerarium*.

Notably, *IP*1's description of the execution of Templar prisoners in the aftermath of the battle of Hattin on 4 July 1187 features an example of 'visionary insurance'. According to *IP*1, for three nights a celestial light could be seen

---

[34] See Tamminen, 'Who Deserves the Crown of Martyrdom?', pp. 309–12.

[35] *IP*1, p. 248: '...mori pro Christo non timuit...' This episode is also discussed by M. Bennett, 'Virile Latins, Effeminate Greeks, and Strong Women: Gender Definitions of Crusade?', in *Gendering the Crusades*, ed. S.B. Edgington and S. Lambert (Cardiff, 2001), pp. 16–30; A. Holt, 'Between Warrior and Priest: The Creation of a New Masculine Identity during the Crusades', in *Negotiating Clerical Identities: Priests, Monks and Masculinity in the Middle Ages*, ed. J.D. Thibodeaux (Basingstoke, 2010), pp. 185–203; Nicholson, '"Martyrum collegio sociandus haberet"', esp. pp. 105–7; and B.C. Spacey, 'Martyrdom as Masculinity in the *Itinerarium Peregrinorum et Gesta Regis Ricardi*,' in *Crusading and Masculinities*, pp. 222–36. On the location of the battle of the Spring of Cresson, see D. Pringle, 'The Spring of Cresson in Crusading History', in *Dei gesta per Francos: Études sur la croisades dédiées à Jean Richard: Crusade Studies in Honour of Jean Richard*, ed. M. Balard, B.Z. Kedar and J. Riley-Smith (Aldershot, 2001), pp. 231–40.

[36] *IP*1, pp. 248–9.

[37] For a discussion of this episode is relation to concepts of masculinity, see Spacey, 'Martyrdom as Masculinity', pp. 227–31.

shining down on the unburied bodies of the holy martyrs.[38] While this is not a case of martyred individuals returning to posthumously guarantee their status in heaven, the description of the light that shone on the unburied bodies functions as proof of the presence of divine grace. In another example of this motif, Alberic of Trois-Fontaines describes in his *Chronica*, in a section drawn from a now unknown source, how light had illuminated the abandoned body of the Latin Emperor Baldwin I following his execution by the Bulgarian emperor Kalojan.[39] The same effect is achieved in the *Historia de expeditione*, where Frederick Barbarossa's watchmen report seeing a flock of bright white birds circling around the crusaders' tents three times before flying to the body of a dying man. The birds remain with the man until he dies, at which point they ascend, 'seeking the upper ether', and disappear from view.[40] The bird, especially the white bird, was a recognised form in which the Holy Spirit might make itself visible, or a human soul might appear after death.[41] Therefore, it is likely that the author intended the ascension of the birds to indicate the dead crusader's soul rising to heaven, itself a motif featured in numerous descriptions of crusader martyrdom, as we have seen. Thus, we can see that authors continued to draw on types of 'visionary insurance' as proofs of the receipt of divine mercy, in order to indicate martyr status, well into the thirteenth century and even within a generation of Thomas Aquinas' influential tract on the subject in his *Summa Theologiae*.[42]

Authenticating Relics and Justifying Translation

One of the ways in which the authors of crusade narrative engage with visionary experiences has clear links with the conventions of hagiographical narrative, namely, visions which demonstrate the authenticity of a relic, the acquiescence of saints to their relic's translation, or the sanctity of individuals associated with relics (often their translators). Indeed, certain texts shade between translation account and crusade narrative at different points in their narratives. The logic of these examples is the same as with other applications of

---

[38] *IP*1, p. 314.
[39] Alberic of Trois-Fontaines, 'Chronica Albrici', p. 885.
[40] *HeFI*, p. 80.
[41] B. Hudson, 'Time Is Short: The Eschatology of the Early Gaelic Church', in *Last Things: Death and the Apocalypse in the Middle Ages*, ed. C.W. Bynum and P. Freedman (Philadelphia, PA, 2000), p. 108; Caesarius of Heisterbach, *Dialogus miraculorum*, vol. 2, p. 112.
[42] See Thomas Aquinas, *Secunda Secundae Summae Theologiae* (Sancti Thomae de Aquino Opera Omnia iussu Leonis XIII P.M. edita, 10; Rome, 1899), q. 124, pp. 27–42. Thomas Aquinas left his *Summa Theologiae* unfinished in 1273. Alberic of Trois-Fontaines did not finish working on his *Chronicle* until 1251.

visionary experience: revelations could legitimise by facilitating direct communication with the divine. In the case of relics and their translation, this usually
involved visions of the saints whose relics were in question. Thus, visions
offered a direct path to authentication and legitimacy. Raymond of Aguilers'
account of events surrounding the discovery of the relic of the Holy Lance at
Antioch is replete with examples of this. The visions that Raymond attributes to
Peter Bartholomew serve to demonstrate the authenticity of the relic on several
levels. For example, no lesser authority figures than the apostle Andrew and
Christ himself advise Peter of the relic's location, while the revelatory significance of those visions is confirmed by the relic's discovery not only in the
location described but on the predicted day. Each of these factors contribute to
a concatenation of authenticating devices.

Raymond's *Historia* offers a raft of corroborative visions pertaining to the
Holy Lance of Antioch that is by no means limited to Peter Bartholomew's
visions of St Andrew and Christ. Notable examples include the posthumous
appearances of the First Crusade's papal legate, Adhémar of Le Puy, which focus
on the bishop's sufferings inflicted upon him in death for harbouring doubts
concerning the Lance.[43] Two days after Adhémar's death, Raymond recounts, the
bishop and St Andrew appeared to Peter. Adhémar explained that:

> I now reside in the heavenly hosts of St Nicholas, but because I hesitated to
> believe in the Lord's Lance, when, I of all people, should have accepted it, I
> was led into hell. The hairs on the right side of my head and one half of my
> beard were singed; and although I am not now chastised, I cannot see the Lord
> clearly until the full growth of my hair and beard returns.[44]

The suggestion that Adhémar's hesitation was punishable through temporary
suffering raises the question of what awaited those who were firmer in their
rejection of the relic, while simultaneously demonstrating not only the authenticity, but also the considerable importance, of the relic. Notably, Raymond's
description of Adhémar as unable to see God clearly employs the logic of St
Augustine's vision hierarchy, in that it implies that the bishop's intellectual
vision, through which the Lord might be perceived, was damaged on account
of his impiety.

---

[43] On the posthumous career of Adhémar in Raymond's narrative, see Kostick, 'The
Afterlife of Adhémar of Le Puy'.

[44] RA, pp. 116–17: 'Ego sum in uno choro cum beato Nicholao, sed quia de lancea
Domini dubitavi, qui maxime credere debuissem, deductus sum in infernum, ubi capilli
mei ex hac parte capitis dextera, et medietas barbe conbusta est. Et licet in pena non
sim, tamen clare Deum videre non potero, donec capilli et barba sicut ante fuerunt,
michi succreverint.' English translation is from Hill and Hill, *Historia Francorum*, p.
96.

Raymond incorporated a further *translatio* narrative into his history of the First Crusade. He records that, while at Antioch, a priest called Peter Desiderius had confided in him that he had experienced a vision. According to Peter Desiderius, an unidentified person had instructed him to visit the church of St Leontios. Once there, he would find the relics of four saints, which he needed to ensure would be transported to Jerusalem with the crusader army.[45] Raymond then reported this story to the bishop of Orange and to the Provençal count, also called Raymond, who proceeded to the specified church in the company of Peter Desiderius. There they found the relics of Sts Cyprian, Epimachus, Leontios and John Chrysostom, alongside some unidentified relics that Raymond of Aguilers himself suggested they leave alone. This soon proved to be a mistake, Raymond explains, as on the following day the unidentified saint visited Peter Desiderius, revealing himself to be St George and demanding to know why they had left him behind. It took a second visit from the saint to convince Peter Desiderius to return for the relics.[46] These repeated visitations from a saint claiming relics as his own allowed for the confident identification of the relics, while simultaneously strengthening the conceptual ties between the warrior saint and the crusaders, whom he had chosen to transport his relics to Jerusalem.

It makes sense that narratives of the Fourth Crusade are particularly rich in visions concerning relic translation given the number of relics transported to Europe in the wake of the 1204 conquest of Constantinople. As we have seen, the primary effect of the vision accounts discussed above pertaining to the relics of the Crucifixion and St George is to offer proof of those relics' authenticity. A particularity of the challenges of narrating the Fourth Crusade, however, manifests itself in the use of visionary authority to emphasise the piety of individual relic translators and saintly acquiescence in the removal of the relic by those persons, largely because of the controversial nature of that crusade, as has been discussed above. A comparison of two narratives elucidates these differences. Gunther of Pairis' *Hystoria Constantinopolitana* and the Anonymous of Langres' *Historia translationum* feature visions in order to communicate subtly different messages to their audiences. The narrative of Gunther's *Hystoria* describes both Abbot Martin of Pairis' involvement in the Fourth Crusade, and his subsequent translation of relics to western Europe.[47] In comparison, the third book of the Anonymous of Langres' *Historia* (the only book concerned with post-1204

---

[45] RA, pp. 131–2. On Peter Desiderius, see Riley-Smith, *The First Crusaders*, p. 216.

[46] RA, pp. 131–4. Peter Desiderius' visions are also discussed in Riley-Smith, *The First Crusade*, p. 94.

[47] For an examination of Gunther of Pairis' representation of Abbot Martin as a way into thinking about the masculinities of monastic crusade participants, see N. Hodgson, 'Leading the People "as Duke, Count, and Father": The Masculinities of Abbot Martin of Pairis in Gunther of Pairis, *Hystoria Constantinopolitana*', in *Crusading and Masculinities*, pp. 199–221.

Constantinopolitan relics) offers a description of the crusader looting of the city and of the resultant relic translations. While both texts certify the provenance of the relics in question, Gunther's text dwells on the divine approval of the theft itself, and of Martin's legitimacy in moving the relics, while the Anonymous' narrative maintains an emphasis on the authenticity of a particular relic.[48]

Gunther of Pairis' *Hystoria Constantinopolitana* is unusual among Fourth Crusade narratives in moving its defence of its key protagonist, Abbot Martin, beyond the use of miracles to the use of visions; Conrad of Krosigk does not receive comparable treatment in the *Gesta episcoporum Halberstadensium*, for example. Even if all the other indications that Abbot Martin's achievements were the product of 'divine dispensation' were false, Gunther states, certain other matters provided clear proof.[49] Those proofs took the form of visions. Three nights before the abbot was due to begin his return voyage, a cleric and friend of Martin's, Aegidius, had a vision of two angels praying over the place where the abbot had hidden the relics, unbeknownst to Aegidius. Gunther presents the evidence in support of this vision's authenticity systematically. First, he argues, Aegidius spoke a different vernacular to Martin, and therefore could only under-stand the abbot when they conversed in Latin. Consequently, he could not have overheard Martin discussing the relics' whereabouts. Further, Gunther guards against accusations that Aegidius was simply dreaming by clarifying that he had been awake at the time, and had seen the angels clearly. Finally, Gunther outlines Aegidius' piety and moral character. After finishing their divine service, the angels encourage one another to call upon God to place the abbot and his companions under divine protection.[50] Gunther reveals the significance of this detail later in the narrative, during his lengthy account of the role of divine clemency in Martin's return journey.

When Aegidius reveals the details of his vision to Martin, the latter divulges that he himself had also experienced a vision on the very same night. It had seemed to Martin, as he slept, that he could see a vastness of clear sky stretching out before him, and that he could clearly see the village of Sigolsheim, which was situated close to his monastery. The sea appeared so calm that Martin had wondered that any ship could fear shipwreck while sailing upon it. Gunther offers the following interpretation: that Martin's eventual safe return should be attributed to 'divine protection', or, in other words, the outcome proved the authenticity of both visions.[51] Thus, the abbot was not only permitted to take and transport the relics, but also, Gunther argues, God actively supported him in the process.

---

[48] See also Perry, *Sacred Plunder*, pp. 88–92.
[49] GP, p. 170.
[50] GP, p. 170.
[51] GP, pp. 170–1.

Notably, the Anonymous of Langres also describes how the ship carrying the priest Walon of Dampierre, erstwhile custodian of the head of St Mammes, set sail under a propitious wind and full sails.[52] However, in this instance a storm arose, threatening the vessel. Appeals to the saint to intercede with God on their behalf and save the ship were successful, and the sea became tranquil at once, to the amazement and joy of all who witnessed it.[53] The emphasis here is on the successful appeal to St Mammes for aid as an indicator that it was indeed his relic on the ship. Unlike Gunther's *Hystoria*, the anonymous author did not write the *Historia translationum* as a defence of a particular 'thief' or act of sacrilege. The relic had been in the possession of Garnier of Troyes because of what David Perry has called a 'second-phase theft', meaning that Garnier had not acquired the relic until after the crusaders had left Constantinople.[54] The relic passed into the custody of the papal legate, Peter Capuano, on the event of Garnier's death. Peter then bestowed the relic upon Walon, who had made an appeal to the legate that he be permitted to take the relic to the cathedral in Langres, as Garnier had putatively wished. Thus Walon, the 'hero' of the narrative, is presented at several removes from the theft itself. Indeed, the anonymous author condemns the looting committed by the crusaders, who 'shamelessly' sacked the city out of their own 'blind cupidity'.[55] This author did not need to use visions and other miraculous themes to navigate the challenge of the contemporaneous censure of the Fourth Crusade. While indirectly legitimising Walon as a worthy custodian of the relic, the *Historia translationum* primarily focuses the efficacy of visionary experience on authentication.

The *Historia translationum* makes a comprehensive case for the authenticity of the relic in question, describing how the relic of St Mammes' head was found with a silver band attached to it, conveniently inscribed with the saint's name. Further, the anonymous author continued, Walon took the relic to the Greek monks from whom it had been taken in order that they might authenticate it.[56] The text's collection of evidence also includes a vision account. One passage describes how Walon, himself plagued by doubt, threatened the relic directly. If it did not prove its authenticity to him soon, he would not take it back to France with him. Shortly afterwards, Walon fell into a state of ecstasy. A beautiful youth appeared to him, holding the head in question. The boy, later revealed to be the saint himself, proceeded to chastise Walon before confirming that this truly was his head.[57] Thus convinced, Walon received permission from Peter Capuano to

---

[52] Anonymous of Langres, 'Historia translationum', p. 31.
[53] Ibid., pp. 31–2.
[54] Perry, *Sacred Plunder*, p. 38.
[55] Anonymous of Langres, 'Historia translationum', p. 28.
[56] Ibid., pp. 28–30.
[57] Ibid., pp. 30–1.

return home with the relic. The remaining proofs are, strictly speaking, miraculous rather than visionary. The saint responds favourably to Walon's appeals for help during a storm at sea, as we have seen. Later, the relic is responsible for the rescue of a village from a great fire, and it withers the hand of a sinful priest before restoring it to functionality upon the demonstration of adequate contrition.[58] However, these later miracles are mainly indicative of the relic's efficacy once removed from Constantinople, and of the saint's acquiescence to the translation. It was the vision account in which St Mammes himself laid claim to the head that offered the clearest proof of the relic's authenticity. Therefore, it is clear that visions can be used to subtly different ends. For the Anonymous of Langres, who was writing to document the provenance of several relics of St Mammes, and did not need to justify the relic's theft as a result of the sack of Constantinople, visions provided a tool for authentication. For Gunther, however, who was writing in support of Abbot Martin's relic thefts while on the Fourth Crusade, visions offered an opportunity to demonstrate divine approval of Martin's actions.

Critical Visions

So far, we have examined visions indicative of divine favour, that legitimise and authenticate. However, visions could reveal the divine disposition whatever its temperament, and an author might therefore draw upon the revelatory potential of visions in the demonstration of divine censure. While it strictly lies outside the bounds of crusade narrative, the author of a notable example nonetheless interpreted it in relation to contemporaneous concerns regarding crusading obligation and the Latin East. In both his *Expugnatio Hibernica* and *De principis instructione*, Gerald of Wales describes a vision that he claims to have experienced himself.[59] On the day of the vision, 10 May 1189, Gerald was in attendance on his ailing king, Henry II, at Chinon. As he slept that night, it seemed to Gerald that he could see a crowd of people gazing up at the sky. Looking up himself, he saw that a brilliant light was breaking through the clouds, which parted to reveal the heavens and the residents of the heavenly court. Suddenly, a terrible armed host surged through the court, wreaking destruction and slaughtering its inhabitants. Gerald looked on as the 'bloodthirsty butchers' set upon 'the Prince of the heavenly host', dragging Christ from his throne and piercing him in his right side. At this, a voice rang out, saying 'Woch, Woch, O Father and Son! Woch, Woch,

---

58 Ibid., pp. 31–3.
59 Gerald of Wales, *Expugnatio Hibernica: The Conquest of Ireland*, ed. and trans. A.B. Scott and F.X. Martin (Dublin, 1978), pp. 212–16; and *Giraldi Cambrensis opera, Vol. VIII: De Principis Intructione Liber*, ed. G.F. Warner (Rolls Series, 21.8; London, 1891), pp. 264–7.

O Holy Ghost!'[60] The voice woke the terrified Gerald, who sat on his bed in a stupor for some time.

Having thus described the experience, Gerald offers his interpretation. In his vision, it may have been that Christ endured suffering while enthroned in majesty, and not on the cross, because of the loss of the relic of the True Cross to Saladin's forces at Hattin in 1187:

> It was as if, now that the cross has been destroyed and removed from among men, His enemies are trying to take from Him the glory of that majesty which He won on the cross.[61]

Gerald then provides a further interpretation:

> Or a more likely explanation is that in that holy land which He finally hallowed by the shedding of His own blood, after it had enjoyed so many wonderful manifestations of His bodily presence, His faithful followers have been suffering, no longer on the cross, but in martial conflict. It has therefore been His wish that His own passion, which He is now somehow enduring through the suffering of His people, in that place where He reigns in majesty with His Father, should be similarly revealed, not on the cross, but amid the fighting and tumult of war.[62]

Thus, Gerald suggests that the suffering of Christians in the Holy Land had so moved Christ that he had determined to reveal his own heavenly passion in analogous terms: in heavenly warfare. Further, Christ had hoped that, by showing suffering on such an enormous scale, he might be able to rouse his followers on earth to take action in the Holy Land.

Gerald then moves on to offer an exposition on the shouted phrase that had awoken him. According to Gerald, the German and Latin of the exclamation ('Woch' being interpreted as a Germanic form of 'Alas!' by Gerald) represented the nations who had proved the most enthusiastic in their planned involvement in the crusades. This is an allusion to Frederick Barbarossa, whose forces had departed for the East from Regensburg on 11 May 1189, which was incidentally

---

[60] Gerald of Wales, *Expugnatio Hibernica*. pp. 212–13: '"Woch, Woch, Pater et Filius! Woch, Woch, Spiritus Sanctus!"'

[61] Ibid., pp. 214–15: 'Qui olim in propria persona passus est pro suis, nunc iterum se pati significat, sed in suis.'

[62] Ibid.: 'tamquam, cruce jam perdita et de medio sublata, illam, quam in cruce sibi acquisierat, hostes ei in majestatis gloriam auferre contendant. Vel potius, sicut in terra illa sacra, quam post tot et tanta corporalis praesentiae suae sacramenta demum proprio cruore consecravit, fideles sui, non in cruce nunc, sed armis et bellico certamine passi sunt, sic suam ipse passionem istam, quam in suis quodam modo nunc sustinet, ubi in majestate Patri conregnat, non in cruce voluit, sed in armis et bellico tumultu declarari.'

the day after Gerald experienced his vision. Indeed, this is not the only occasion on which Gerald had praised Frederick for his 'praiseworthy haste' in undertaking the expedition.[63] Until this point, the versions of Gerald's vision are largely the same in both his *Expugnatio Hibernica* and *De principis instructione*. However, in his later *De principis*, Gerald adds an additional passage explaining that, after the event, it was clear that the lamentation in the two languages was a reference to the future destruction of that people along with their leader. Here, *De principis* alludes to Frederick's death in June 1190 while on campaign, and the inefficacy of his forces in rendering aid to the Latin East. According to Gerald's interpretation, the vision had demonstrated the significance of crusading endeavour in the Holy Land by reinforcing the conceptual link between earthly and heavenly Christendom. If this vision were to be believed, then Christian travails in the Holy Land were of paramount significance to Christ himself. The implication of this, which Gerald made clearer through the discussion of the mysterious voice, is criticism of those who exhibited tardiness in their response to the Latin East's plight: namely, Henry II.

The first suggestion that contemporaries expected Henry to render aid to the Holy Land came as early as the 1160s. As discussed above, Henry took a crusade vow in 1172, but failed to set out for the Holy Land. A critical moment, however, came in 1185, when patriarch Heraclius of Jerusalem travelled to Henry's court to appeal for aid directly. In a rather lacklustre response, Henry promised financial aid to the Latin East. When news of Saladin's 1187 conquest of Jerusalem reached Europe, Henry took a crusade vow alongside Philip Augustus of France, at Gisors in 1188 (Henry's son Richard had shown greater promise by taking the cross at Tours in 1187). Henry also commissioned Archbishop Baldwin of Canterbury to undertake a crusade preaching tour of Wales during Lent 1188, on which Gerald himself accompanied the archbishop. However, tensions between the two kings delayed the expedition. It was in the context of protracted delay that Gerald experienced his vision. Gerald probably wrote the earlier of these two works, his *Expugnatio Hibernica*, between the spring of 1188 and the summer of 1189, and it appears that he still clung to the hope that his king would fulfil his crusade vow. For example, in the *Expugnatio Hibernica*, he rationalises that, perhaps, God was reserving the king for the restoration of the Latin East until it was completely destroyed in order that he may gain the greater glory.[64] However, Gerald extinguishes any sense of optimism in *De principis*, which he began working on in the years after his departure from the Angevin court in 1194, and completed in around 1216. In the intervening years, Henry had died (July 1189). Gerald articulated his frustration explicitly in this later text:

---

[63] Ibid., p. 210.
[64] Ibid., p. 206.

Immediately I fell from my whole hope, which before I had indulged, great as it was, with earnest desire; for I had hoped that [Henry] would deliver Israel in our day; and I call the Lord to witness that I had desired that thing with great earnestness, as well on account of the retention of the Holy Land, and the deliverance of it from the hands of the infidels, as on account of the honour of our own kingdom and nation. That same thing, also, the whole English people desired with the utmost earnestness.[65]

Thus, while in the *Expugnatio* Gerald's vision represents part of a brief narrative interlude concerning Heraclius' embassy to Henry, in the *De principis*, it becomes one part of a broader narrative agenda criticising Henry and demonstrating God's instrumentality in the punishment of the late king in the final years of his life. It is Gerald's vision at Chinon, however, that provides the proof that, by failing to undertake the crusade to the Holy Land in person, Henry had forsaken his kingly duty to render aid to Christ's patrimony in its hour of need.

The Absence of Visions from Second Crusade Narrative

This chapter's discussion has not drawn on material from narrative histories of the Second Crusade. This is because, aside from brief allusions, none of the sources analysed in this book engage with visions in relation to that crusade. The only fleeting reference to visions in relation to the Second Crusade can be found in the *De expugnatione Lyxbonensi* which, as we have seen, engages with miraculous themes throughout in its construction of the Lisbon campaign as a legitimate action. The *De expugnatione* describes how the crusaders endured a storm, or more precisely an act of divine chastisement, on the night of 29 May 1147. Having confessed their sins and sought atonement, the crusaders received many heavenly favours, 'to such an extent that it would be tedious to relate in detail the divine miracles which were revealed in visions'.[66] And so, Raol's narrative moves on, having sufficiently indicated the scale of divine support without having to provide the details.

It is a striking absence: visions and dreams were certainly part of these authors' narrative repertoires. We find an illustrative example of this in Helmold

---

[65] Gerald of Wales, *De Principis Instructione*, p. 208: 'His autem auditis, statim a spe decidi tota, quam ante quidem magnam et cum desiderio magno conceperam. Speraveram enim quod ipse diebus nostris redempturus esset Israel; et Deum testem invoco quoniam, tam propter terrae sacrae retentionem et ab impiorum manibus liberationem, quam ob regni quoque nostri et gentis honorem, illud magno opere concupiram. Id ipsum quoque totus Anglorum populus cum summa voluntate desiderabat.' English translation is from J. Stevenson, trans., *Concerning the Instruction of Princes* (Felinfach, 1991), p. 44.

[66] *DeL*, pp. 60–1.

of Bosau's *Chronica Slavorum*, a text which documents crusading activity in the Baltic, Iberia and eastern Mediterranean in and around 1147. The absence of miraculous themes pertaining to these various elements of the Second Crusade (with the exception of his discussion of Bernard of Clairvaux's preaching and a punitive miracle, as has been discussed above) contrasts with the abundance of such material elsewhere in the source. In particular, Helmold's description of the life and posthumous miracles of Bishop Vicelin of Oldenburg (*c.* 1090–1154), also in the *Chronica*, is punctuated with detailed accounts of Vicelin's numerous posthumous appearances.[67] This hagiographical material constitutes a *vita* of Vicelin incorporated into the chronicle, the visions of which function to demonstrate Vicelin's sanctity. Helmold had probably known Vicelin. He had been part of the latter's community at Segeberg, and may have fled with Vicelin to Wippenthorp (later Neumünster) following Pribislav of Lübeck's destruction of Segeberg in 1138.[68] Born in Hameln, Vicelin studied in Laon before returning to Saxony (*c.* 1125) in order to preach the gospel among the Abodrites. Following this commission, he based himself at Faldera (1127) in order that he might preach among the nearby Wends. A house of regular canons was soon founded at Faldera, Segeberg and Lübeck. In 1149 the archbishop of Hamburg-Bremen appointed Vicelin as the bishop of the revived see of Oldenburg, which he presided over until his death in late 1154.[69] Thus, Vicelin gained a reputation as one of the few in this period who sought to facilitate the conversion of pagan peoples through peaceful means. Indeed, Helmold describes Vicelin's ability to move the Nordalbingian people with his preaching as a miracle.[70] In contrast, Helmold concluded his account of the 1147 crusade against the Wends thus:

> Finally, when our men were weary, an agreement was made to the effect that the Slavs were to embrace Christianity… Many of them, therefore, falsely received baptism… Thus that great expedition broke up with slight gain. The Slavs immediately afterward became worse: they neither respected their baptism nor kept their hands from ravaging the Danes.[71]

---

[67] HB, pp. 146–7.

[68] HB, pp. 19–26; S. Rossignol, 'Bilingualism in Medieval Europe: Germans and Slavs in Helmold of Bosau's *Chronicle*', *Central European History*, 47 (2014), 528.

[69] See I. Fonnesberg-Schmidt, *The Popes and the Baltic Crusades, 1147–1254* (Leiden, 2007), pp. 49–50; and R.A. Fletcher, *The Barbarian Conversion: From Paganism to Christianity* (New York, NY, 1997), p. 446.

[70] HB, p. 93.

[71] HB, p. 123: 'Ad ultimum nostris iam pertesis conventio talis facta est, ut Slavi fidem Christianam reciperent… Multi igitur eorum falso baptizati sunt… Taliter illa grandis expedicio cum modico emolumento soluta est. Statim enim postmodum in deterius coaluerunt; nam neque baptisma servaverunt nec cohibuerunt manus a depredacione Danorum.' English translation is from Tschan, *The Chronicle of the Slavs*, pp. 180–1.

Helmold's emphasis on the sanctity of the missionary Vicelin and the inability of the crusade to achieve genuine conversion mirrors his usage of the miracles and visions in the *Chronica Slavorum*. In other words, he creates a contrast between preaching and crusade that is supported through his use of the miraculous. In the case of Helmold's *Chronica*, therefore, the absence of the miraculous in its sections of crusade narrative is indicative of a differing narrative agenda. While it may well have been the case that there were simply no accounts of visions associated with the events of the Second Crusade for authors to work with, or that an awareness of a negative outcome undermined the use of visions, the example of Helmold's *Chronica* reveals that it is possible to detect significance in silences.

Conclusion

Provided that it was viewed as legitimate, a vision communicated divine truths. Consequently, visionary experience represented a valuable persuasive tool for medieval authors. This included those who produced narrative histories of crusades, phenomena defined by their perceived association with God's will. Thus, visions offered narrative solutions for authors who sought to demonstrate the legitimacy of particular expeditions, ambiguous dogma or problematic *furta sacra*. As we have seen, however, visions, or indeed the lack thereof, could also reinforce critical constructions, drawing upon the revelatory potential of the visionary to demonstrate divine censure, or focusing the implications of visionary experience away from particular themes. Therefore, visions, like their related phenomena the miracle and the sign, represent valuable lenses through which to examine the narrative agendas and priorities of the medieval Latin Christian historians of crusade narrative.

PART III

Signs and Augury

5

Ways of Knowing

Miracles and visions were not the only means by which the divine might communicate with humankind. Rather, to those of a more Augustinian worldview, God had imbued the entirety of Creation with communicative potentiality, an intrinsic ability to serve as a sign. Thus, while both miracles and visions could signify, so could the unusual or uncanny, such as solar and lunar eclipses or earthquakes. However, Christian theologians since the early Church grappled with the long, pre-Christian history of signs and other 'ways of knowing', and the association between certain practices and Islam, classical antiquity, and ancient Mesopotamia. Additionally, the increasing scope allowed for naturalising explanations and the pursuit of causation in the Latin Christian intellectual landscape of the twelfth and thirteenth centuries shrank the scope of the potentially significant. A lunar eclipse could be indicative of an impending clash between kingdoms, or it could just be a manifestation of the routine cycle of the planets, signifying nothing. In this chapter, it will be argued that tensions between theologically licit and illicit ways of knowing surface at intervals in crusade narrative, often in discussions of the legitimacy of certain practices or in descriptions of perceived Others. These examples reveal a blurred, shifting boundary between legitimate and illegitimate practice, which authors were required to navigate in order to effectively engage with signs in their narratives.

Interpreting Signs in Medieval Latin Christendom

God's communication with humankind had considerable scriptural precedent. As the twelfth-century polymath John of Salisbury comments in his *Policraticus*, one should not doubt that certain astounding things can be signs, since Christ advises in the Gospel of Luke that 'there shall be signs in the sun and in the moon and in the stars', and 'there shall be great earthquakes in divers places, and pestilences, and famines, and terrors from heaven; and there shall be great signs.'[1] These sorts of signs, often presented in the form of natural phenomena such as earthquakes, were indicative of events temporally past, present and future, and spatially near and far. For example, William of Poitiers records how an appearance of Halley's comet foretold the defeat of Harold Godwinson in 1066.[2] However, signs were

---

[1] Luke 21.11, 25; John of Salisbury, *Policraticus*, p. 89.
[2] William of Poitiers, *Gesta Guillelmi*, pp. 140–3. For other near-contemporary

not the only way of accessing this sort of knowledge: there were other, more theologically questionable, methods, such as astronomy, astrology, horoscopy, and prophecy. To the more intellectually conservative Latin Christians of the twelfth century, many of these means of reckoning were problematic because of their origins or association with the pre- and non-Christian intellectual traditions that were becoming increasingly accessible in Latin Christendom in this period.[3] It is important to sketch out the key contemporaneous discourses on these themes in what follows, because discussions of these various ways of knowing can be found in crusade narrative.

Some of the most spectacular signs of crusade narrative are celestial in nature. However, the study of the celestial bodies, or more specifically, the use of knowledge about those celestial bodies to divine temporal affairs, was something of a concern for Christian theologians. It should be noted that the modern conceptual distinction between the practices of astronomy and astrology does not directly map onto the Latin terms *astronomia* and *astrologia* as they were understood in medieval Latin Christendom. It is not unusual to see *astronomia* and *astrologia* used interchangeably or with varying degrees of subtlety in texts from this period. Generally speaking, however, in the twelfth century, *astronomia* indicated aspects of the science that were calculated using an instrument, such as an astrolabe or quadrant.[4] *Astrologia*, by contrast, could be used to denote both natural astrology on the one hand, which sought to understand the nature of God's creation and incorporated meteorology and medical astrology, and superstitious (or what modern scholars refer to as judicial) astrology on the other, which was concerned with horoscopic predictions regarding the subtleties of the human life course.[5] The former, theologically licit form of *astrologia* roughly corresponds to our modern understanding of the science of astronomy. Henceforth, therefore, 'astronomy' is used to denote both *astronomia* and natural *astrologia*. 'Astrology' will correspond to judicidial *astrologia*, or, in other words, horoscopy. This dichotomy most closely reflects the twelfth-century Latin Christian distinction between the theologically licit and illicit.

Late antique and early medieval theologians were unsettled by the implicit and inextricable ties between 'pagan' culture past and present and both astronomy and astrology. Rooted in a Babylonian past and entirely separate from any

---

interpretations of the comet, see especially E. van Houts, 'The Norman Conquest through European Eyes', *The English Historical Review*, 110.438 (1995), 832–53.

[3]   On Arabic learning and astrology in the twelfth-century intellectual landscape of Latin Christendom, see R. Kieckhefer, *Magic in the Middle Ages*, 2nd edn (Cambridge, 2014), pp. 116–31.

[4]   C. Burnett, 'Adelard, Ergaphalau and the Science of the Stars', in *Adelard of Bath: An English Scientist and Arabist of the Early Twelfth Century* (London, 1987), p. 138.

[5]   K. von Stuckrad, 'Interreligious Transfers in the Middle Ages: The Case of Astrology', *Journal of Religion in Europe*, 1 (2008), 49.

Jewish, pre-Christian, tradition, horoscopic astrology in particular represented a vessel for the continuation of pagan traditions.[6] Yet astronomy was taught in the universities of western Europe as part of the *quadrivium*, alongside arithmetic, geometry and music. The related science of *computus* had played an important role in Catholicism for centuries as a means of time reckoning; the chief feast of the liturgical year was computed calendrically according to the lunar cycle, for example.[7] Bede (d. 735), in his *De temporum ratione*, had utilised the zodiacal method in his computation of the Church calendar in the eighth century.[8] Thus, while the gaze of ecclesiastical censure came to rest more firmly upon astrology – as a superstition – than astronomy, the Church's relationship with these sciences remained complicated.

One cause for concern regarding the legitimacy of astronomy and astrology was the Greek and Arabic intellectual heritage of much of this learning. The Umayyad emirate (756–929), and later caliphate (929–1031), of Cordoba in Iberia had come to rival Baghdad as a centre for astronomical and astrological research at a time when the Islamic scientific corpus integrated and built upon Hellenistic, Persian, Indian and Jewish traditions.[9] As the eminence of Cordoban astronomers increased, other cities of the Iberian peninsula, including Seville and Toledo, were encouraged to become centres for the study of the celestial bodies.[10] When the forces of Alfonso VI of León-Castile brought the *taifa* of Toledo under Christian rule in May 1085, it became an important locus for the translation of Arabic texts into Latin.[11] These translation initiatives reached their apogee in the twelfth century, and led to the incorporation of Greco-Arabic scientific learning into the Christian corpus of astrological knowledge. The Iberian Peninsula was not the only route by which this intellectual cargo entered into a Latin Christian milieu; the cultural dialogue brought about by the establishment of the polities of the Latin East facilitated further exposure of the western intellectual tradition

---

[6] N. Campion, *The Great Year: Astrology, Millenarianism and History in the Western Tradition* (London, 1994), p. 353; S. Page, *Astrology in Medieval Manuscripts* (London, 2002), p. 7.

[7] Bartlett, *Gerald of Wales*, pp. 104–5.

[8] Page, *Astrology*, pp. 41–2.

[9] On Iberia as a centre for astrological sciences in this period, see von Stuckrad, 'Interreligious Transfers', pp. 39–40, and *Locations of Knowledge in Medieval and Early Modern Europe: Esoteric Discourse and Western Identities* (Leiden, 2010), pp. 124–6.

[10] Von Stuckrad, 'Interreligious Transfers', p. 46.

[11] See especially M.-T. d'Alverny, 'Translations and Translators', in *Renaissance and Renewal in the Twelfth Century*, ed. R.L. Benson, G. Constable and C.D. Lanham (London, 1991), pp. 421–62. On the importance of Toledo as a centre for Arabic–Latin translation, see C. Burnett, 'The Coherence of the Arabic-Latin Translation Program in Toledo in the Twelfth Century', *Science in Context*, 14.1–2 (2001), 249–88.

to that of the Greek and Arab world.[12] Therefore, it is significant that crusade narratives were being produced in a period of intellectual enrichment that was received defensively in some quarters; as it will be argued in this chapter, we can see evidence of this ambivalence in crusade narrative.

Despite the abovementioned concerns, theologians accepted that the study of the heavenly bodies was a means of fostering an appreciation of God's creation. The subsequent application of that knowledge, however, raised questions about causation and agency. To Augustine of Hippo, there was a fine line between seeing celestial phenomena as indicative of change and as prescriptive agents of change:

> We, too, deny the influence of the stars upon the birth of any man; for we maintain that, by the just law of God, the free-will of man, which chooses good or evil, is under no constraint of necessity. How much less do we subject to any constellation the incarnation of the eternal Creator and Lord of all! When Christ was born after the flesh, the star which the Magi saw had no power as governing, but attended as witness... Christ was not born because the star was there; but the star was there because Christ was born.[13]

According to Augustine, the concept of the predetermined life course central to judicial astrology was incompatible with the principle of humankind's free will and God's omnipotence.[14] Isidore of Seville echoes Augustine's conclusions in his influential treatise, the *Etymologies*:

> Astronomy concerns itself with the turning of the heavens, the rising, setting, and motion of the stars, and where the constellations get their names. But astrology is partly natural, and partly superstitious... It is natural as long as it investigates the courses of the sun and the moon, or the specific positions of the stars according to the seasons; but it is a superstitious belief that astrologers (*mathematici*) follow when they practice augury by the stars, or when they associate the twelve signs of the zodiac with specific parts of the soul or body,

---

[12] Von Stuckrad, 'Interreligious Transfers', p. 52.

[13] Augustine of Hippo, 'Contra Faustum Manichaeum', cols. 212–13: 'Et nos quidem sub fato stellarum nullius hominis genesim ponimus, ut liberum arbitrium voluntatis, quo vel bene vel male vivitur, propter justum judicium Dei ab omni necessitatis vinculo vindicemus: quanto minus illius temporalem generationem sub astrorum conditione credimus factam, qui est aeternus universorum Creator et Dominus? Itaque illa stella quam viderunt Magi, Christo secundum carnem nato, non ad decretum dominabatur, sed ad testimonium famulabatur... non ideo Christus natus est quia illa exstitit, sed ideo illa exstitit quia Christus natus est.' English translation is from *NPNF*, 2.5, p. 158.

[14] V.I.J. Flint, 'The Transmission of Astrology in the Early Middle Ages', *Viator*, 21 (1990), 1.

or when they attempt to predict the nativities and characters of people by the motion of the stars.[15]

In this work, Isidore condemned astrology, yet recognised the utility of portents and medical astrology. Thus, both Augustine and Isidore, two of the most influential authorities on the subject for the duration of the early and central Middle Ages, acknowledged the value of moving beyond the simple observation of the celestial spheres.

Continued efforts to reconcile Christianity and astrology hint at the enduring appeal of the latter. That the Dominican friar and scholar of Aristotle Thomas Aquinas was writing treatises engaging with these issues demonstrates astrology's continued relevance even by the later thirteenth century. Indeed, astrologers could be found at the heart of European intellectual and political establishments throughout the central and later Middle Ages.[16] The career of the philosopher Adelard of Bath (died *c.* 1152) is a pertinent example, not only of the role of astrology in political contexts, but also of the influence of Arabic learning upon Latin Christian intellectuals in the twelfth century.[17] After studying at Tours, Adelard visited southern Italy, Sicily and Antioch, and it was while he was living at Monte Cassino that he translated twenty Arabic medical texts. As an independent mathematician, astronomer and astrologer in western England in the 1120s, Adelard produced Latin translations of two Arabic works on astronomy and three on astrology.[18] His last known work is his treatise on the astrolabe, dated to *c.* 1150, which he dedicated to the future Henry II of England, who appears to have been his patron at the time. It has even been suggested that Adelard's astrological skills were called upon during the Anarchy.[19] Yet Adelard's career stands in contrast with John of Salisbury's *Policraticus,*

---

[15] Isidore of Seville, *Etymologiae*, 3.27: 'Inter Astronomiam autem et Astrologiam aliquid differt. Nam Astronomia caeli conversionem, ortus, obitus motusque siderum continet, vel qua ex causa ita vocentur. Astrologia vero partim naturalis, partim superstitiosa est. Naturalis, dum exequitur solis et lunae cursus, vel stellarum certas temporum stationes. Superstitiosa vero est illa quam mathematici sequuntur, qui in stellis auguriantur, quique etiam duodecim caeli signa per singula animae vel corporis membra disponunt, siderumque cursu nativitates hominum et mores praedicare conantur.' English translation is from S.A. Barney et al., *The Etymologies of Isidore of Seville*, p. 99.

[16] Campion, *The Great Year*, pp. 347–53.

[17] D. Metlitzki, *The Matter of Araby in Medieval England* (London, 1977), pp. 26–30.

[18] M. Gibson, 'Adelard of Bath', in *Adelard of Bath: An English Scientist and Arabist of the Early Twelfth Century*, ed. C. Burnett (London, 1987), pp. 7–16; C. Burnett, 'Adelard of Bath', in *Medieval Science, Technology and Medicine: An Encyclopedia*, ed. T.F. Glick, S.J. Livesey and F. Wallis (London, 2005), pp. 5–6. On Adelard and the dissemination of Arabic astrology beyond clerical and into courtly spheres in the twelfth century, see von Struckrad, *Locations of Knowledge*, p. 132.

[19] See Campion, *The Great Year*, p. 353.

in which he identifies 'astrologers' (*mathematici* or *horoscopi*) as a type of 'magician' (*magus*), alongside 'soothsayers' (*aruspices*), 'dream interpreters' (*coniectores*) and 'fortune tellers' (*sortilegi*).[20] While theoretical treatises like John of Salisbury's attempted to carve out astrology as the most problematic of the astronomical sciences, it would appear that, in practice, idiosyncratic perceptions of the legitimacy of astronomy and astrology were commonplace at the time that authors were writing the crusade narratives examined in the present book.

As we have already seen, the study of the celestial bodies was not the only way of understanding the otherwise unknowable, and other ways of knowing, such as augury, are discussed in certain crusade narratives. John of Salisbury juxtaposes several illicit practices with divine signs in his commentary, including augury:

> Although I assert that all omens are meaningless and credence should not be given to augury, I do not condemn the authenticity and value of those signs which have been conceded by divine ordinance for the guidance of man. In manifold ways indeed [Heb. 1.1] God instructs his creatures; now by the sound of the elements, now by signs of animate and inanimate nature he makes manifest what is to come in accord with what he knows to be expedient for the elect. Certain preceding signs foretell the coming of storms or of fine weather, that man who is born for toil [Job 5.7] may in accord with these regulate his activities.[21]

Here, John of Salisbury distinguishes between the vanities of augury, a practice with ancient pre-Christian associations, and the divine origin of signs by specifying that God sends signs for the benefit of humankind. In an echo of Augustine and Isidore's consideration of astrology, John concedes that while augury may appear to offer some semblance of truth, it is ultimately meaningless superstition and its predictions should not be heeded.[22]

Otto of Freising discusses the legitimacy of prophecy, a way of knowing conceptually linked to signs but with a more precise focus on future events, at length and with frequent recourse to early Christian authorities in his *Historia*.[23]

---

[20] John of Salisbury, *Policraticus*, pp. 57–60.

[21] Ibid., p. 74: 'Non tamen, licet omina uana esse fidemque auguriis asseram non habendam, ideo signorum quae a dispositione diuina ad erudiendam creaturam concessa sunt fidem et fructum euocauo. Multipharie siquidem multisque modis suam Deus instruit creaturam, et nunc elementorum uocibus nunc sensibilium aut insensibilium rerum indiciis, prout electis nouerit expedire, quae uentura sunt manifestat. Futuras itaque tempestates aut serenitates signa quaedem antecedentia praeloquuntur, ut homo, qui ad laborem natus est, ex his possit exercitia sua temperare.' English translation is from Pike, *Policraticus*, pp. 57–8.

[22] John of Salisbury, *Policraticus*, pp. 71–2.

[23] On Otto's sources, see Mierow, *The Two Cities*, pp. 23–46.

In particular, Otto concentrated his efforts on demonstrating the legitimacy of pre-Christian prophecies. In the prologue to the fifth book of his *Historia*, Otto discusses how knowledge of such subjects as arithmetic, astronomy and philosophy was passed between pre-Christian civilisations over time. According to Otto, God enabled certain men to 'foresee' (*praevidere*) and be divinely inspired, as if dreaming.[24] Further, after a consideration of the prophecies of Hosea and Isaiah, Otto includes a passage on the Erythraean Sibyl of classical antiquity and her acrostic prophecy regarding Christ's incarnation, passion and second coming.[25] Otto pre-empts any reservations that his audience might harbour regarding the legitimacy of Sibylline prophecy by stating that Augustine came to believe that she, and others of the 'Gentiles', did belong to the City of God.[26] Indeed, Isidore of Seville also comments on how the Sibylline prophecies contained material about God and Christ, and concludes his section on the Sibyls by noting that the Erythraean was the more celebrated and noble.[27] Otto continues his defence of their significance by noting that not only have prophetically inspired individuals from among 'our' (*noster*) people foreseen the destruction of the world, but some of the 'Gentiles', relying on human aspects, were able to dream and thus prophesy it. Additionally, in another nod to the legitimacy of Sibylline prophecy, Otto notes that the Erythraean Sibyl had clearly referred to the final fire and judgement, and therefore her predictions parallel those of the Christian tradition.[28] As will become clear below, parallel discussions of the legitimacy of particular ways of knowing, and of the ability of certain individuals to interpret signs, also surface in crusade narrative.

Besides the abovementioned anxieties surrounding certain traditions and practices, another theological challenge relating to signs came from the increasing popularity of naturalising explanations in the twelfth century, as has already been discussed in relation to the miraculous and marvellous. Naturalising explanations of eclipses, including the idea that a solar eclipse can only naturally occur on a new moon, had entered the intellectual landscape of Latin Christian Europe centuries earlier via the works of Pliny the Elder and Isidore of Seville.[29] The latter clearly sets out the causes of solar and lunar eclipses in his *Etymologies*:

---

[24] OFC, p. 374.
[25] OFC, pp. 112–14. Mischa Hooker has demonstrated how Augustine came to view Sibylline oracles as a legitimate, albeit inferior, form of prophecy, and that this became the prevalent view in the Middle Ages. See M. Hooker, 'The Use of Sibyls and Sibylline Oracles in Early Christian Writers', PhD diss., University of Cincinnati, 2007, esp. pp. 343–97.
[26] OFC, p. 112.
[27] Isidore of Seville, *Etymologiae*, 8.8.
[28] OFC, p. 598.
[29] See I. Draelants, 'Le Temps dans les Textes Historiographiques du Moyen Âge', in *Le temps qu'il fait au Moyen Âge: phénomènes atmosphériques dans la littérature,*

An eclipse of the sun occurs whenever the moon, on the thirtieth lunar day, comes to that line where the sun travels, and by interposing itself before the sun, conceals it. Thus to us the sun appears to vanish when the orb of the moon is set before it… An eclipse of the moon occurs whenever the moon runs into the shadow of the earth. The moon is thought not to have its own light, but to be illuminated by the sun; hence it disappears if the earth's shadow comes between it and the sun… This happens to the moon on the fifteenth lunar day.[30]

Isidore, who was writing in the seventh century, does not use this naturalising explanation to undermine the potential for eclipses to act as signs. However, there are twelfth-century examples which do reveal the desacralising effect that these sorts of explanations could have. We find a particularly illustrative example in Richard of Devizes's account of a solar eclipse that occurred on 23 June 1191:

Those who do not understand the causes of things marvelled greatly that, although the sun was not darkened by any clouds, in the middle of the day it shone with less than ordinary brightness. Those who study the working of the world, however, say that certain defects of the sun and moon do not signify anything.[31]

Carl Watkins has discussed this passage as part of his consideration of Richard's 'epistemological pragmatism', concluding that his focus on demystification reveals how we can find challenges to Augustinianism beyond the immediate influence of the schools.[32] As part of the narrative that Richard's *Chronicon* offers, which includes a rather scattered account of Richard I's exploits on the Third Crusade, this passage serves to mock the credulity of those who believed that eclipses could be significant, while fashioning an image of the narrator – who is presented as being Richard himself – as learned. Indeed, Robert Bartlett has demonstrated how the ability to predict eclipses has contributed to narratives of

---

    la pensée scientifique et religieuse, ed. J. Ducos and C. Thomasset (Paris, 1998), pp. 91–138.

[30] Isidore of Seville, *Etymologiae*, 3.58–9: 'Eclipsis solis est, quotiens luna trigesima ad eandem lineam, qua sol vehitur, pervenit, eique se obiiciens solem obscurat. Nam deficere nobis sol videtur, dum illi orbis lunae opponitur… Eclipsis lunae est, quotiens in umbram terrae luna incurrit. Non enim suum lumen habere, sed a sole inluminari putatur, unde et defectum patitur si inter ipsam et solem umbra terrae interveniat. Patitur autem hoc quinta decima luna eo usque.' English translation is from S.A. Barney et al., *The Etymologies of Isidore of Seville*, p. 103.

[31] Richard of Devizes, *Chronicon*, p. 35: 'Mirati sunt qui causas rerum nesciunt; nullis obstantibus soli nubibus, medio die solis radios solito lucere debilius, sed hii quos agitat mundi labor dicunt solis et lune defectus facere aliquid non significare.' The eclipse of 23 June 1191 is also documented by Henry of Livonia, *Chronicon Livoniae*, ed. L. Arbusow and A. Bauer (MGH SSRG, 31; Hanover, 1955), p. 4.

[32] Watkins, *History and the Supernatural*, pp. 35–8.

societal and cultural superiority and rationality in this period.[33] The scorn demonstrated by Richard in the abovementioned passage certainly appears to tap into these sorts of derogatory discourses.[34]

It is important to view crusade narrative against this contextual backdrop of theological ambivalence towards certain practices, and the growing influence of desacralised approaches to nature. This perspective enables us to more clearly understand the implications of discussions of signs and prophetic practices in relation to, for example, interpretative responsibility and representations of the Other, and to situate these discussions within the intellectual landscape that produced them, as we shall see.

Ways of Knowing and Interpretive Responsibility in Crusade Narrative

According to Otto of Freising, the ability to accurately interpret signs was a God-given gift that came with enormous responsibility. In his discussion of the Old Testament Joseph, son of Jacob, Otto quotes Paulus Orosius, a student of Augustine of Hippo, and identifies Joseph as the first to be granted the ability to interpret dreams and prodigies.[35] Those skills were divinely bestowed upon Joseph. Further, he describes how Elijah and Elisha received their ability to interpret miracles, prodigies and signs directly from God because of their virtuous lives.[36] Consequently, Otto imposes an exclusivity on interpretive agency that is indicative of the perceived significance of prophecy and signs; the ability to accurately decipher the prophetic was not universal.

This notion of interpretive exclusivity is voiced in crusade narrative and is often visible in the proofs that the narrator offers regarding the authority of a given interpreter. Many of the proofs that accompany discussions of the interpreters of signs align with those that often feature alongside representations of visionaries, such as an assertion of good character. However, when it came to the interpretation of celestial signs authors often included a statement regarding the interpreter's intellectual credentials. For example, according to Guibert of Nogent, the ability to reliably read and interpret the movements of the celestial bodies came from 'knowledge of the stars', and such individuals should be consulted in the event of a potential sign.[37]

---

[33]   Bartlett, *The Natural and the Supernatural*, pp. 52–61.
[34]   Elsewhere in Richard of Devizes's *Chronicon*, witnesses marvelled at a bat that flew through Westminster Abbey on the day of Richard I's coronation, and the absence of bells until compline is presented as a sign. Richard of Devizes, *Chronicon*, pp. 3–4.
[35]   OFC, p. 78; Cf. Paulus Orosius, 'Historiarum Libri Septem', *PL*, 31, 1.8, cols. 709–12.
[36]   OFC, p. 100.
[37]   GN, pp. 318–19.

Ralph of Caen discusses the interpretation of celestial signs in similar terms. Ralph's *Tancredus* is unusual, however, in its consistent framing of crusade narrative in terms more analogous to classical literature and history. Indeed, he incorporated references to Virgil, Ovid, Livy, Caesar, Lucan and Sallust, among others, into his *Tancredus*, and offers relatively little discussion of divine agency as it is discussed in other crusade narratives.[38] The influence of these authorities is manifest in discussions of signs which employ the terminology indicative of precisely the sort of pre-Christian 'superstitions' that John of Salisbury would criticise later in the twelfth century. For example, after describing how the crusader army had prepared to sally out of Antioch to meet Kerbogha's forces on 28 June 1098, Ralph interrupts the chronology of his narrative to discuss the events of the previous night. According to Ralph, a certain man had roused the crusaders because the stars heralded their imminent victory.[39] Ralph explains that this man had learnt to read the order of the stars and what they portend as a child. He then embarks upon a discussion of the constellations and signs of the zodiac. Ralph engages with horoscopic imagery here, and in doing so reflects the influence of various classical authors upon his writing. The individual who was, according to Ralph, schooled in reading the stars therefore had adequate interpretative authority to be taken seriously. Ralph then turns to discuss Arnulf of Chocques, who he also describes as having been instructed in the art of reading the stars.

The consistency with which Ralph applies a classicising stylistic veneer to the First Crusade is evidenced in discussions of signs elsewhere in the *Tancredus*. For example, after describing the crusader conquest of Antioch (minus the citadel), the *Tancredus* offers an anecdote concerning Bohemond, whose wiles had facilitated the crusaders' entry into the city. According to Ralph, the crusade leaders had met for dinner one evening, when they became unsettled by Bohemond's unusual behaviour. He had drawn his sword and declared that he would cut one of the candles, which was much larger than the others in the room, in half with a single blow. Having achieved this, Bohemond and the others watched as both halves of the candle spontaneously reignited. However, the flame on the piece of candle that had remained standing went out suddenly. This, Ralph laments, was a 'sad augury' because the wax and the flame had not become exhausted at the same time. According to the soothsayers, this augured that though there was hope that Bohemond might have children in the future, they would soon die. Having quoted Virgil's *Aeneid*, Ralph adds that Virgil had said other things which served as a prophecy regarding the fate of Bohemond the Younger, the future Bohemond II of Antioch, who would be killed in 1130. The event is described as a 'wonder', a 'prodigy' or 'omen', and an 'augury', and the interpretation of the event is

---

[38] See Bachrach and Bachrach, *The Gesta Tancredi of Ralph of Caen*, pp. 4–5.
[39] RC, p. 73.

allegedly that of 'soothsayers', the latter three of which all bear an uncomfortable association, as far as authorities like John of Salisbury were concerned, with pre-Christian superstition.[40]

Ralph's framing of these discussions in classical terms does not necessarily mean that he himself perceived such phenomena in this way; it is entirely possible that he chose to write *as if* he did. Indeed, Ralph had studied under the instruction of Arnulf in Caen, who in turn had been tutored by Lanfranc at Caen in the 1060s, and it seems unlikely that he would have been unaware of contemporaneous discourses surrounding the theology of signs, or at least with the negative connotations of zodiacal reckoning.[41] Rather, Ralph's discussion of ostensibly illicit practices represents an aspect of the classicising veneer that he applies to his narrative wherein Bohemond, and especially Tancred, are portrayed in terms analogous to Virgil's Aeneas. This is a significant technique given the importance of Troy and the descendants of Aeneas to the concepts to Normanness that Ralph was navigating in his *Tancredus*.[42] Thus, within the classicising narrative of the *Tancredus*, the suggestion that a crusader camp might contain soothsayers, or that augury was a legitimate method of precognition, was perfectly reasonable.

To return to Ralph's portrayal of celestial signs, it is worth noting that his representation of Arnulf as a churchman in possession of a level of *scientia astrorum* is not unusual. According to Orderic Vitalis, Bishop Gilbert of Lisieux was an elderly physician with a comprehensive knowledge of the stars.[43] Gilbert

---

[40] RC, p. 66. Cf. Virgil, *Bucolics, Aeneid, and Georgics Of Vergil*, ed. J.B. Greenough (Boston, MA, 1900), 6.869–70, Perseus Digital Library, http://data.perseus.org/ citations/urn:cts:latinLit:phi0690.phi003.perseus-lat1:6.854-6.892 (accessed March 28, 2019). On Bohemond II, see T. Asbridge, *The Creation of the Principality of Antioch, 1098–1130* (Woodbridge, 2000), esp. pp. 89–91, 146–7. On the impact of Bohemond II's death in the context of the principality of Antioch, see A.D. Buck, *The Principality of Antioch and its Frontiers in the Twelfth Century* (Woodbridge, 2017), esp. pp. 22–7, 68–73, 221–30.

[41] See D.S. Spear, 'The School of Caen Revisited', *The Haskins Society Journal*, 4 (1992), 55–66.

[42] On Norman identity and Virgil, see P. Bouet, 'De l'origine troyenne des Normands', in *Mélanges René Lepelley: Recueil d'études en homage au Professeur René Lepelley*, ed. C. Bougy, P. Boissel and B. Garnier (Caen, 1995), pp. 401–13; and E. Albu, *The Normans in their Histories: Propaganda, Myth and Subversion* (Woodbridge, 2001), esp. pp. 12– 20. On Ralph of Caen and Norman identity, see N. Hodgson, 'Reinventing Normans as Crusaders? Ralph of Caen's *Gesta Tancredi*', *Anglo-Norman Studies*, XXX (2008), 117–32; and L. Ní Cléirigh, 'Gesta Normannorum? Normans in the Latin Chronicles of the First Crusade', in *Norman Expansion. Connections, Continuities and Contrasts*, ed. K.J. Stringer and A. Jotischky (Farnham, 2013), pp. 207–26, esp. pp. 221–5.

[43] Gilbert Maminot was bishop of Orderic's own diocese. Marjorie Chibnall has suggested that while it is unlikely that Orderic ever conversed with Gilbert at any length, stories about him may have circulated at Orderic's monastery. This story is one

would often plot the course of the stars through the heavens. One night, at around the time of the Council of Clermont in November 1095, he beheld a particular 'prodigy of the stars' and drew it to the attention of Walter of Cormeilles, who was on watch while the others at court were asleep. Gilbert asked Walter if he could see the sign and Walter confirmed that he could but was unable to tell what it portends. Gilbert advised that, in his opinion, it prefigured the migration of peoples to other kingdoms. The implication here is that Gilbert had interpreted the sign as portending the expedition to Jerusalem, thus framing the crusade within a context of divine predestination.

An individual's learning is a key aspect of each of the abovementioned descriptions of the interpreters of celestial signs; the ability to responsibly read signs was derived in part from the possession of specialist knowledge. The importance placed on an interpreter's credentials is further emphasised by negative discussions of the interpretation of signs. As we have already seen, Richard of Devizes mocked the alleged propensity of certain people to see perfectly explicable phenomena as signs.[44] Guibert of Nogent, in his narrative of the First Crusade, also critiques invented significance and incorrect interpretation. Unlike Richard, however, Guibert was not criticising people for their ignorance in the face of contemporaneous advances in the study of the natural order. Rather, he was concerned that the ubiquity of signs would dilute their significance and thus draw attention away from that which truly was divine. Indeed, fabrication of the sacred and the gullibility of the masses (as he would have it) appear to have been particular concerns for Guibert, who wrote an extended piece on the falsification of relics in the *De pignoribus sanctorum*.[45] It is striking that, in a history designed to foreground the divine architecture of the First Crusade, Guibert expended so much effort in criticising those who, in his opinion, desired to see signs everywhere. For example, in one passage, Guibert recalls how, one day when he was living in Beauvais, it was popularly claimed that a cross had appeared in the sky. However, Guibert states that the clouds had formed no such shape.[46] Regardless of whether Guibert's testimony is reflective of a genuine atmosphere of hysteria experienced at this time, as has been suggested by Jay Rubenstein, Guibert's careful exposition of the issue fosters confidence in his identification

---

of the examples which she uses to support this argument. See Chibnall, *The World of Orderic Vitalis*, p. 186.

[44] Richard of Devizes, *Chronicon*, p. 35.

[45] Guibert of Nogent, *De Pignoribus Sanctorum*, ed. R.B.C. Huygens (CCCM, 127; Turnhout, 1993), pp. 79–175.; On Guibert's attitude towards the cult of saints, see especially C. Morris, 'A Critique of Popular Religion: Guibert of Nogent on *The Relics of the Saints*', in *Popular Belief and Practice*, ed. G. J. Cuming and D. Baker, (Studies in Church History, 8; Cambridge, 1972), pp. 55–60; and Yarrow, *Saints and their Communities*, pp. 70–5.

[46] GN, p. 330.

of other phenomena as authentic signs.[47] Indeed, he counterbalances his criticism of credulity with a defence of true signs. In an echo of St Augustine, Guibert argues that the Magi would not have known of Christ's nativity, or that he was both God and man, had they not questioned the significance of the 'lofty light' in the sky.[48] This defence is situated after the discussion of several signs, each of which Guibert presents as indicative of the crusade's place in sacred history, as will be discussed in further detail in the next chapter. For the present purposes, however, it is enough to conclude that Guibert's discussions of the misidentification of signs represented a form of self-fashioning analogous to that which we have already seen in certain representations of the miraculous. By investing in his audience's conceptualisation of the author as a trustworthy interpretive agent, Guibert strengthens the foundations of his narrative agenda, namely, demonstrating that the First Crusade was indeed an act of God.

The most common 'way of knowing' in crusade narrative is the interpretation of signs, many of which come in the form of earthly or celestial phenomena. As has already been shown, crusade narratives emphasise the importance of the responsible interpretation of signs, preferably by individuals known to have a good amount of knowledge of the type of sign in question. A less common means of prognostication was derived from the exposition of scripture for the purposes of calculating sacred history. At the heart of this, and other, licit ways of knowing was divine edification: that those signs were provided by God for the benefit of humankind. Certain narratives, as we shall see, hint at the vanity inherent in the pursuit of knowledge about the future. While a sign was bestowed, the active search for information could smack of superstition. Not so, however, in Roger of Howden's representation of Richard I's meeting with Joachim of Fiore (*c.* 1135–1202) in 1190.

Rather than discredit Richard, Roger's lengthy description of the king's consultation with the renowned Calabrian abbot and theologian is laudatory. According to Roger, who had been travelling with Richard to the Holy Land, the king arranged to meet Joachim at Messina soon after Christmas Day, shortly before their departure for the eastern Mediterranean.[49] Joachim was a controversial figure both in life and for centuries after his death; Marjorie Reeves has called him 'a man with two reputations'.[50] On the one hand, he was a man

---

[47] Rubenstein, 'How, or How Much, to Reevaluate Peter the Hermit', pp. 60–1, and *Armies of Heaven*, p. 47.

[48] GN, p. 321.

[49] For a discussion of this episode in relation to Joachim's broader ideas regarding crusade and Apocalypse, see Rubenstein, *Nebuchadnezzar's Dream*, pp. 181–207.

[50] M. Reeves, *Joachim of Fiore and the Prophetic Future* (London, 1976), p. 28. On Joachim of Fiore, see especially the collection of essays by Emmett Randolph Daniel in *Abbot Joachim of Fiore and Joachinism* (Farnham, 2011). For a useful survey of scholarship on the Jews in Joachim of Fiore's predictions, see B. Whalen, 'Joachim of

with acute spiritual vision renowned for his exegesis on the Apocalypse and theses on the patterns of history. On the other, his views on the dual procession of the Holy Spirit and his three-*status* model of history were posthumously condemned by the papacy on two occasions: first by the Fourth Lateran Council in 1215, when Peter Lombard's trinitarian doctrine was upheld; and again in 1254 during the so-called 'scandal of the Eternal Evangel'.[51] Joachim's beliefs concerning the nature of the Trinity – that the Spirit was derived equally from the Father and the Son – was inextricably linked with his three-*status* model of history. Each *status* corresponded to an aspect of the Trinity. History could only progress into the final age of the Spirit once the Antichrist had been defeated. Inherent within the third and final *status*, that of Spiritual Intelligence, was a challenge to the Latin Church as an institution, as the *ecclesia activa* would be replaced by the *ecclesia contemplativa*.

Roger's portrayal of Joachim is undoubtedly a positive one. According to Roger, Joachim possessed the 'spirit of prophecy' and was capable of foretelling things to come.[52] The ascription of the prophetic spirit appears to be a reference to Joachim's interpretation of John's visions in Revelation, from which the phrase itself is drawn: 'it is the Spirit of prophecy who bears testimony to Jesus'.[53] Indeed, it may have been Joachim's expositions on the Apocalypse and the concordances he identified between figures in the Old and New Testaments (for example, Isaac and Jacob are identified with John the Baptist and Jesus Christ),[54] and in turn with his own contemporaries (for example, Bernard of Clairvaux as Moses),[55] that drew Richard to him. Roger suggests that Richard wanted himself and his crusade to be situated within Joachim's eschatological schema. Whatever the reality of the encounter, if it ever occurred, Roger's account of the interview with Joachim is not only an example of contemporary acceptance of Joachim's ideas in the final decade of the twelfth century, but also demonstrates that Roger considered Richard's desire to seek out Joachim's

---

Fiore, Apocalyptic Conversion, and the "Persecuting Society"', *History Compass*, 8.7 (2010), 682–91.

[51] Reeves, *Joachim of Fiore*, p. 26.

[52] *Chronica* 3, p. 75; *GR*2, p. 151.

[53] Revelation 19.10: 'Testimonium enim Iesu est spiritus prophetiae.'

[54] E.R. Daniel, 'Joachim of Fiore: Patterns of History in the Apocalypse', in *The Apocalypse in the Middle Ages*, ed. R.K. Emmerson and B. McGinn (London, 1992), p. 79; reprinted in E.R. Daniel, *Abbot Joachim of Fiore and Joachinism* (Farnham, 2011), 4, p. 79.

[55] E.R. Daniel, 'A New Understanding of Joachim: The Concords, the Exile, and the Exodus', in *Gioacchino da Fiore tra Bernardo di Clairvaux e Innocenzo III: Atti del V Congresso Internationale di Studi Gioachimiti (San Giovanni in Fiore, 16–21 September 1999)*, ed. R. Rusconi (Rome, 2001), p. 218; reprinted in E.R. Daniel, *Abbot Joachim of Fiore and Joachinism* (Farnham, 2011), 5, p. 218.

advice to have been an indicator of Richard's diligence as king. Consequently, this episode lends itself to Roger's broader narrative agenda aimed at a positive portrayal of Richard.[56]

According to Roger, Joachim responded to Richard's request by way of a brief exposition of the twelfth chapter of Revelation, in which the penultimate, or sixth, head of the red dragon, the sixth great persecutor of the Church, was identified as Saladin. The sixth head would soon be defeated, though this was dependent, Joachim noted, upon Richard's perseverance.[57] Notably, in his later *Chronica*, Roger alters the prediction, postponing the predicted victory over Saladin. It is likely that Roger made these edits in response to the crusade's failure to capture Jerusalem or defeat Saladin.[58] Thus, unaware of how controversial a figure Joachim would become (Roger died in 1201), Roger's account of Richard's encounter with Joachim contributed to his representation of Richard as the proactive and diligent crusader king, fated to play an instrumental role in the advancement of sacred time. At a time when contemporaries looked upon Joachim's ideas favourably, Richard's pursuit of information about his future relies on the study of scripture, itself a sign provided for the edification of humankind.

In each of the examples discussed above, authors have discussed the credentials of the interpreters of signs: they are often wise or learned, or, in the case of Joachim of Fiore, in possession of the 'spirit of prophecy'. The presentation of these qualities enables an author to proffer convincing expositions on the significance of signs. In each case, with the notable exception of Ralph of Caen's classicising representation, the discussions echo contemporaneous theological stances regarding the legitimacy of certain ways of knowing, eschewing superstition and horoscopy and focusing on the nature of signs as God-given. However, as we shall see, crusade narratives also feature considerations of other, less theologically savoury practices.

---

[56] Richard was not the only individual who sought out Joachim on account of his reputation as a prophet of the Apocalypse. In 1184 Pope Lucius III asked Joachim to interpret Sibylline prophecies, and in 1198 Adam of Persigny sought him out in order to discuss his prophetic gift. See Reeves, *Joachim of Fiore*, pp. 2, 24.

[57] *Chronica* 3, pp. 75–86; *GR2*, pp. 151–5.

[58] E.R. Daniel uses Roger's description of this encounter to suggest that Joachim had been unsure regarding the utility of crusading against the perceived threat of Islam. Any wavering on Joachim's part was soon ended by the Third Crusade's failure to defeat Saladin or recapture Jerusalem. See E.R. Daniel, 'Apocalyptic Conversion: The Joachite Alternative to the Crusades', *Traditio*, 25 (1969), 127–54; reprinted in E.R. Daniel, *Abbot Joachim of Fiore and Joachinism* (Farnham, 2011), 11, pp. 127–54.

Superstition and the Religious Other

Latin Christian crusade narratives occasionally map the abovementioned anxieties surrounding illicit ways of knowing onto their caricatures of religious Others. By tapping into an audience's anticipated association between certain practices, often astrology and augury, and pagan idolatry, an author might add layers of meaning to othering representations.[59] John Tolan has argued that several Latin Christian narratives of the First Crusade portray Muslims as pagan idolaters as a way of justifying the crusade.[60] However, an examination of the use of superstitious practices in the representation of Muslims reveals that this technique was not universally othering, but could be used to subtly different ends.

Walter the Chancellor, who wrote the *Historia Bella Antiochena* around two decades after the capture of Jerusalem by the First Crusade, declares in his narrative that the sultan of Khorasan (by which he probably meant the Seljuk sultan Ghiyath al-Din Muhammad) had heeded 'the auguries of sun and moon' when planning an invasion of northern Syria in 1115.[61] Walter returns to this imagery later when he notes that the forces of Bursuq, the Turkish emir of Hamadan, consulted 'the augury of the crescent moon' while in the region of Shaizar.[62] Here, Walter appears to anticipate that his audience would be suffi-ciently familiar with the association between judicial astrology, superstition and

---

[59]   See especially J. Flori, 'La caricature de l'Islam dans l'Occident médiéval. Origine et signification de quelques stéréotypes concernant l'Islam', *Aevum*, 66 (1992), 245–56; J.V. Tolan, 'Muslims as Pagan Idolaters in Chronicles of the First Crusade', in *Western Views of Islam in Medieval and Early Modern Europe*, ed. D.R. Blanks and M. Frassetto (Basingstoke, 1999), pp. 97–117, *Saracens: Islam in the Medieval European Imagination* (New York, NY, 2002), pp. 105–34, and *Sons of Ishmael: Muslims through European Eyes in the Middle Ages* (Gainesville, FL, 2008). For a useful survey of key scholarship on medieval Christian representations of Islam, see M. Pages, 'Medieval Roots of the Modern Image of Islam: Fact and Fiction', in *Bridging the Medieval-Modern Divide: Medieval Themes in the World of the Reformation*, ed. J. Muldoon (London, 2013), pp. 23–44. On Christian perceptions of Muslims in First Crusade texts, see especially A. Holt, 'Crusading Against Barbarians: Muslims as Barbarians in Crusades Era Sources', in *East Meets West in the Middle Ages and Early Modern Times, Transcultural Experiences in the Premodern World*, ed. A. Classen (Berlin, 2013), pp. 443–56; and N. Morton, *Encountering Islam on the First Crusade* (Cambridge, 2016). Jacqueline de Weever has identified a similar 'erasure of alterity, of otherness' in her exploration of representations of 'Saracen' women as heroines in *chansons de geste*, see J. de Weever, *Sheba's Daughters: Whitening and Demonizing the Saracen Woman in Medieval French Epic* (London, 1998), p. xxv. On medieval European representations of Islam more broadly, see S.C. Akbari, *Idols in the East: European Representations of Islam and the Orient, 1100–1450* (Ithaca, NY, 2009).

[60]   Tolan, 'Muslims as Pagan Idolaters'; and in his *Sons of Ishmael*, p. 67.

[61]   Walter the Chancellor, *Bella Antiochena*, ed. H. Hagenmeyer (Innsbruck, 1896), p. 66.

[62]   Ibid., p. 90: '...crescentis lunae augurium exspectabant...'

Islam for it to represent an appropriate element of his representation of a Muslim emir. In a similar vein, in *IP*1, Saladin consults a 'Syrian soothsayer' regarding his future. The soothsayer suggests to Saladin that he will obtain a vast kingdom and that he would rule over Damascus and 'Babylon' (presumably meaning Cairo).[63] The fact that Saladin did indeed become sultan of Syria and Egypt proves the accuracy – if not the legitimacy – of the prediction. Indeed, as discussed above, even authorities such as Augustine and Isidore had conceded that the predictions of superstitious practices were occasionally accurate. In *IP*1, this is a formative moment of Saladin's career that galvanises him in the course of action that would see him become 'the great persecutor of the Christian name'.[64] Here, Saladin is not only associated with superstitious practices, but his very pursuit of power is attributed to them.

An author might throw superstitious practices into sharper relief by pitching them against the powers of more legitimate methods. According to Rahewin, the continuator of Otto of Freising's *Gesta Frederici*, a 'prophetic counsellor' had provided Frederick Barbarossa with a particularly detailed prognostication. An elderly, one-eyed and foul-faced person would visit the emperor's court with twenty disciples. The stranger would, Rahewin continued, be either a Spaniard, an Arab or a 'Saracen', who lived in contempt of death and excelled in the art of sorcery and evil counsel. He and his followers sought fame and profit through Frederick's murder, which they would achieve by offering him poisoned gifts. Thus informed, Frederick has the 'magician' crucified.[65] Rahewin concludes that this affair was proof that God was Frederick's preserver. The abilities of Frederick's prophetic counsellor – portrayed as entirely licit in his practices and correct in his prognostications, even if no detail is actually provided on what form this might have taken – far outweigh those of the magician. Indeed, the counsellor's predictions triumph over the magician's superstitious arts even though the latter was, allegedly, unusually skilled in such wiles. Thus, Frederick emerges from the episode as the beneficiary of divine counsel, while the outcome

---

[63] *IP*1, pp. 250–1.

[64] *IP*1, p. 249: 'Verum ut tantus christiani nominis persecutor cupide posteritati plenius innotescat...' This is aligned with other contemporary representations of Saladin following the battle of Hattin and the conquest of Jerusalem. See for example Gregory VIII, 'Audita tremendi', p. 6. It contrasts, however, with another prevalent representation of Saladin as noble, evidenced in various *chansons de geste* and in Ambroise's *Estoire de la Guerre Sainte*, also a participant narrative of the Third Crusade. See M.J. Ailes, 'The Admirable Enemy? Saladin and Saphadin in Ambroise's *Estoire de la Guerre Sainte*', in *Knighthoods of Christ: Essays on the History of the Crusades and the Knights Templar, Presented to Malcolm Barber*, ed. N. Housley (Aldershot, 2007), pp. 51–64.

[65] OFGF, pp. 284–5.

reinforces the perceived superiority of his own advisor's prophetic methods; the implication is that this is a distinctly Christian triumph.

The caricature of the superstitious 'Saracen' appears to have been rather plastic, meaning that it was possible for authors to play with the blurred boundaries of the superstitious in their representations of the ostensibly Other. While John Tolan and others have identified the othering mechanisms employed in certain First Crusade narratives, the following will demonstrate how alterity might be partially erased in order that a typically superstitious prognostication might be legitimately incorporated into a narrative agenda.[66]

Despite their association with pre-Christian and Islamic learning, prognostications derived from practices such as astrology might still have a claim to authority. Guibert of Nogent admitted that knowledge of the stars was 'thinner and less plentiful' among 'westerners' (*Occidentales*) than 'easterners' (*Orientales*), where the science had originated.[67] He also describes a prophecy that had existed among the 'Gentiles', which predicted their subjugation by the Christian people. However, because their skill in the art of reading the stars was incomplete, they had been unable to calculate the date of the prophesied events.[68] The implication is that, had they correctly calculated the date, it would have corresponded to the events of the First Crusade. According to Guibert, the prophecy was ubiquitous in the East, such that Robert I of Flanders, while on pilgrimage to Jerusalem in 1083, had encountered a 'holier Saracen' ('sanctioris Sarracenum') who had explained that a council had been held to discuss that same portent. Thus, Guibert describes how a prophecy originating among Muslims in 'the East' and calculated according to the positioning of the stars had predicted (unbeknownst to them) the crusader conquest of Jerusalem in 1099. Further, the prediction had been in circulation over a decade before the events themselves. Here, Guibert indicates that astrological predictions could not only be correct, as others such as Isidore had conceded, but that they can, in certain circumstances, be communicative of sacred history, a context in which Guibert was undoubtedly trying to situate the First Crusade. The astrological prediction of crusade victory is thus absorbed into Guibert's narrative agenda, demonstrating the ineffable significance of the First Crusade. In light of this, Guibert's portrayal of the Muslim who spoke with the elder Robert of Flanders as 'holier' is significant, as it makes Robert's ostensibly friendly conversance with him, and the origins of the prediction itself, more palatable for the intended audience of a narrative predicated on the legitimacy of violence against adherents of Islam.

Another important example of this moderated othering occurs during a conversation alleged to have taken place between Kerbogha, *atabeg* of Mosul,

---

[66] Tolan, *Saracens*, pp. 109–20.
[67] GN, pp. 318–19.
[68] Ibid.

and his mother at some point before the battle of Antioch.[69] Kerbogha's mother, who goes unnamed in the Latin histories, but is called 'Calabre' in the *Chanson d'Antioche*, advised her son not to engage the Christian army in combat, because 'their god fights for them'.[70] According to the *Gesta Francorum*, the *atabeg*'s mother had acquired knowledge of the impending crusader victory from the consultation of 'our page' ('nostra pagina'), and the 'books of the gentiles' ('gentilium voluminibus').[71] The implication here is that she had consulted the sacred texts of Islam and Christianity. Indeed, she makes several references to the Old and New Testaments in her speech to her son, often quoted incorrectly, which may have been a deliberate device employed by the author to indicate a clumsy acquaintance with Christian scripture.[72] Additionally, according to Peter Tudebode, she had gazed 'upon the stars of heaven … shrewdly speculating and thoroughly examining with inquisitive mind the planets of the skies and the twelve signs of the zodiac and countless omens'.[73] Despite the various parallels between her alleged practices and the typically condemned practice of astrology and particularly horoscopy, her portrayal in these texts is not damning; the authors pass no judgement on her. The logic of her otherness is unbalanced by her familiarity with Christian scripture and firm belief in the superiority of the Christian god but is simultaneously reinforced by her horoscopy.[74]

---

[69] Rosalind Hill describes the episode as 'camp gossip' in *GF*, p. xvi; Yuval Noah Harari has discussed this episode in relation to the status of the *Gesta Francorum* as an 'eyewitness' narrative, Y.N. Harari, 'Eyewitnessing in Accounts of the First Crusade', *Crusades*, 3 (2004), 89–90. On the story of Kerbogha's mother as a source for understanding how non-Christian women and motherhood were perceived and represented in crusade narratives, see N. Hodgson, 'The Role of Kerbogha's Mother in the *Gesta Francorum* and Selected Chronicles of the First Crusade', in *Gendering the Crusades*, ed. S.B. Edgington and S. Lambert (Cardiff, 2001), pp. 163–76, and *Women, Crusading and the Holy Land in Historical Narrative* (Woodbridge, 2007), pp. 190–6.

[70] GF, p. 53. Cf. PT, pp. 93–6. Kerbogha's mother is called 'Calabre' on two occasions in the *Chanson d'Antioche*, laisses 33, 218, pp. 248, 606.

[71] *GF*, p. 55.

[72] Rosalind Hill commented, in her translation of the *Gesta Francorum*, that these misquotes are indicative of a devout lay author recalling passages from memory (*GF*, pp. 54–5, n. 9). However, these misquotes only occur in the direct speech attributed to Kerbogha's mother, and, as more recent scholarship has shown, the author of the *Gesta Francorum* was more likely a cleric. See C. Morris, 'The *Gesta Francorum* as Narrative History', *Reading Medieval Studies*, 19 (1993), 55–71; and C. Kostick, 'A Further Discussion on the Authorship of the *Gesta Francorum*', *Reading Medieval Studies*, 35 (2009), 1–14.

[73] PT, p. 95: '...in qua spiculando atque ingeniose rimando respexi in cęlorum astra, atque ingeniando sagaciter ac mente sedula scrutando cęlorum planetas, ac in xii polorum signa, sive in sortes innumeras...' English translation is from Hill and Hill, *Historia de Hierosolymitano itinere*, p. 71. Cf. *GF*, p. 55.

[74] On the otherness of Kerbogha's mother as a means of making her role as an intelligent,

Notably, each of the 'theologically refined' Benedictine texts made significant alterations to their own portrayals of Kerbogha's mother, augmenting both the positive and negative elements of her portrayal in the *Gesta Francorum*. Robert the Monk, for example, elaborates on her prophetic practices, rendering her association with superstition and augury explicit.[75] In Robert's history, Kerbogha's mother describes how oracles cast lots and scrutinised the entrails of animals, while she herself 'examined the courses of the stars, the seven planets and the twelve signs... [and] cast lots with the soothsayers'.[76] Despite this, she makes repeated reference to the Old Testament.[77] While the version provided by Baldric of Bourgueil does associate Kerbogha's mother with augury, he does not go to the same lengths as Robert. Baldric grants her the ability to foretell future events and knowledge of the stars gleaned from the study of the constellations. Additionally, Baldric presents her as a soothsayer learned in many disciplines. A notable deviation in Baldric's version is his description of Kerbogha's mother as 'old and full of days', an allusion to Old Testament descriptions of Isaac and Job that emphasises her perceived wisdom.[78] In typical style, Guibert of Nogent discusses the episode at length. In his *Dei gesta*, Guibert draws a link between Kerbogha's mother's prophecy and the prophecy relayed by the 'holier Saracen' to Robert I of Flanders, that the Christians would subjugate the 'Gentiles'.[79] According to Guibert, she had tested that prediction using her skills in astronomy. Strikingly, Guibert describes her advice to Kerbogha as 'miraculous', and augments the scriptural allusions made during her speech.[80] Each of these authors, then, adjusted the image of Kerbogha's mother as conversant with Christian scripture and superstitious practices, indicating the perceived relevance of these themes to the desired narrative effect of the passage.

The story of Kerbogha's mother only appears in the First Crusade narratives that are known to have drawn upon the *Gesta Francorum* or its derivatives, though the narratives of Raymond of Aguilers and Fulcher of Chartres, which

---

religiously informed woman more believable, see Hodgson, *Women*, pp. 190–6.

[75] RM, pp. 61–5.

[76] RM, p. 63: 'Cum astrologis siderum cursus, VII scilicet planetas et XII signa, sapienter contemplata sum, et quidquid phisiculari potest cum aruspices, extis et armis pecudum. Cum sortilegis sortes temperavi...' English translation is from Sweetenham, *Robert the Monk's History of the First Crusade*, pp. 156–7. The *Chanson d'Antioche* appears to follow Robert the Monk here, even comparing her to the Arthurian enchantress Morgan le Fay. See *Chanson d'Antioche*, laisse 218, pp. 604–6.

[77] Particularly to Deuteronomy (10.17, 32.30, 39 and 41–2) and Exodus (23.20–3).

[78] BB, p. 64. Cf. OV, vol. 5, p. 96. Scriptural allusions in Baldric's version of her speech includes reference to 1 Kings 8.41 (BB, p. 64).

[79] GN, p. 215. Cf. GN, p. 319.

[80] GN, pp. 212–14. Scriptural allusions include references to Matthew 15.16, Isaiah 49.26, Psalms 20.13, 78.6, 81.8, 112.3–4, Romans 8.15, 9.25, and Genesis 18.10, 14.

hint at an intertextual connection with the *Gesta Francorum*, do not include the scene. Orderic Vitalis, writing nearly four decades after the events of the First Crusade, condensed the story significantly by removing the direct speech and, by extension, excising the scriptural allusions and their implications for how Kerbogha's mother is perceived. Consequently, in Orderic's history, she is simply a prophetic woman with knowledge of the stars.[81] Writing a further forty years after Orderic, William of Tyre omitted the episode from his narrative altogether. He did, however, follow Raymond of Aguilers in describing how, during the siege of Jerusalem, two witches were brought out onto the walls in order that they might render the siege machine powerless through their magic incantations.[82] A projectile flung from the very siege machines they had been attempting to bewitch promptly crushed the two women and the three girls attending them. This is certainly a more straightforward employment of othering superstitious imagery than we find in the various discussions of Kerbogha's mother.

These representations of Kerbogha's mother are fascinating for numerous reasons. As far as its engagement with discourses on ways of knowing is concerned, it speaks to expectations surrounding the association of the religious Other with superstitious practices. At the same time, however, it is forced to reconcile this with a central narrative aim of the anecdote: the demonstration of the divine support of the crusaders, and the predestined nature of their victories on that expedition. Moderated representations of Kerbogha's mother, which dilute the motif of the 'Saracen' sorceress by situating her prognostications in more legitimate methods (namely, the consultation of Christian scripture), speak to concerns – possibly those of the anticipated audience – regarding the legitimacy of certain methods of precognition. In other words, the various representations of Kerbogha's mother are indicative of a multiplicity of understandings regarding the accuracy and, more importantly, the validity, of the sorts of practices that John of Salisbury condemns in his *Policraticus*.

Conclusion

Many Latin Christian crusade narratives reflect a belief in God's ability to communicate with and through Creation using phenomena known as signs. Events spatially and temporally distant could be presaged by significant or uncanny natural phenomena, though as several narratives reveal, there was great responsibility in the interpretation of these signs. However, the boundaries between signs, and other ways of knowing, and practices condemned by the Latin Church, such as augury and horoscopy, were blurry and shifting. Thus, we

[81] OV, vol. 5, p. 96.
[82] WT1, pp. 406–7. Cf. RA, p. 149.

find that discussions of signs in crusade narratives engage with these theological discourses of ambivalence. They reflect on the importance of misidentification or misrepresentation and draw upon, and occasionally push against, traditions associating particular practices with perceived Others. This is visible when authors take steps to navigate that boundary between the licit and illicit and pre-empt their audience's attitudes towards certain practices. They did this in order that they might more confidently employ signs, and other ways of knowing, in service of their narrative agendas, and it is to the function of these themes that the following chapter will turn.

6

Signs of the Times

Signs were another means by which God might communicate with humankind, harnessing the proclivities of Creation to arouse wonder and encourage reflection. This logic implies that God had a vested interest in matters provoking signs, a concern or investment significant enough to prompt the provision of said sign. By recognising this aspect of the implications of signs, we are able to see how they function in parallel with miracles and visions as indicators of divine approval or chastisement, or of futures good or ill. Indeed, it is the predictive capabilities of signs, their ability to indicate the spatially or temporally distant, which allowed them to embed a particular event within sacred history. For, as diverse signs had foretold the coming of Jesus Christ according to the Gospel of Luke, so too might other signs predict other momentous events.

It will be argued in this chapter that signs in crusade narrative can work to situate the relevant expedition alongside what contemporaries viewed as appropriately momentous events, and to flag the divine disposition regarding the events narrated. It will also be shown how the use of signs to indicate divine approbation contributes to the preponderance of positively interpreted signs in this corpus, meaning signs that are accompanied by interpretations explaining that they communicated victory, or other positive outcomes, rather than, for example, destruction or famine. The role that signs of divine approval play in First Crusade narratives will be examined first, followed by signs of divine wrath across a broader range of sources. Two case studies will then be discussed, allowing an exploration of the ways in which signs, and related ways of knowing, might be employed in a justificatory capacity, and how discussions of signs might be seen to tap into contemporaneous hopes and anxieties surrounding crusading and the Latin East.

Signs of Divine Approval

The signs of First Crusade narrative are usually astronomical in nature, and contribute to the idea that the First Crusade was divinely predestined. Much like miracles and visions, an author might incorporate such phenomena into a narrative with or without an accompanying exposition regarding its significance. Robert the Monk describes how a great fire, visible in the sky over Antioch in June 1098, fell into the Turkish camp on the night after the discovery of the relic of the Holy Lance. This, Robert explains, was a message from God that signified his wrath come from the West in the form of the Christian army.[1] Robert also describes a comet that was seen in the sky on the morning the crusader army entered the city (3 June 1098). It gave off a reddish glow, and heralded change within the 'kingdom' (*regnum*).[2] Thus, Robert voices the appropriate responses to the phenomena in the narrative, thereby harnessing descriptions of both a falling fire and a red comet to demonstrate divine investment in the fate of the First Crusade. The absence of explicit interpretation in other examples does not render signs devoid of implication, however. Often, the narrative logic of the events surrounding the sign nudges an audience towards a particular interpretation. Beyond the cue offered by a narrative's 'order of meaning', an audience's interpretation of an account of a sign may also depend on governing external discourses, for example, that earthquakes bring grave tidings, according to John of Salisbury.[3] Such traditions would have been manifold and contradictory, however: Albert of Aachen describes how an earthquake occurred in affirmation of the popular response to Peter the Hermit's message, and that it should be interpreted as 'predicting nothing other than' the mobilisation of armies from numerous Latin Christian kingdoms.[4] Fulcher of Chartres describes a 'marvellous redness' in the sky over Antioch, though unlike both phenomena described by Robert, this was seen before the crusaders had entered the city.[5] While Fulcher offers no interpretation, he situates the event between descriptions of crusader famine and suffering, the expulsion of the women from the crusader camp, and an earthquake. It is difficult to discern whether Fulcher intended his audience to interpret this as a good or ill omen, but we can at least conclude that the story of the red sky contributes towards the creation of an atmosphere in which one might expect events of great significance to occur.

Other First Crusade narratives discuss the various signs seen over Antioch in the summer of 1098; namely the red sky witnessed during the crusader siege of the city, and the falling fire and red comet during their subsequent travails inside the city. Raymond of Aguilers, who presents himself as being at Antioch at the time, records a red sky in late December 1097, which places the event during the crusader siege of the city, like Fulcher's 'marvellous redness'.[6] Also like Fulcher, Raymond describes the phenomenon during his account of the suffering experienced by the crusaders during the initial eight-month siege of the city, and immediately after his description of an earthquake. However, Raymond's version

---

[1] RM, pp. 69, 71.

[2] RM, pp. 54–5.

[3] John of Salisbury, *Policraticus*, pp. 68–70. I follow Hayden White's usage of 'order of meaning'. See H. White, 'The Value of Narrativity in the Representation of Reality', *Critical Inquiry*, 7.1 (1980), 9.

[4] AA, p. 8.

[5] FC, p. 244.

[6] RA, p. 54.

is distinctive because of its clear negative interpretation. The sky turned red in the north during the first watch of the night, as though dawn were coming. This, Raymond continues, should be interpreted as divine chastisement from God that did not succeed in wresting the minds of many from sinful occupations. It was at this time, Raymond continues, that Adhémar of Le Puy prescribed fasts, prayers, alms and processions that God might end the crusaders' current tribulations.[7] As part of Raymond's narrative, the red sky at Antioch contributes to the series of events leading up to the discovery of the Holy Lance at Antioch, helping Raymond to build the atmosphere of crisis and divine punishment into which Peter Bartholomew's revelations would be introduced.

Signs contribute to the anticipation of the Holy Lance's discovery elsewhere in Raymond's narrative. For example, he describes an event that parallels Robert's description of the falling fire. One night, a great star appeared over Antioch before splitting into three parts and descending on the Turkish camps.[8] Raymond draws an explicit link between this phenomenon and the discovery of the Holy Lance, as promised by Peter Bartholomew and discussed above. According to Raymond, this sign strengthened the will of the crusaders, who waited in anticipation for the fifth day and the coming of God's mercy in the form of the recovery of the Holy Lance (from which it can be deduced that the star was seen around 9 June).

Guibert of Nogent, who follows Fulcher in describing a fiery red sky witnessed during the crusader siege of Antioch, also clearly integrates the sign into his narrative agenda. In his version, however, the red light took the form of a cross:

> Some of the wise men there related the fire to future battles, and said that the appearance of a cross was a sign of certain salvation and victory to come. We do not call this an error, for many witnesses confirm this testimony.[9]

Here, Guibert appears to be drawing on the story of the cross that Constantine and his army had seen in the sky, as famously described in the *Vita Constantini* of Eusebius and later associated with the Battle of Milvian Bridge (312).[10] By evoking this imagery, Guibert nudges his description of the sign towards

---

[7]   Ibid.

[8]   RA, p. 74.

[9]   GN, p. 333: 'Quod quique illic sapientium incendium ad bella retulere future, ubi tamen esset – quod crux videretur innuere – certa salus et successura victoria. Hoc non refellimus, id plane uberrimis testimoniis approbatur, hoc, inquam, rimarum plenus poterit tacuisse Parmeno.' English translation is from Levine, *The Deeds of God through the Franks*, p. 157. Cf. EA, p. 18, and *HeFI*, p. 62.

[10]   Eusebius, *Life of Constantine*, trans. A. Cameron and S.G. Hall (Oxford, 1999), p. 81. See G. Constable, 'The Cross of the Crusaders', in *Crusaders and Crusading*, p. 84. For a useful summary of Eusebius, his life and works, see T. Barnes, *Constantine: Dynasty, Religion and Power in the Later Roman Empire* (Chichester, 2014), pp. 9–13.

a recognisable motif associated with a well-known precedent for divinely sanctioned warfare. Notably, the account of Frederick of Swabia's fourth sortie from Adrianople on 1 February 1190, as described in the *Historia de expeditione*, also draws on this motif. Those accompanying the duke witnessed a 'remarkable sign' in the form of a huge, blood-red cross glittering in the sky.[11] According to the *Historia de expeditione*, witnesses interpreted it as a benevolent sign, perhaps indicative of future good fortune, and thus they celebrated by singing and chanting their thanks to God. Given the appearance of the celestial knight motif in the *Historia de expeditione*, as has already been discussed, it is possible that this episode is similarly indicative of the influence of First Crusade histories on the narrativisation of later crusade enterprises, though we should be cautious in this instance, given the limited circulation of Guibert's First Crusade history, and the relative ubiquity of the story of Constantine.

Signs could take on distinctly martial implications by means other than reference to well-known precedents like Constantine. In his discussion of a similar sign, Fulcher describes how a brilliant white sword had been visible in the sky over Heraclea pointing towards the East.[12] As with his account of the red sky at Antioch, he does not provide an interpretation. Possible interpretations include: that the sword was pointing the way for the crusaders; that it was indicative of divine approval of the violent nature of the endeavour; that it was a sign of impending crusader victory in the East (as in Guibert's account of the cross in the sky over Antioch); or a combination of these. However unreachable such specific interpretations may be, its inclusion in Fulcher's text nonetheless reveals a belief that the crusade merited the provision of signs for the edification of its participants, and that this sign has a distinctly martial quality.

One might anticipate that a monastic author would be more inclined to offer specific interpretations of signs, in order to shepherd his intended audience's perception of the divine significance of the expedition. While this does appear to have been the case with Guibert, who, as we have seen, goes to some length to offer precise interpretations for such phenomena, it is not so with Baldric of Bourgueil's history of the First Crusade. After describing that many people chose to take the cross, Baldric notes that many reported signs from heaven at this time.[13] For example, on 4 April in 1095 a hail of countless stars was seen falling over France.[14] Baldric admits that stars had been known to fall from

---

[11] *HeFI*, pp. 62–3.

[12] FC, pp. 203–5. Cf. William of Malmesbury, *Gesta Regum Anglorum*, p. 630.

[13] BB, p. 141.

[14] BB, pp. 140–1. *Grando* can be translated figuratively as meaning 'multitude'; however, given the immediate context (i.e. Baldric's discussion of these stars as having fallen), I believe the literal translation of 'hail' or 'hailstorm' to be a more accurate reflection of the intended meaning.

heaven in this way, thereby anticipating those of his audience who might have been more inclined to reach for a natural explanation for the phenomenon. While Baldric clearly frames this event as a sign, he does not venture an interpretation of what the phenomenon portended, concluding rather that the mysteries of God are unknown. This phrase, indicating humility in the face of Creation, prompts the audience to reflect on what the significance of that event might have been, while excusing Baldric from committing to an interpretation himself. In Baldric's narrative, the story of the falling stars occurs after his version of Urban II's sermon at the Council of Clermont (27 November 1095), and a description of how Adhémar of Le Puy and Raymond of Saint Gilles took the cross. This means that Baldric's narrative momentarily looks back in time from the council in November to the sign of the previous April. The implications of this order of meaning is that the sign should be read in light of the events of that November, if not foreshadowing them then at least contributing to Baldric's portrayal of those times as significant.

Order Vitalis, who drew on Baldric's work for sections of his chronicle in *c.* 1135, frames the same event in more definite terms. Orderic describes how a shower of stars was seen by many in France in April 1095. These stars could have been mistaken for hail, he continues, had they not shone so brightly.[15] In an addition to Baldric's version, Orderic then notes that many had interpreted the sign as an indication of the imminent fulfilment of Scripture: namely, that the sixth seal of the Apocalypse had been opened and that the stars would fall from heaven. Jay Rubenstein has argued that such apocalyptic interpretations of signs are indicative of a popular contemporaneous conceptualisation of the First Crusade as the End Times: 'The words of prophecy had become the language of current events'.[16] Whatever the reality of Orderic's ideas regarding the First Crusade and Apocalypse, its evocation as part of his narrative certainly serves to enhance the crusade's status as a crucial moment in sacred history.

Such language is also used in Ekkehard of Aura's narrative of the First Crusade. Relying heavily on the 1106 Continuations of the chronicle of Frutolf of Michelsberg, Ekkehard devotes a significant proportion of his narrative to signs that occurred around the time of the crusade's preaching. According to Ekkehard and his anonymous source, at the time of the emperors Henry IV and Alexios Komnenos, nation rose against nation as foretold by the Gospels. Earthquakes, famine, pestilence and great signs from heaven occurred all around the known world.[17] There were so many events indicative of the eschatological significance

---

[15]   OV, vol. 5, p. 8.
[16]   Rubenstein, *Armies of Heaven*, p. 44.
[17]   EA, p. 12; Cf., *Frutolfi Chronici Continuationes*, p. 19. URL: http://www.mgh.de/
fileadmin/Downloads/pdf/Bamberger_Weltchronistik/Continuatio_I_und_II/

of the time, Ekkehard continues, that he may only record the 'most useful'.[18] Presumably, utility lies in the ability to demonstrate the importance of the crusade. Indeed, the aggregate of these anecdotes clearly conveys the perceived significance of the events subsequently narrated, namely the First Crusade. For example, Ekkehard follows his source in claiming to have witnessed a comet in the shape of a sword in the southern sky in early October 1096.[19] He also describes seeing 'bloody clouds' coming together from both the East and the West; and on another occasion, at midnight, Ekkehard and many others (again, the implied involvement of the narrator is lifted directly from the anonymous continuation) observed fiery torches flying through the air from the north.[20] The parallels between these accounts and those of, for example, Fulcher, discussed above, are striking, particularly in their discussion of the signs taking on the shapes of swords, of their red colouring, and of their directional indication (on an East–West alignment). Having described what he himself had supposedly witnessed, Ekkehard records several signs seen – or so it is implied – by acquaintances of his. For example, a priest named Siggerius witnessed two horsemen fighting in the sky, and another priest, named Gaius, saw a sword 'of marvellous length' lifted to imperceptible heights by a sudden wind.[21] Further indicative events include a woman who, after a two-year pregnancy, gave birth to a son who could already speak, animals that were born with two heads, and mares that gave birth to foals with the teeth of much older animals.[22] Thus, Ekkehard concludes, all of Creation was exerting itself to rouse potential participants to involvement in the expedition.

As we have already seen, Albert of Aachen wrote his narrative account of the First Crusade independently from the written traditions of, for example, the *Gesta Francorum*. It is striking, therefore, that the descriptions of signs contained in his work bear many similarities to those of other authors. For example, after his account of the victory at Antioch and the activities of Baldwin at Edessa, Albert describes how those on watch one evening saw the stars first grouping together and shining brightly, before circling the heavens and breaking up. According to Albert, witnesses interpreted this in different ways, but the true meaning, he argues, turned out to be far better. The crusade leaders, who had been scattered after the victory at Antioch, reunited and continued their journey to Jerusalem.[23] This imagery, of a star that broke up in the sky, is reminiscent of

---

Satzlauf_2018-08-09T0918/Frutolf-Fortsetzungen_bis_1101_und_1106_
Satzlauf_2018-08-09T0918.pdf.

[18] EA, p. 18; Cf., *Frutolfi Chronici Continuationes*, p. 27.
[19] EA, p. 18; Cf., *Frutolfi Chronici Continuationes*, p. 27.
[20] EA, p. 18; Cf., *Frutolfi Chronici Continuationes*, pp. 27–8.
[21] EA, p. 18; Cf., *Frutolfi Chronici Continuationes*, pp. 28–9.
[22] EA, p. 18; Cf., *Frutolfi Chronici Continuationes*, p. 29.
[23] AA, pp. 366–8.

the falling stars described by Raymond, Robert and Baldric. We also find familiar imagery – namely the reddening of celestial bodies – in Albert's description of an eclipse witnessed by the crusaders as they drew close to Jerusalem. According to Albert, the eclipse turned the moon blood red.[24] Those with knowledge of the stars comforted the fearful, explaining that the portent was a good one for the Christians because it indicated the destruction of the 'Saracens'. Should an eclipse of the sun occur, however, it would spell disaster for the Christians.[25] Given the independence of Albert's account, his reliance on oral testimony, and the parallels across the texts, we can conclude that stories involving signs of this type would likely have been familiar to many crusaders and Latin Christian onlookers at the time, and in the wake, of the First Crusade. Therefore it is possible to discern a much broader belief that the crusade prompted edificatory signs beyond the worlds of individual narratives or clusters of traditions.

We must temper such an observation, however, with the fact that the *Gesta Francorum*, a text that influenced so many others in this corpus, makes no mention of celestial phenomena like those mentioned above (e.g. eclipses, shootings stars). This is striking considering the important role of such signs in Guibert, Baldric and Robert's narratives (and indeed in the participant narratives of Fulcher of Chartres and Raymond of Aguilers). While it has already been shown how the three Benedictine authors refined the *Gesta Francorum*'s treatment of miracles and visions, in the case of signs, this constitutes an insertion of material rather than a fine-tuning of the work's existing content. While Guibert appears to have drawn some of the signs contained in his work from Fulcher's account, many of the signs contained in the monastic works appear to derive from traditions unattested elsewhere in the sources. The fact of their insertion into texts intended as more theologically sensitive retellings of the First Crusade highlights the importance of signs for communicating divine significance, while hinting at a popular anticipation, among the intended audiences of these works, that an account of those events should include reference to these sorts of phenomena.

Positively interpreted signs are rare outside the narrative corpus pertaining to the First Crusade. Aside from the example from the *Historia de expeditione*, discussed above, a striking exception to this rule in Raol's *De expugnatione*. As we have seen, this text delivers a concerted celebration and justification of the 1147 Lisbon campaign, drawing upon the justificatory capabilities of miracles. Signs, as devices indicative of divine predestination, are also an important aspect of this narrative agenda, while simultaneously bearing some interesting similarities to First Crusade examples. An example is the 'wonderful sign' witnessed by the fleet as it entered the Tagus estuary, wherein two clouds – one representing the crusaders and one their enemies – clashed in a celestial battle. The

---

[24]   Albert may be referring to a total lunar eclipse that occurred on 5 June 1099.
[25]   AA, p. 398.

crusaders' cloud is described as having travelled with them from parts of Gaul (*Gallia*) before colliding with the opposing cloud from the mainland.[26] The directional quality of this phenomenon is reminiscent of the Easterly pointing sword described in Fulcher's history of the First Crusade, and the clouds identified as Eastern and Western in Ekkehard's, though there is insufficient evidence to argue that this is deliberate evocation. Witnesses believed, Raol alleges, that the perceived triumph of the crusaders' cloud foreshadowed their impending victory at Lisbon. Thus, the decision to involve the crusaders in affairs in Portugal is presented as in line with divine communications.

Therefore, it is clear that celestial signs represent important aspects of First Crusade narrative in particular, contributing to narrative agendas aimed at highlighting the significance of the crusade in the trajectory of sacred time. Signs indicated importance, and brought with them the implication that God had deigned to employ Creation in the provision of said sign. The signs of crusade narrative did not need to be accompanied by explicit interpretation in order to communicate these ideas; it is often the case that the location of the sign in the narrative sequence provides the audience with enough of a cue for them to associate it with a given event, as in Baldric's narrative. There is also the possibility that an author could reasonably anticipate that certain types of sign would be interpreted as positive or negative by his intended audience, though these discourses are difficult for us to access with any degree of certainty.

Ill Omens

Not all the signs of crusade narrative were interpreted positively, as indicative of coming victory or aid. Indeed, the miracle of the bloody host included in Raol's account of the crusaders' preparations for the siege of Lisbon in 1147 has already been discussed in a previous chapter. Raol suggests that the miracle had occurred as a sign of God's wrath directed at the Flemings in response to their impious motivations for participating in the siege, a concern which fits into Raol's broader focus on the importance of right intention.[27] Other narratives of mid-twelfth-century crusading endeavours also describe ill omens. Rather than disassociating particular groups of crusaders from behaviours presumably condemned by God, as in Raol's *De expugnatione*, the following example exonerates the crusaders as a whole by blaming crusader setbacks on Greek malfeasance.

There is only one sign in Odo of Deuil's *De profectione*. Odo describes how the French and German armies left Constantinople and proceeded into Asia Minor in the autumn of 1147, leaving the French king behind to continue negotiations

---

[26] Ibid.
[27] *DeL*, pp. 134–5.

with the Byzantine Emperor Manuel Komnenos. It was around this time that the crusaders witnessed a solar eclipse in the form of half a loaf of bread for a great part of the day.[28] Odo records the initial interpretation that circulated among the French crusaders, who feared the eclipse signified the betrayal of their king by the Greeks, a recurring theme in the *De profectione*, as we have already seen. However, Odo revises this with the benefit of hindsight. The French contingent later discovered that the sign had signalled the misfortune of the German army instead, who had advanced ahead of the French and had been attacked by Turks. Odo explains that the celestial portent should be interpreted as a manifestation of this betrayal, and that the French and German armies comprised the light of one sun, being of the same faith. The darkened half of the sun had represented the German defeat and retreat (which Odo still considered to be the result of Greek betrayal), whereas the light half was indicative of the French army continuing towards its destination.[29] The implications of either interpretation are similar, as the sign demonstrates God's desire to warn the crusader army of Greek treachery via celestial portent. Additionally, the offering of this sign at the expense of the Greeks implies that divine approbation rested firmly with the followers of the Latin Church. Odo makes it clear throughout his account of Louis VII's crusade that he considered the Greeks to be at least partially responsible for the setbacks experienced during that undertaking, and his use of signs to denigrate the Byzantine emperor should certainly be viewed in light of this.

The eclipse described in such unusual terms by Odo was probably the same as the one that occurred on 26 October 1147 and documented in various European annals. The *Annales Magdeburgenses* discusses it alongside a brief description of the crusading events of that year. It records that the sun was visible in the shape of a sickle while a terrible darkness covered the world, denoting a time of human bloodshed.[30] We find a similar interpretation of the event in the *Annales Sancti Iacobi Leodiensis*, probably written in *c.* 1174.[31] Notably, the only reference to solar eclipses in the corpus of Latin narrative histories of the First Crusade, contained in Albert of Aachen's *Historia Ierosolimitana*, comments that a solar eclipse would spell disaster for the crusaders.[32] It would appear, therefore, that these authors were participating in a broader discourse in which eclipses of the sun were viewed as ill omens. This tradition, as it existed among the clerical and

---

[28] OD, p. 82. This episode is also discussed in Bartlett, *The Natural and the Supernatural*, pp. 63–5.

[29] OD, p. 82.

[30] 'Annales Magdeburgenses', *MGH SS*, 16, p. 188. See F.R. Stephenson, *Historical Eclipses and Earth's Rotation* (Cambridge, 2008), p. 418. This eclipse is also mentioned in the 'Annales Palidenses', *MGH SS*, 16, p. 83; and the 'Annales Brunwilarenses', *MGH SS*, 16, p. 727.

[31] 'Annales Sancti Iacobi Leodiensis', *MGH SS*, 16, p. 641.

[32] AA, p. 398.

monastic authors discussed here, may have been influenced by, in the words of Robert Bartlett, a 'persistent set of beliefs, according to which an eclipse was caused either by the incantations of magicians or by monsters devouring the heavenly bodies', albeit reimagined within the conceptual frameworks of the Latin Church.[33] In Odo's crusade narrative, the negative associations of solar eclipses work to add another layer to his representation of the impact of Greek treachery on the Second Crusade, one in which divine support of the expedition is revealed in edificatory signs at the expense of the narrative's malefactors.

The 'Toledo Letter' and the Planetary Conjunction of 1186

Gerald of Wales reflects in his *De principis instructione* that it was no wonder that the earth's surface quaked when the relic of the True Cross was lost at Hattin in 1187.[34] Indeed, several Latin Christian sources from the late twelfth and thirteenth century associate Saladin's successes in the Latin East in the late 1180s with signs. The implication of this is that some contemporaries viewed, or at least decided to represent, Latin setbacks and defeats in the eastern Mediterranean as momentous losses that inspired signs. This is especially clear in the case of several discussions of a fascinating letter, allegedly sent by Toledan astrologers to Pope Clement III (d. 1191). The letter was purported to contain a detailed horoscopic prediction, whereby a planetary alignment in Libra in September 1186 would bring with it destruction, famine and war. As we shall see, the differing treatments of this prediction reveal varied approaches to the problem of narrating controversial practices, while also showing how authors might reshape their representations of predictions in light of a contradictory outcome.

The so-called 'Toledo Letter' has been identified as one of the most renowned prophecies of the Middle Ages, and its dissemination in Latin, Greek, Persian, Syriac, Arabic and Hebrew texts during the medieval and early modern periods has received much attention, primarily in the German-speaking world.[35] Of the

---

[33] Bartlett, *The Natural and the Supernatural*, p. 58.

[34] Gerald of Wales, *De principis instructione*, p. 243.

[35] H. Grauert has traced the intercontinental dissemination of the letter and this article remains the authority on the 'Toledo Letter' in H. Grauert, 'Meister Johann von Toledo', *Sitzungsberichte der königlich bayerischen Akademie der Wissenschaften*, 2 (1901), 111–325. For an English summary of Grauert's findings, see M. Gaster, 'The Letter of Toledo', *Folklore*, 13.2 (1902), 115–34. On the hypothesised Jewish origins of the prediction, which are now largely discredited, see F. Baer, 'Eine jüdische Messiasprophetie auf das Jahr 1186 und der dritte Kreuzzug', *Monatsschrift für Geschichte und Wissenschaft des Judentums*, 3 (1926), 155–65. For more recent scholarship on the 'Toledo Letter', see D. Weltecke, 'Die Konjunktion der Planeten im September 1186: Zum Ursprung einer globalen Katastrophenangst', *Saeculum*

main Latin chronicles that discuss the planetary conjunction, some of which also contain crusade narrative, are several interpretations of the sign's significance in relation to events in the Latin East on the eve of the Third Crusade.[36] Analysis of the discussions of the 1186 planetary conjunction reveals something of the perceived place of crusading and the Latin East in the hierarchy of Latin Christendom's affairs. Interestingly, the source materials are such that we are also able to see how the loss of Jerusalem in 1187, and the anticlimactic outcome of the Third Crusade, shaped the ongoing representation of the Toledo Letter.

During a brief report of events in the Latin East between 1187 and 1189, *IP*1 – likely compiled by an English participant of the Third Crusade – discusses the conjunction predicted in the Toledo Letter alongside several other phenomena.[37] These events include famine, earthquakes, and lunar and solar eclipses and are all presented as indicators of future destruction.[38] *IP*1 explains that the planetary coincidence would cause a strong wind, indicating that the world would soon suffer from 'strife and battles'. Here, the conceptual link between the planetary conjunction and the fate of the Latin East is clear: it is one of several phenomena which contribute to the narrative of decline and defeat in the Latin East, mainly at the hands of Saladin, against which its account of the Third Crusade is set.

Other accounts of the period, such as Roger of Howden's *Gesta Regis* and *Chronica*, and Gerald of Wales's *De instructione principis*, dwell on the predicted planetary conjunction in more detail, though the following discussion will focus on Roger's especially rich considerations of these events.[39] Indeed, Roger's discussion of these events is of such length that his nineteenth-century translator described it as an 'astrological parade', suggesting that the passage is of no greater significance than as a demonstration on Roger's part of his own knowledge of astrology.[40] More recently, this section of Roger's work has led John Gillingham to describe Roger more generously as 'a man of marked eschatological interest'.[41]

    Jahrbuch für Universalgeschichte, 54 (2003), 179–212; and G. Mentgen, *Astrologie und öffentlichkeit im Mittelalter* (Stuttgart, 2005).

[36] For a list of the early sources for the letter, see Appendix 2 of Weltecke, 'Die Konjunktion', pp. 209–12. Nicholas Paul has analysed an early version of the 'Toledo Letter' in the context of Clement III's appeals for Alfonso II of Aragon to undertake crusading activity in Iberia, and in association with other 'doom-laden' letters copied by the monks of Ripoll. See Paul, *To Follow in Their Footsteps*, pp. 285–90.

[37] See Nicholson, *The Chronicle of the Third Crusade*, p. 10.

[38] *IP*1, p. 247.

[39] *Chronica* 2, pp. 290–8 and *GR*1, pp. 324–7; Gerald of Wales, *De principis instructione*, pp. 242–3.

[40] H.T. Riley, trans., *The Annals of Roger de Hoveden: Comprising the History of England and Countries of Europe from A.D. 732 to A.D. 1201* (London, 1853), p. 45, n. 52.

[41] J. Gillingham, J., 'Roger of Howden on Crusade', in *Richard Cœur de Lion: Kingship, Chivalry and War in the Twelfth Century* (London, 1994), p. 151.

According to Roger, Spanish and Sicilian 'astrologers' (*astrologi*), as well as Greek and Latin 'soothsayers' or 'diviners' (*conjectores*), had all predicted a planetary conjunction.[42] Gerald, employing terminology less likely to conjure associations with superstitious practices, attributes the predictions to Toledan and Apulian philosophers and astronomers.[43] According to these authors, the letter inspired widespread anxiety throughout Europe. The annals of the Augustinian abbey of Marbach in Alsace, the *Annales Marbacenses* (written *c.* 1230), describe the letter at some length. According to the *Annales Marbacenses*, the prediction had been made by a Toledan astronomer named John and detailed a planetary conjunction which 'heralded the advent of the Antichrist'.[44] The chronicle continues by noting that all of the astronomers, philosophers and wise men were in agreement over its significance, whether Christian, 'Gentile' or Jewish. The *Annales Marbacenses* record that the people of the region received the news with such fear that they built underground dwellings while many churches organised processions, litanies and fasts.[45] The passage concludes by noting that the predictions amounted to nothing in order 'that the wisdom of this world may be proven to be foolish before God'.[46] This final comment reads as a push back against increasing interest in natural causation in the period, and as an exercise in re-establishing the unknowable mysteries of God's Creation. By contrast, Roger of Howden frames the predictions as legitimate interpretations of the divinely predestined. For example, in a letter which Roger includes in both his *Gesta Regis* and *Chronica*, and attributes to a 'certain astrologer' named Corumphira, it is noted how 'Almighty God knows, and the science of numbers showed' that the planets would come into conjunction in Libra in September 1186.[47] Here, Roger reconciles God's will with astrological prediction by acknowledging God's ultimate authority, and by presenting the study of the celestial bodies as a route to understanding the divine will.

Corumphira's letter, as incorporated into the works of Roger of Howden, states that the year of the planetary conjunction would also be marked by a partial solar and a total lunar eclipse, and that a 'powerful wind' would blacken the air and corrupt it with its stench.[48] This is the same wind that the

---

[42] *Chronica* 2, p. 290.

[43] Gerald of Wales, *De principis instructione*, p. 242.

[44] *Annales Marbacenses qui dicuntur*, ed. H. Bloch (MGH SSRG, 9; Hanover, 1907), p. 56. See also, Mentgen, *Astrologie*, pp. 20–1.

[45] *Annales Marbacenses qui dicuntur*, p. 56. Cf. Gerald of Wales, *De principis instructione*, p. 243; and Roger of Wendover, *Rogeri de Wendover Liber qui dicitur flores historiarum*, ed. H.G. Hewlett (Rolls Series, 84.2; London, 1887), p. 357.

[46] *Annales Marbacenses qui dicuntur*, p. 56: 'Sed ut probaretur sapientia huius mundi stulticia esse apid Deum'.

[47] *Chronica* 2, pp. 290–1.

[48] *Chronica* 2, p. 291.

author of *IP*1 describes in similarly alliterative terms, and is a key motif of the tradition. According to Roger, Corumphira interpreted this event as signifying, God willing, the change of kingdoms, the superiority of the Franks, and the destruction of the 'Saracens'.[49] However, rather than being a forecast of Saladin's military advances in Syria, it predicts Christian victory in the East, possibly as an outcome of an impending crusade.

Notably, Roger's works offer us the opportunity to compare two discussions of the prediction composed on either side of the Third Crusade, and the differences are intriguing. Roger returned from the Third Crusade in 1191. Soon after, probably in 1192, he finished work on his *Gesta Regis* and began composing his *Chronica*. Gillingham has identified a certain 'optimism' in the earlier work, which was later expunged in the *Chronica* through the alteration, augmentation and omission of certain passages from the *Gesta*.[50] The consideration of the planetary conjunction contained in the later *Chronica* is comprised of four letters, while the earlier *Gesta* contains only two. While Corumphira's letter is included in both, the later *Chronica* also includes a letter fundamentally undermining the significance of the Toledo Letter. Roger attributes the contradictory letter to a certain Pharamella, of Arab descent and the son of Abd Allah of Cordoba, to John, bishop of Toledo.[51] In it, 'western astrologers', presumably meaning those responsible for the Toledo Letter, are criticised for their imprecise predictions. This has the effect of undermining the scale of the predicted natural disasters and emphasising the superiority of the Islamic mastery of astrology. Pharamella allegedly learnt about the predictions from a Frank held in captivity 'with us', the implication here being that this Frank, named Ferdinand, was being held captive in Muslim Spain. The astrologers of the West are described as false and ignorant, and Pharamella is incredulous that even the supposedly wise among Christ's followers believed their inaccurate interpretations.[52] He then points out that this planetary alignment occurs every thirty years, and therefore either such pestilential winds would have occurred many times before, or have not and would not occur. Roger describes this letter as a comfort to those who were alarmed by previous astrological predictions, but offers no further exposition.

When viewed alongside Roger's amending of the passage in which Richard meets with Joachim, whereby the predicted victory over Saladin is postponed, as has been discussed above, it becomes clear that we are seeing Roger responding

---

[49] Ibid.

[50] Gillingham, 'Roger of Howden on Crusade', p. 149.

[51] *Chronica* 2, p. 297. Gerald of Wales, in his consideration of the Toledo Letter contained in his *De principis instructione*, discusses a letter similar to Pharamella's, attributed instead to 'a certain philosopher'. See Gerald of Wales, *De principis instructione*, p. 64.

[52] *Chronica* 2, p. 297.

to the Third Crusade's failure to amount to much more than the acquisition of the port cities of Acre and Jaffa. This repositioning of supposedly prophetic predictions in the face of contradictory outcomes looks similar to what Richard Landes has called 'apocalyptic jazz' in reference to the changing expectations of Latin Christian society in the first decades of the eleventh century.[53] This is not to say that Roger fabricated Pharamella's letter, but that its incorporation is part of an effort in his later *Chronica* to iron out some of the more problematic, or optimistic, predictions concerning the Third Crusade and Latin East presented in his *Gesta*. Indeed, in the *Gesta*, the discussion of the Toledo Letter is immediately followed by a consideration of Patriarch Heraclius' 1185 embassy to Henry II on behalf of Baldwin IV of Jerusalem, which strengthens the conceptual association between the letter's predictions and the push to render aid to the Latin East. In the *Chronica*, however, this section is separated from the Toledo Letter by other details of Henry's reign, thereby severing the order of meaning between the dramatic prognostications of Frankish victory in the East and the patriarch's appeals to Henry II for aid and an answer to the kingdom of Jerusalem's succession question.

The differing representations of the Toledo Letter are revealing. Not only do they tap into contemporaneous ambivalence surrounding astrology and its association with Islam, but they also reveal how authors might reshape the content of their narratives in response to contemporaneous events. Prophetic motifs were plastic, especially when it came to their implications, which could be altered as easily as changing the material immediately surrounding the prediction in a narrative. The Toledo Letter appears to have been a particularly attractive example of this, especially in relation to crusading and the Latin East, as Roger of Wendover (d. 1236), who utilised various works including Roger of Howden's, would also weave it into his defence of Frederick II's negotiated Christian occupation of Jerusalem in 1229.[54]

Prophecy and the Crusader Sack of Constantinople, April 1204

Signs and portents could demonstrate an event's status as a manifestation of the divine plan. Latin Christian narratives of the Fourth Crusade contain many examples of this, drawing on prophetic themes to emphasise the legitimacy of the campaign. By demonstrating that the crusader conquest of Constantinople was divinely preordained, these texts situate the crusaders as instruments of

---

[53] R. Landes, 'The Birth of Heresy: A Millennial Phenomenon', *Journal of Religious History*, 24.1 (2000), 38.

[54] Roger of Wendover, *Flores Historiarum*, p. 369.

God's will. In the words of Innocent III in his letter to the crusade army, dated 13 November 1204:

> Now behold, brothers and sons, you can openly reap because finally God brings to divine completion through you in our time the already mentioned mystery, which He foresaw from all eternity and foreshadowed in the Gospel, though you understand that God produces this mystery through your ministry not as if it were by fortuitous chance but, to be sure, by an exalted plan so that in the future there might be one flock and one pastor.[55]

The curia's response, before its views were changed by the news of the brutality of the crusader sack of the city, was that the crusaders were enacting God's plan to unite the Greek and Latin Churches. While the papal perspective on the conquest of Constantinople soon soured, Latin Christian authors continued to produce texts emphasising the predestination and legitimacy of the Fourth Crusade, often with recourse to themes pertaining to signs and portents. Gunther of Pairis, in his narrative history of the Fourth Crusade, commented that 'all things that God wills happens, and things foreordained become reality'.[56] This conceptual alignment of things prophesied with things divinely willed is evidenced throughout the texts examined below.

The section of the *Gesta episcoporum Halberstadensium* documenting the events of the Fourth Crusade is thought to have been composed in around 1209 and follows the involvement of Conrad of Krosigk, bishop of Halberstadt. The relevant section of the work was likely composed by a single author, who may well have been a cleric working under the supervision of Conrad himself, who at that time had retired to the monastery at Sittichenbach, despite having been forbidden to do so by papal legates on two occasions.[57] In the *Gesta episcoporum*, therefore, the demonstration of the legitimacy of the Fourth Crusade was of especial importance to its *apologia* of Conrad. The narrative construction of Conrad thus includes an account of his consultation of prophecies. According to the *Gesta episcoporum*, the bishop received a prophecy from a hermit whom

---

[55] *Die Register Innocenz' III, 7. Band, 7. Pontifikatsjahr, 1204–1205, Texte und Indices*, ed. O. Hageneder, A. Sommerlechner, H. Weigl, C. Egger and R. Murauer (Wien, 1997), 7.154, p. 264: 'Ecce iam, fratres et filii, colligere potestis aperte, quia Deus, quod ab eterno previdit et in Evangelio presignavit, per vos tandem in nobis sacramentum adimplet superius prelibatum, ut intelligatis, quod non quasi casu fortuito sed alto quidem consilio Deus hoc misterium per vestrum ministerium operatur, quatinus decetero sit unum ovile et unus pastor.' English translation is from Andrea, *Contemporary Sources*, pp. 125–6.

[56] GP, p. 158: 'Cunctaque proveniunt, que vult Deus, et rata fiunt.' English translation is from Gunther of Pairis, *The Capture of Constantinople*, p. 109.

[57] Andrea, *Contemporary Sources*, p. 240.

he had met as the crusade army passed Ragusa (now Dubrovnik). The hermit, identified as Count Burchard of Halremont, prophesied the crusader sack of Constantinople.[58] Later, during Conrad's temporary governance in Tyre, the bishop had the future events of his life revealed to him by a certain philosopher.[59] This passage is situated within the immediate context of other notable events which reflect positively on the character of the bishop; the very next sentence details how Conrad was 'divinely cured' of quartan fever in the church of Blessed Mary in Tortosa, for example.[60] The predictions of the hermit and philosopher are therefore part of a collection of phenomena indicative of the bishop's sanctity in both character and deed. The descriptions of Conrad's interest in prophecy bear similarities to Richard I's interview with Joachim of Fiore as described by Roger of Howden, discussed above, and these representations of Conrad and Richard both draw upon the theme of consultation with legitimate sources of prophecy as a means of praising the 'heroes' of their narratives and highlighting the significance of their actions.

Another tradition concerning the predestination of the crusader conquest of Constantinople in 1204 is attested across four histories of that event, namely the Old French accounts of Geoffrey of Villehardouin and Robert of Clari, and the Latin narratives of Gunther of Pairis and Ralph of Coggeshall. Each of these works describe either one or both historiated columns allegedly situated within the city of Constantinople and foretelling the climactic events of the Fourth Crusade. The columns referred to in these texts stood in the forum Tauri and the forum of Arcadius (or the Xerolophos).[61] The descriptions of these columns as they appear in the western crusade narratives are particularly concerned with the Greek response to the allegedly prophetic carvings on those columns. Robert of Clari describes the columns thus:

> On the outside of these columns were depicted and written out as prophecies all the events and conquests which have happened in Constantinople or which were to happen, nor could anyone know the event before it happened... even the conquest when the Franks conquered it was written about and depicted there, and the ships with which they attacked and through which the city was taken... When it had happened, they went to look at and reflect on these columns and so they found that the letters which had been written on the painted ships said

[58] 'Gesta episcoporum Halberstadensium', p. 118.
[59] Ibid., p. 119.
[60] Ibid.
[61] R. Macrides, 'Constantinople: The Crusaders' Gaze', in *Travel in the Byzantine World. Papers from the Thirty-fourth Spring Symposium of Byzantine Studies, Birmingham, April 2000*, ed. R. Macrides (Aldershot, 2002), p. 204.

that out of the west would come a people with hair cut short and iron hauberks who would conquer Constantinople.[62]

Gunther of Pairis, who describes only one column, discusses it in similar terms, including a description of the ladders on board the ships of the depicted conquerors, which he identifies as the particular characteristic which allowed the Greeks to identify that the scene depicted the crusader conquest.[63] Gunther identifies this as the structure from which Alexios V Doukas was flung during his execution. The irony that the emperor from whom the crusaders took the city should fall to his death from atop a Greek structure presaging the Latin conquest would likely not have been lost on Gunther's audience. According to Villehardouin, the column from which Alexios was thrown was decorated with an image of a falling emperor, thereby prophesying that event also.[64]

Ruth Macrides has shown that these accounts reflect the active process by which contemporary Greeks sought to interpret the meaning of the columns, as it was communicated to the crusaders from instances of interaction between the army and the Greek and Latin inhabitants of the city following its conquest.[65] Beyond allowing for an appreciation of the interpretative responses of the city's residents, these passages also reveal certain aspects of the utility of the prophetic for authors. Gunther wastes no time in putting the story of the columns to work in support of his broader desire to portray the crusader conquest of Constantinople as preordained and, by extension, to underline the legitimacy of Abbot Martin's participation. He notes the futility of the Greeks' attempts to reverse the prophecy by defacing the carvings on the column: 'this was an absolutely vain hope, and the foreordained outcome of events demonstrated that the aforementioned sculpture had been a token of truth.'[66] Thus, Gunther uses the attempts to expunge the prophecy to attribute the Greek populace with a certain naivety in the face of divinely ordained events.

---

[62] Robert of Clari, *La Conquête de Constantinople*, pp. 108–9: '...[p]ar dehors ches columbes si estoient pourtraites et escrites par prophetie toutes les aventures et tout les conquestes qui sont avenues en Coustantinoble, ne qui avenir i devoient, [n]e ne pooit on savoir l'aventure devant la qu'ele estoit avenue... nis cheste conqueste que li Franchois le conquisent i estoit escrite et pourtraite, et les nes dont on assali par coi le chités fu prise... Et quant che fu avenue, si ala on warder et muser en ches colombes, si trova on que les letres, qui estoient escrites seur les nes pourtraites, disoient que de vers Occident venroient une gent haut tondue a costeles de fer, qui Constantinoble conquerroient.'

[63] GP, p. 166.

[64] Geoffrey of Villehardouin, *La Conquête de Constantinople*, vol. 2, p. 116.

[65] Macrides, 'Constantinople', pp. 202–12.

[66] GP, p. 166: 'Que spes omnino utique cassa fuit et prefatam sculpturam veri significativam extitisse certus rei exitus declaravit.' English translation is from Gunther of Pairis, *The Capture of Constantinople*, p. 117.

Notably, Gunther attributes the subject matter of the carvings to Sibylline prophecies.[67] Consequently, Gunther was participating in a tradition of continued interest in the prophecies of the Sibyls in medieval Europe, in the company of such notable theologians as Peter Abelard (d. 1142) and Peter Comestor (d. *c.* 1178), and, as is discussed in the previous chapter, Otto of Freising.[68] Gunther's engagement with the theme is probably closer to what Anke Holdenried has characterised as a less sophisticated level of dialogue stemming from the use of the motif's 'Christological poignancy', in contrast to that of contemporary theologians.[69] This does not necessarily mean that Gunther did not have access to such considerations of the Sibylline prophecies. Garnier of Rochefort (later bishop of Langres), who is known to have discussed the role of the Sibylline prophecies as a pagan witness to Christ's incarnation in a sermon, was both a contemporary of Gunther's, and a fellow Cistercian.[70] Garnier preached the Third Crusade in France, and took the Cross at the Chapter General of 1198 at which Fulk of Neuilly unsuccessfully petitioned for Cistercian aid in the preaching of the Fourth Crusade.[71] Therefore, Gunther was writing within an intellectual environment where Sibylline prophecy was presented as a legitimate, non-Christian prediction, and its integration into his discussion of the Constantinopolitan columns therefore represents a move to align their predictions with a non-Christian provenance that was nonetheless theologically valid.

Ralph of Coggeshall also describes a column associated with a prophecy regarding the fate of the city. Ralph comments that the column was erected in the city in ancient times by a certain prophetic individual versed in the mechanical arts, who constructed it in such a way that its base was in constant motion.[72] Above the capital were the images of three emperors, one of which looked towards Asia, the other to Europe, and the third to Africa. A circle could be seen above the heads of these images, on which could be read a statement in Greek which predicted that, after three emperors named Alexius had reigned in Greece, the empire of the Greeks would fall into the hands of another people. Another figure stood above

[67] GP, p. 166.
[68] A. Holdenried, *The Sibyl and Her Scribes: Manuscripts and Interpretation of the Latin Sibylla Tiburtina c. 1050–1500* (Aldershot, 2006), p. 54.
[69] Ibid., p. 57.
[70] Garnier of Rochefort, 'Sermo XL. De Arca Spirituali', *PL*, 205, col. 825.
[71] N.M. Haring, 'The Liberal Arts in the Sermons of Garnier of Rochefort', *Mediaeval Studies*, 30 (1968), 47. At the time of the Chapter General in 1198, Garnier was acting under the shadow of an accusation of 'dilapidatio et insufficientia' from Pope Innocent III. He was to be suspended from his position as bishop of Langres on 31 December of that year, and later resigned his position voluntarily. See E.A.R. Brown, 'The Cistercians in the Latin Empire of Constantinople and Greece, 1204–1276', *Traditio*, 14 (1958), 66, n. 14.
[72] Ralph of Coggeshall, *Chronicon Anglicanum*, pp. 150–1.

the heads of the others, appearing more lofty and eminent, and to be looking towards the western 'quarter' of the world while extending its hand towards the West. Ralph's description of this uppermost figure is reminiscent of the statue of Athena which, according to Niketas Choniates, was demolished by a Greek mob in 1203 because it appeared to them to be looking towards and beckoning the West and its armies.[73] Robert of Clari describes this statue as one of a pair, both of which were twenty feet in height. According to Robert, the following was written on the statue which held her hand outstretched to the West: 'Out of the West will come those who will conquer Constantinople.'[74] These descriptions of prophetic historiated columns and statues, presumably transmitted to the authors of these works via residents of Constantinople, though this is uncertain, enable their narratives to tap into the association between the foretold and the divinely willed, and thereby contribute to the portrayal of the Fourth Crusade as a legitimate manifestation of the divine plan.

Conclusion

Signs implied divine investment; God stirred Creation in order that humankind might be alerted to an event. On one level, therefore, the signs of crusade narrative helped communicate the divine agency that was so important to many Latin Christian conceptualisations of those expeditions. These signs could be indicative of divine approbation or wrath, or serve to alert crusaders of the wrongdoings of others. In the case of the Toledo Letter, we can see how signs, identified through the often problematic practice of astrology, were integrated into discussions of Saladin's key victories in 1187, and can reflect the shifting hopes held by Latin Christian onlookers that effective aid might be rendered to the Latin East. Signs, and related ways of knowing, also play an important role in narratives of the Fourth Crusade, enabling authors to highlight the perceived legitimacy of the 1204 conquest of Constantinople. Signs therefore represented another useful tool for authors who sought to communicate divine agency in their narratives, alongside miracles and visions, albeit one with a problematic relationship to theologically questionable practices.

---

[73] Niketas Choniates, *O City*, pp. 305–6.
[74] Robert of Clari, *La Conquête de Constantinople*, pp. 108–9: 'De vers Occident venront chil qui Constantinoble conquerront.' On the statue, see also R.J.H. Jenkins, 'The Bronze Athena at Byzantium', *The Journal of Hellenic Studies*, 67 (1947), 31–3; and Macrides, 'Constantinople', p. 206.

Conclusion

Divine will represented the theoretical keystone for Latin Christian justifications of the crusading movement. It was the belief that God 'willed it', in the minds of contemporaries, that elevated crusading above internecine and inherently sinful warfare. Consequently, in narrative accounts of crusades, miracles, visions and signs were among the most effective means of communicating the divine agency that lay at the heart of conceptualisations of such endeavours. This is because the phenomena were by definition reliant on divine power; in order for the miraculous to occur, Creation had to be harnessed by its creator. Thus, divine potency was a common feature of miracle and crusade. Indeed, it is this principle of God's agency that enabled the authors of crusade narrative to portray crusades as miracles.

I have argued in this book that authors employed miracles, visions and signs, as instances of visible (and sometimes tangible) and communicative divine agency, in the service of varying narrative agendas. The implications of these findings are significant, as they reveal that the crusades, or rather, contemporaneous perceptions of crusading, presented particular challenges for authors for which the miraculous offered solutions. Miracles and other divine phenomena could answer questions about the divine disposition in relation to a particular campaign, demonstrating the legitimacy of a given expedition and its participants. Through their implied association with the divine, they were powerful tools for authors who sought to compose panegyrics or defensive records of an individual's deeds. They could offer proofs of the otherwise unknowable, such as the reality of crusader martyrdom and the condition of a crusader's soul after death. They could situate events within the trajectory of sacred history and authenticate relics. In short, they were multifaceted, plastic narrative tools for the authors of crusade narrative.

A recurring theme in this book has been the ways in which the authors of crusade narrative drew upon and applied theoretical authorities pertaining to the miraculous. Examining different authors' recourse to these authorities – mainly Augustine, Macrobius and Isidore of Seville – has made it possible to situate these narratives in relation to their intellectual milieu. Importantly, it has also allowed this book to demonstrate how these authors might evoke these authorities in the support of their narrative agendas, as when Gunther of Pairis draws heavily of Macrobian dream theory in support of his justification of Abbot Martin of Pairis' actions on the Fourth Crusade. In other words, the authors of crusade narrative often draw upon authorities in their works in order to make their own discussions of the miraculous more convincing and thereby more effective in the service of a given narrative agenda.

In approaching the miraculous as a narrative ingredient, this book does not focus on the lived experiences, or beliefs, of crusade participants or contemporaries. However, its findings do speak to medieval, Latin Christian attitudes towards the miraculous in one key way: in examining what an author might anticipate his audience to find convincing or problematic. The ability of the miraculous to serve a narrative agenda relies on its being convincing to a reader or audience. It is that act of belief that enables the miraculous episode to communicate divine agency. Without it, the utility of these themes collapses, and their inclusion in narrative becomes problematic. Therefore, it has certainly not been the intention of this book to divorce the miraculous of crusade narrative from medieval belief; rather, it is acknowledged that it is this ability to believe in the genuine nature of these events that allows them to function so effectively.

This book presents the abovementioned arguments and conclusions thematically. However, it is important that I now draw together some of the intra-thematic patterns revealed in the above. If we look chronologically across the themes: miracles and marvels, visions and dreams, and signs and augury, we can identify a peak in the use of the miraculous at a very early stage, followed by something of a dip, and concluding with another, albeit inferior, peak. The first, highest peak represents the narrative renderings of the First Crusade, in which the miraculous is a recurring, and often integral, theme. The narrative histories of the Second and Third Crusades, with some notable exceptions, make far less consistent use of the miraculous. Then, finally, the narrative histories of the Fourth Crusade, in their response to the controversial nature of that undertaking, and as a result of the many *translatio*-type narratives produced in its wake, constitute the final peak.

For many of the narratives of the First Crusade, the demonstration that the crusade was itself a miracle was paramount. This is seen most clearly in the Benedictine narratives which drew on existing narratives like the *Gesta Francorum*. In their accounts, the crusade as miracle represented a sort of metanarrative, with constituent miraculous episodes representing the columns that supported this edifice. The examination of the terminology used in the representation of the miraculous has revealed that the Benedictine authors – Robert the Monk, Guibert of Nogent, and Baldric of Bourgueil – revised their source materials at that micro level, and often in ways which hint at broader theoretical concerns regarding the genuinely miraculous. These findings therefore support Jonathan Riley-Smith's model of 'theological refinement'; these authors were framing the miraculous in more theologically sensitive, and convincing ways in support of their broader communication of the crusade's significance.[1]

---

[1] Riley-Smith, *The First Crusade*, pp. 135–52.

The miraculous of First Crusade narratives is overwhelmingly positive, meaning that it mainly comprises constructive interventions or signs indicative of divine approbation, all of which culminate in victory at Jerusalem and Ascalon in 1099. In narratives of the Second Crusade campaign to the eastern Mediterranean, however, we begin to see punitive miracles directed at crusaders. As this book has argued, the miraculous metanarrative of so many of the narratives of the First Crusade could not be applied to the events of the Second Crusade, which ended in an ignominious retreat from Damascus in July 1148. The only exception to this rule is the *De profectione* of Odo of Deuil, the narrative of which does not extend beyond the early summer of 1148, and therefore functions without knowledge of the crusade's outcome. The influence of narrative histories of the First Crusade is clear in Odo's account, and this extends to his use of miraculous motifs like the celestial knight. Other narratives of the Second Crusade, however, contain isolated accounts of miracles with much reduced implications, such as indicating the sanctity of Bernard of Clairvaux, for example.

Another important exception to the abovementioned rule regarding the lack of miracles in narrative histories of the Second Crusade is the *De expugnatione*, an account of the 1147 siege of Lisbon. Notably, that campaign culminated in victory, and the longest narrative account, which is commonly attributed to Raol, represents both a celebration and justification of that victory which evokes the miraculous metanarrative of many First Crusade narratives. However, these exceptions, the *De profectione* and *De expugnatione*, prove the rule that crusades that contemporaries believed to be failures presented a challenge to those who sought to compose narratives about them; defeat challenged the logic of the miraculous, for how could God have willed a crusade that ultimately failed?

The Third Crusade was not viewed as the resounding disaster that the Second Crusade represented for Latin Christian contemporaries. After all, it had secured key port cities which could be used as important staging posts for future expeditions. However, it had not succeeded in capturing Jerusalem, which – as has been demonstrated – several contemporaneous texts reveal a discomfort about. By stepping outside what can be called strictly crusade narrative, it has been demonstrated how miraculous themes were employed in discussions of anticipated crusades and the fate of the Latin East. It is in these examples, like the Toledo Letter, that we can view changing Latin Christian understandings of the miraculous in the face of the rise of natural philosophy and exposure to Greco-Arabic learning most clearly. As with the narrative histories of the Second Crusade, however, there are some narratives of the Third Crusade which engage with the miraculous more profoundly, mainly surrounding the expedition of Frederick Barbarossa and the siege of Acre, though these represent exceptions rather than the norm.

The Fourth Crusade posed different challenges for authors. It had culminated in victory at Constantinople in 1204, and the establishment of the Latin Empire of Constantinople. However, it remained a controversial expedition on account of its targeting of Christian cities and failure to render significant aid to the Latin East via Egypt. Many of the narratives examined in this book were written with the intention of defending relic thefts or authenticating Constantinopolitan relics that were transported to Europe after the crusade. Consequently, these narratives shade between narrative history and *translatio* account. This means that we should attribute in part the increased presence of miraculous themes in these narratives to this influence. This observation does not account for all the miraculous themes discussed in narrative histories of the Fourth Crusade, however. For example, signs and prophecy play an important role across several of the texts as a means by which that campaign might be portrayed as divinely foreordained and, by extension, legitimate.

Thus, as the fortunes of the crusading movement changed over the course of the twelfth and into the thirteenth century, so too did the employment of the miraculous in crusade narrative.

Many scholarly considerations of the miraculous in crusade narratives have been piecemeal. By looking beyond individual episodes or crusades, this book has offered the first far-reaching analysis of the miraculous in crusade narratives pertaining to the crusades of 1096 to 1204. This approach has revealed that stories of miracles and related phenomena often represent part of broader narrative agendas, many of which draw upon different aspects of the miraculous. By highlighting the role of the miraculous in crusade narrative, it has been demonstrated that crusade sources represent an enormously rich repository of material for the study not only of the crusades, but of the medieval miraculous, and medieval historiography, more broadly. The sources consulted in the preparation of this book are products of the Latin Christian intellectual landscape of the late eleventh to mid-thirteenth centuries, and there is much instructive work still to be done to situate medieval crusade historiography within this broader context.

Over the course of the last two decades or so, the miraculous of crusade narrative has moved from representing an overlooked, problematic symptom of an 'Age of Faith' towards a viable area of study in its own right. This book has argued that rather than representing an ornament of crusade narrative, the miraculous in fact offered authors a vital and multifaceted narrative tool that was uniquely situated for tapping into contemporaneous conceptions of crusading as divinely sponsored. Thus, when Orderic Vitalis attributed the origins of the First Crusade to God, he was evoking the same notion of divine agency that was central to contemporaneous understandings of the miraculous. As this book has argued, it is clear that miracles and related phenomena were of considerable importance to the narrativisation of the crusades, and they deserve to be treated as such.

Appendix: The Sources

The following appendix is intended to provide a short overview of the main sources used in this book, for the benefit of those who may be unfamiliar with the Latin Christian primary sources for the crusades of 1096 to 1204.

Generally speaking, the sources discussed in this book are either dedicated crusade histories – texts produced with the express purpose of documenting a crusade, often beginning with its preaching and ending with its perceived climax, or the return of participants to their homes in western Europe – or larger chronicles which feature a crusade account within a broader narrative, often tracing the affairs of particular kings or polities. As will become clear in the following, the scale of the textual response to the First Crusade was not matched by that of the Second, Third or Fourth, and there are markedly fewer dedicated histories of these later campaigns. For the Fourth Crusade, this book makes use of several *translatio* narratives, sources documenting the removal of relics in the wake of the sack of Constantinople in 1204 and their transportation to and distribution in western Europe, often including descriptions of parts of the campaign. It should also be noted that, while this book focuses on the corpus of prose narratives written or compiled in Latin, it also draws upon evidence from Old French prose and verse sources at points.

The first-hand account contained in the *Gesta Francorum et aliorum Hierosolimitanorum* is at the centre of the narrative histories of the First Crusade.[1] It is believed to have been completed within months of the narrative's symbolic end point: the crusader victory against an Egyptian force at Ascalon in August 1099.[2] The author, if indeed it is the product of one singular author,

---

[1] For useful overviews of the Latin Christian sources for the First Crusade, see S.B. Edgington, 'The First Crusade: Reviewing the Evidence', in *The First Crusade: Origins and Impact*, ed. J.P. Phillips (Manchester, 1997), pp. 207–27; and M. Bull, 'The Western Narratives of the First Crusade', in *Christian-Muslim Relations: A Bibliographical History. Volume 3 (1050–1200)*, ed. D. Thomas, A. Mallett et al. (Leiden, 2011), pp. 15–25.

[2] GF. It should be noted that, regrettably, certain crusade narratives have remained outside the scope of this book, particularly in the case of the First Crusade, for which Latin narrative histories are relatively plentiful. In particular, the anonymous Monte Cassino chronicle, also known as the *Historia Belli Sacri*, is not discussed here. On this text, see especially L. Russo, 'The Monte Cassino Tradition of the First Crusade: From the *Chronica Monasterii Casinensis* to the *Hystoria de Via et Recuperatione Antiochiae atque Ierusolymarum*', in *Writing the Early Crusades*, pp. 53–62. For a

remains anonymous, though it is likely that he was a cleric attached for a time to the contingent led by Bohemond of Taranto before departing from Antioch with the rest of the crusade army as it progressed towards Jerusalem.[3] A closely related text is the participant narrative of a Poitevin priest named Peter Tudebode, who relied on a version of the *Gesta Francorum*, or a text very similar to it.[4]

Two further histories are believed to have been written by First Crusade participants: the *Historia Francorum qui ceperunt Iherusalem* of Raymond of Aguilers and Fulcher of Chartres's *Historia Hierosolymitana*.[5] Raymond of Aguilers, a southern French cleric in the entourage of the Provençal count, Raymond IV of Toulouse, completed his *Historia* soon after the events it narrates (*c.* 1101). He had co-authored the work with Provençal knight Pons of Balazun until the latter's death during the siege of Arqah (February–May 1099). Fulcher of Chartres was a northern French cleric who travelled east with the armies of Duke Robert II of Normandy and Count Stephen of Blois before becoming chaplain to Count Baldwin of Boulogne at Edessa in October 1097. His *Historia* begins with a

---

Latin edition, see *Hystoria de via et recuperatione Antiochiae atque Ierusolymarum (olim Tudebodus imitatus et continuatus): Normanni d'Italia alla prima Crociata in una cronaca cassinese*, ed. E. D'Angelo (Florence, 2009).

[3] Formerly thought to have been the work of a lay crusader, Colin Morris has made a convincing case that the *Gesta Francorum* was in fact written by a cleric. See Morris, 'The *Gesta Francorum* as Narrative History'. Morris's arguments have been problematised recently by Kostick, 'A Further Discussion on the Authorship of the *Gesta Francorum*'.

[4] PT. On the relationship between the *Gesta Francorum* and the *Historia de Hierosolymitana itinere*, see especially J. France, 'The Anonymous *Gesta Francorum* and the *Historia Francorum qui ceperunt Iherusalem* of Raymond of Aguilers and the *Historia de Hierosolymitana itinere* of Peter Tudebode: An Analysis of the Textual Relationship between Primary Sources for the First Crusade', in *The Crusades and Their Sources: Essays Presented to Bernard Hamilton*, ed. J. France and W.G. Zajac (Aldershot, 1998), pp. 39–69; J. Rubenstein, 'What is the *Gesta Francorum*, and Who was Peter Tudebode?', *Revue Mabillon*, 16 (2005), 179–204; M.G. Bull, 'The Relationship between the *Gesta Francorum* and Peter Tudebode's *Historia de Hierosolymitano Itinere*: The Evidence of a Hitherto Unexamined Manuscript (St. Catharine's College, Cambridge, 3)', *Crusades*, 11 (2012), 1–17; and S. Niskanen, 'The Origins of the *Gesta Francorum* and Two Related Texts: Their Textual and Literary Character', *Sacris Erudiri*, 51 (2012), 287–316. On the relationship between the *Gesta* and non-participant narratives, see especially Riley-Smith, *The First Crusade*, pp. 135–52.

[5] RA; FC. Reference is also made in this book to a text derived from an early recension of Fulcher's *Historia*, known as the *Gesta Francorum Iherusalem expugnantium*. For a Latin edition, see Bartolf of Nangis, 'Gesta Francorum Iherusalem Expugnantium', pp. 491–543. On this text and its relationship to Fulcher's work, see S.B. Edgington, 'The *Gesta Francorum Iherusalem expugnantium* of "Bartolf of Nangis"', *Crusades*, 13 (2014), 21–35.

narrative of the crusade, begun probably *c.* 1101, followed by an account of the years until 1127 which Fulcher spent living in Jerusalem.

Three crusade narratives produced in the first decade of the twelfth century declare themselves reworkings of the *Gesta Francorum*, or of a text very similar to it. Their Benedictine authors, Baldric of Bourgueil, Guibert of Nogent and Robert the Monk, each sought to represent the events of the First Crusade in terms deemed more theologically apposite for the narration of such significant events.[6] Baldric of Bourgueil began work on his *Historia Ierosolimitana* in 1105 while he was abbot of the Benedictine abbey of St Peter at Bourgueil. Two years later, he was made archbishop of Dol, at which point be made some revisions to the work.[7] Guibert of Nogent wrote his *Dei gesta per Francos* between 1107 and 1108 while exiled from his abbacy of Notre-Dame de Nogent.[8] Other than revising the *Gesta Francorum*, which Guibert decried as unsophisticated, he also appears to have come across and critically received a version of Fulcher of Chartres's crusade narrative towards the end of the production of his own. In contrast to Baldric and Guibert, little is known about Robert the Monk (also known as Robert of Rheims).[9] His *Historia Iherosolimitana* is thought to have been completed in *c.* 1110 and is known to exist in over eighty extant manuscript witnesses from the twelfth to sixteenth centuries: a remarkable number.[10]

Another crusade narrative was written by an individual who had been in the Levant soon after the establishment of the Latin polities of Outremer: the *Tancredus* (better known as the *Gesta Tancredi* from its title in the Recueil edition) of Ralph of Caen.[11] Ralph, who had been schooled at Caen under the tutelage of Arnulf of Chocques, chaplain of Robert of Normandy on the crusade and later patriarch of Jerusalem, joined the entourage of Bohemond as chaplain in *c.* 1106 while Bohemond was in Europe raising reinforcements for his campaign against the Byzantine Empire.[12] Ralph later transferred his services to

---

[6]   See Riley-Smith, *The First Crusade*, pp. 135–52. Jay Rubenstein has since argued that Riley-Smith's term, 'theological refinement', should be nuanced to incorporate broader narrative refinements in these texts. See Rubenstein, 'Miracles and the Crusading Mind'.

[7]   BB. On Baldric and his crusade history, see S. Biddlecombe, *The Historia Ierosolimitana of Baldric of Bourgueil*, pp. xi–cvii, and 'Baldric of Bourgueil and the *Familia Christi*', in *Writing the Early Crusades*, pp. 9–23.

[8]   GN. On Guibert and his crusade history, see J. Rubenstein, *Guibert of Nogent: Portrait of a Medieval Mind* (New York, NY, 2002).

[9]   RM. On Robert's crusade history, see also Sweetenham, *Robert the Monk's History of the First Crusade*; M.G. Bull, 'Robert the Monk and his Source(s)', in *Writing the Early Crusades*, pp. 127–39; and Kempf, 'Towards a Textual Archaeology'.

[10]   Bull and Kempf, *The Historia Iherosolimitana*, pp. ix–x.

[11]   Ralph of Caen, 'Gesta Tancredi in expeditione Hierosolymitana', *RHC Oc.*, 3, pp. 587–716. For a more recent edition, see RC.

[12]   Arnulf of Chocques was chaplain to Robert of Normandy during the First Crusade.

Bohemond's nephew Tancred in Antioch, and began his prosimetric history of the crusade after the latter's death in December 1112, probably while living in Jerusalem where the then Patriarch Arnulf was able, or so the text claims, to cast a critical eye over it.[13] He had likely completed it before mid-1118.

Two further narratives offer a decidedly German perspective on the First Crusade: Ekkehard of Aura's *Hierosolymita* and Albert of Aachen's *Historia Ierosolimitana*.[14] As Thomas McCarthy has recently argued, Ekkehard's account of the First Crusade is derived from the 1106 Continuation of Frutolf of Michelsberg's chronicle. At some point between 1108 and his death in *c.* 1130, Ekkehard drew material from the 1106 Continuation's narrative of the First Crusade, including an account the expedition of 1101, on which the Continuation's author is believed to have been a participant, and appended it – with some adaptations – to his own work under the title *Hierosolymita*.[15]

Albert's *Historia Ierosolimitana* is an enormously rich and valuable narrative of the First Crusade. It is an important source for two main reasons: first, unlike so many of the narratives outlined above, its version of the First Crusade makes no reference to the *Gesta Francorum* tradition and constitutes a synthesis of oral testimony gleaned from returning participants; and second, it is by far the longest and most detailed of the contemporary narratives. Albert is thought to have begun preparing the first six books of the *Historia* from *c.* 1102, and the remaining six from *c.* 1120.[16] While Albert may not have used the *Gesta Francorum*, it is thought that he did draw upon an early version of the vernacular *Chanson d'Antioche*, an epic account of the First Crusade until the battle of Antioch in June 1098 and attributed to Richard the Pilgrim.[17] Richard's *Chanson* survives as a late

---

After his election as patriarch of Jerusalem in 1099, he was challenged by Daimbert archbishop of Pisa and deposed. He resumed the office in 1112 until his death in 1118. On Arnulf's career, see B. Hamilton, *The Latin Church in the Crusader States* (London, 1980), esp. pp. 61–4; and N. Hodgson, 'Reputation, Authority and Masculine Identities in the Political Culture of the First Crusaders: The Career of Arnulf of Chocques', *History*, 102.353 (2017), 889–913.

[13] See Bachrach and Bachrach, *The Gesta Tancredi of Ralph of Caen*, p. 4.

[14] EA; AA.

[15] The 1106 Continuation has been commonly misattributed to Ekkehard of Aura. For the argument that the 1106 Continuation was prepared by a monk from Michelsburg and later used by Ekkehard, see T.J.H. McCarthy, trans., *Chronicles of the Investiture Contest: Frutolf of Michelsberg and his Continuators* (Manchester, 2014), and *The Continuations of Frutolf of Michelsberg's Chronicle* (Monumenta Germaniae Historica Schriften, 74; Wiesbaden, 2018).

[16] AA, pp. xxi–xxvi.

[17] See AA, pp. xxvi–xxviii; and S.B. Edgington, 'Albert of Aachen and the *Chansons de Geste*', in *The Crusades and their Sources, Essays Presented to Bernard Hamilton*, ed. J. France and W.G. Zajac (Farnham, 1998), pp. 23–37. For an Old French edition with French translation, see *La Chanson d'Antioche*.

twelfth-century reworking by Graindor of Douai, who added it to reworkings of the *Chanson des Chétifs* and the *Chanson de Jérusalem* to create what are now known as the central pieces of the Old French Crusade Cycle.[18]

Finally among the sources for the First Crusade discussed in this book is the *Historia Ierosolymitana* of archbishop William of Tyre.[19] While the *Historia* is concerned with the affairs of the kings of Jerusalem over a lengthy period (614–1184), it contains a long and detailed account of the First Crusade derived in large part from the *Gesta Francorum* and the works of Raymond of Aguilers, Fulcher of Chartres, Baldric of Bourgueil and Albert of Aachen.[20] William, who was born in the Latin kingdom of Jerusalem, rose to prominence in the court of King Amalric of Jerusalem (d. 1174) and wrote his *Historia* between 1170 and 1184.[21]

The Holy Land expedition of the Second Crusade can boast only one dedicated treatment of the type represented by many of the narrative histories of the First Crusade: Odo of Deuil's (d. 1162) *De profectione Ludovici VII in Orientem*, written in the form of a letter addressed to Abbot Suger of Saint-Denis.[22] Odo, monk and later abbot of Saint-Denis near Paris and chaplain of King Louis VII of France during the Second Crusade between 1147 and 1149, ended his account at the point at which the remains of Louis' army reached Antioch in early 1148. Consequently, it does not describe the army's subsequent efforts in the East, most notably the failed siege of Damascus in July 1148.[23]

The other main source for the expedition to the East is Otto of Freising's *Gesta Frederici* (written 1157–8), a work which was continued upon Otto's death in

---

[18] For Old French editions of the *Chétifs* and *Jérusalem*, see *La Chanson de Jérusalem*; and *Les Chétifs*, ed. G.M. Myers, *The Old French Crusade Cycle*, vol. 5 (Tuscaloosa, AL, 1981). For English translations, see C. Sweetenham, trans., *The Chanson des Chétifs and Chanson de Jérusalem: Completing the Central Trilogy of the Old French Crusade Cycle* (Crusade Texts in Translation, 29; Farnham, 2016).

[19] WT.

[20] Edbury and Rowe, *William of Tyre*, pp. 45–6.

[21] Ibid., p. 26.

[22] Odo intended the letter, so the text claims, to provide Suger with material that he might use to inform a *Life* of the French king. OD, pp. 2–4. See Phillips, 'Odo of Deuil's *De profectione*', p. 80. An alternative interpretation of *De profectione* can be found in B. Schuste, 'The Strange Pilgrimage of Odo of Deuil', in *Medieval Concepts of the Past: Ritual, Memory and Historiography*, ed. G. Althoff, J. Fried and P.J. Geary (Cambridge, 2002), pp. 253–78.

[23] Virginia Berry has argued that Odo's reference to how 'the flowers of France withered before they could bear fruit at Damascus' (OD, p. 118) could indicate that he was writing between the defeat on the Cadmos Mountain in January 1148 and the end of the siege of Damascus in July 1148. See OD, p. xxiii; However, Henry Mayr-Harting has argued for a composition date in early 1150. See Mayr-Harting, 'Odo of Deuil,' pp. 230–1. Recently, Marcus Bull has argued that the text's metaphorical linkage between the act of writing and the journey itself supports the argument that Odo was writing in mid-1148. See Bull, *Eyewitness and Crusade Narrative*, pp. 161–8.

1158 by a certain Rahewin.[24] In contrast to the relatively obscure Odo, Otto was the son of Margrave Leopold III of Austria and of Agnes, daughter of Emperor Henry IV. Otto was therefore the half-brother of King Conrad III and the uncle of Frederick Barbarossa, about whom this work was written as a panegyric. Initially educated by the Augustinian canons of Klosterneuburg, Otto joined the Cistercian Order in 1132 before becoming abbot of Morimond and bishop of Freising in 1138. While Otto was also a participant on the crusade, the events in the East only comprise a small part of the *Gesta Frederici*, and an even smaller proportion of his *Historia duabus civitatibus* (written 1143–7), extant only in a later (1157) recension dedicated to Frederick Barbarossa.[25]

The conquest of Lisbon on 24 October 1147 by a coalition of north-western European crusaders and the forces of King Afonso Henriques of Portugal (1128–85) has been considered the only Christian success to result from the series of almost concurrent endeavours now known as the Second Crusade.[26] The crusaders who joined the forces of the recently styled king of Portugal in the siege had embarked from Dartmouth in England in May, and were principally Anglo-Norman, Flemish and Rhenish. The text known as the *De expugnatione Lyxbonensi* is the longest and most detailed of the limited extant sources relating to the event.[27] It takes the form of a letter, attributed to a Norman-French priest named Raol and addressed to Osbert of Bawdsey, a cleric in the employ of the East Anglian Glanvill family.[28] He is believed to have completed his account during the winter of 1147–8, and to have participated in the events he narrates.[29]

There are several shorter sources for the 1147 conquest of Lisbon which will feature in the following discussion: namely a collection of short, contemporary letters known as the Lisbon Letter or the 'Teutonic Source'.[30] The original version

---

[24] OFGF.

[25] OFC.

[26] For a narrative of the conquest of Lisbon, see Phillips, *The Second Crusade*, pp. 136–67.

[27] *DeL*. On the *De expugnatione*, see especially Livermore, 'The "Conquest of Lisbon" and its Author'; and Phillips, 'Ideas of Crusade and Holy War'.

[28] On the identification of the 'R' of the text's opening address as Raol – a conclusion that is generally accepted – see Livermore, 'The "Conquest of Lisbon" and its Author'. For a useful reminder that Livermore's conclusions depend in large part upon the implied author of *DeL*, see Bull, *Eyewitness and Crusade Narrative*, pp. 129–30. The Glanvill connection is significant; the leader of the Anglo-Norman contingent was one Hervey de Glanvill. On the association between Raol and Hervey, and on the Glanvill family more broadly, see David, 'The Authorship of the *De Expugnatione Lyxbonensi*'.

[29] Livermore, 'The "Conquest of Lisbon" and its Author', p. 16; Constable, 'The Second Crusade', in *Crusaders and Crusading*, p. 236; *DeL*, p. 146, n. 3; Phillips, *The Second Crusade*, p. 161.

[30] Phillips, 'St Bernard of Clairvaux, the Low Countries, and the Lisbon Letter'; Edgington, 'Albert of Aachen, St Bernard and the Second Crusade'; Constable, 'The

of the letter was written by a contemporary named Winand, a priest, for Arnold, archbishop of Cologne.[31] Included in the five other extant versions of the Letter are two first-person 'customisations', attributed to one Duodechin, also a priest, to Abbot Cuno of Disibodenberg, and Arnulf, who was writing to Milo, bishop of Thérouanne. Winand, Duodechin and Arnulf are all understood to have been participants in the campaign at Lisbon.[32]

Sources for the northern crusades of this period are somewhat less detailed than those for crusading in Iberia, and even in the East. There are no extant pieces dedicated to the events of the Wendish Crusade of 1147, however reference to the northern expeditions can be found in chronicles written a generation or two after the events themselves, such as the northern German *Annales Magdeburgenses* and *Annales Palidenses*.[33] The Saxon chronicler Helmold of Bosau (d. *c.* 1177) is believed to have written his *Chronica Slavorum* between *c.* 1167 and 1171 in Schleswig-Holstein.[34] His chronicle traces the Christianisation of the Polabian Slavs from the ninth century until his own time, drawing heavily on the work of Adam of Bremen for information about the period before his own lifetime. Despite writing his account of the Wendish Crusade of 1147 around two decades after the events took place, Helmold's work offers an invaluable insight, not only into northern crusading activity, but also into how these events were perceived in relation to crusading efforts in the Holy Land and Iberia.[35]

As with many of the sources for the Second Crusade, we are often reliant on texts which only discuss disparate elements of the series of events now known as the Third Crusade. For example, a work might treat both the German expedition of Frederick Barbarossa (1189–90) and the later Anglo-Norman campaign of Richard I of England (1190–2) in relation to one another, or explore one series of events in isolation, or incompletely. We are similarly reliant upon texts in which the Third Crusade comprises only a small portion of a whole concerned with a much broader temporal and geographical span.

The first set of Third Crusade narratives can be grouped together because of their ties to Angevin crusading interests, and intention to document either Richard's participation in the Third Crusade or his father Henry II's failure to act

---

Second Crusade', in *Crusaders and Crusading*, pp. 237–9. For a Latin edition of the letter, see Edgington in 'The Lisbon Letter of the Second Crusade', pp. 336–9; translated in 'Albert of Aachen, St Bernard and the Second Crusade', pp. 61–70.

[31] Edgington, 'Albert of Aachen, St Bernard and the Second Crusade', p. 61.
[32] Ibid., pp. 56–7.
[33] 'Annales Magdeburgenses', p. 188; 'Annales Palidenses', p. 82.
[34] Constable, 'The Second Crusade', in *Crusaders and Crusading*, p. 239; Phillips, *The Second* Crusade, p. 228. For a Latin edition, see HB.
[35] On Helmold's understanding of crusading in Iberia, the Baltic and the Holy Land as linked, see especially Constable, 'The Second Crusade', in *Crusaders and Crusading*, p. 239.

upon his crusade vow.[36] A key source for the Third Crusade is in fact a compilation, edited by William Stubbs in the nineteenth century as the *Itinerarium Peregrinorum et Gesta Regis Ricardi* and attributed to one Richard de Templo, canon of the Augustinian priory of Holy Trinity in London.[37] Book One, also known as *IP*1, is comprised of an account of the years 1187–9, a description of Frederick Barbarossa's crusade expedition, and a section on the siege of Acre (1189–91). Later, Richard de Templo added *IP*1 to other materials on the Third Crusade, including the work of Ralph of Diceto, Roger of Howden, and a Latin translation of Ambroise's *Estoire de la Guerre Sainte* to create the *Itinerarium* (also known as *IP*2), probably between *c.* 1216 and 1220.[38]

There are further extant sources written by individuals who are known to have taken part in the Third Crusade. Roger of Howden (d. 1201), former clerk to Henry II of England, went on crusade in the entourage of the latter's son, and by then king, Richard. He remained only briefly in the Holy Land, leaving Acre for Europe in the company of the French king Philip Augustus in August 1191, having spent thirteen months with the army.[39] Roger is thought to have finished work on his *Gesta Regis Henrici Secundi* soon after his return from crusade, when he began working on his more ambitious *Chronica* (a treatment of English history from 732 to 1201).[40]

While he did not participate in the Third Crusade, the prolific Cambro-Norman writer Gerald of Wales (d. 1223) did accompany Baldwin of Ford, archbishop of Canterbury (1184–90) on his crusade preaching tour of Wales in 1188.[41] He completed his account of this tour, the *Itinerarium Kambriae*, by the end of

---

[36] On contemporary attitudes towards Henry II's failure to take the cross, see Paul, *To Follow in Their Footsteps*, pp. 207–50.

[37] *IP*2.

[38] *IP*1 was coined by Hans Eberhard Mayer and its usage has been continued by Nicholson in her translation. See *IP*1. Book One can be separated using Stubbs' chapter numbers (which are followed by Mayer and Nicholson), as comprising chapters 1–17, 18–24, and chapters 25 to the end. On this and the dating of the text, see Nicholson, *The Chronicle of the Third Crusade*, esp. pp. 10–11. See also Staunton, *The Historians of Angevin England*, pp. 142–9; and Bull, *Eyewitness and Crusade Narrative*, pp. 222–3.

[39] For Roger's participation in the Third Crusade, see Gillingham, 'Roger of Howden on Crusade'.

[40] On Roger's career and works, see Staunton, *Historians of Angevin England*, pp. 51–66.

[41] P.W. Edbury, 'Preaching the Crusade in Wales', in *England and Germany in the High Middle Ages*, ed. A. Haverkamp and H. Volrath (Oxford, 1996), pp. 221–33. On Gerald's career and works, see especially Bartlett, *Gerald of Wales*; Staunton, *Historians of Angevin England*, esp. pp. 95–107; and A.J. McMullen and G. Henley, eds., *Gerald of Wales: New Perspectives on a Medieval Writer and Critic* (Cardiff, 2018).

1191.[42] His account contains discussions of miraculous themes, occasionally in a crusading context. The others of Gerald's works discussed in this book are his *Expugnatio Hibernica*, which was probably written between the spring of 1188 and the summer of 1189, and his *De Principis Instructione*, which he was in the prolonged process of composing from around 1190 until 1217.[43] Again, while these are not crusade narratives *per se*, they do contain important critical material regarding Henry II's failure to adequately prepare for and embark upon crusade, a point that Gerald reiterates with recourse to the miraculous.

Additionally, a brief and incomplete narrative of the Third Crusade is contained in Winchester monk Richard of Devizes' *Chronicon*, written in the early 1190s and possibly within one year of Richard I's departure from the Holy Land in 1192, the event with which the chronicle ends. It is comprised of a description of affairs in England during the first three years of Richard's reign, interspersed with anecdotes relating to the Third Crusade.[44]

This book also makes reference to two works relating specifically to the ill-fated expedition of Frederick Barbarossa (Barbarossa famously died attempting to cross the river Göksu in Asia Minor on 10 June 1190). The longest and most detailed of these is the composite *Historia de expeditione*, believed to have been completed by *c.* 1200 by a compiler who was possibly working in the Passau region of Bavaria.[45] The majority of the text concerning the crusaders' passage across Asia Minor appears to have been written by a participant. It also closely resembles (particularly during the section concerning 16 May to 9 June 1190, the eve of Frederick's death) a source written by a Bavarian cleric named Tageno.[46] The second source for Barbarossa's expedition, which makes extensive use of the *Historia de expeditione*, is the *Historia Peregrinorum*, also thought to represent a composite work, albeit of shorter length than the *Historia de expeditione*, compiled in around 1200.[47] Graham Loud has argued that the author/compiler of

---

[42] Ibid., p. 221. For a Latin edition, see *Itinerarium Kambriae*.

[43] Bartlett, *Gerald of Wales*, p. 62. For a Latin edition, see Gerald of Wales, *De Principis Instructione*.

[44] Appleby, *The Chronicle of Richard of Devizes*, p. xviii. On Richard and his *Chronicon*, see Staunton, *Historians of Angevin England*, esp. pp. 129–34. On the at-times eccentric qualities of the *Chronicon*, see especially N. Partner, *Serious Entertainments: The Writing of History in Twelfth-Century England* (London, 1977), pp. 143–79, and 'Richard of Devizes: The Monk Who Forgot to be Medieval', in *The Middle Ages in Text and Texture: Reflections on Medieval Sources*, ed. J. Glenn (Toronto, ON, 2011), pp. 231–44.

[45] Loud, *The Crusade of Frederick Barbarossa*, pp. 1–7. For a Latin edition, see *HeFI*.

[46] Dean of the cathedral of Passau who died in Tripoli later in 1190. See Loud, *The Crusade of Frederick Barbarossa*, pp. 3–5, especially for details of the relationship between the two texts.

[47] The *Historia Peregrinorum* is extant in only a single thirteenth-century manuscript. For a Latin edition, see *HP*.

the *Historia Peregrinorum* should be identified as a Cistercian monk of Salem Abbey (Salmansweiler) in Swabia.[48]

Many of the narrative histories of the Fourth Crusade follow, and often defend, the deeds of a particular participant. The history of the so-called Anonymous of Soissons is based, or so the text claims, on the testimony of one Nivelon de Chérisy, bishop of Soissons and chief prelate of the crusading army.[49] Because the text presents Nivelon as still alive, its composition has been dated to between Nivelon's return to Soissons from Constantinople on 27 June 1205 (at which point Nivelon would presumably have related the information to the Anonymous), and his death in Apulia on 13 September 1207.[50]

Alfred Andrea has observed that Germans produced three of the most important histories of the Fourth Crusade, despite only comprising around ten percent of the crusade host.[51] The highest ranking German cleric on the expedition, Conrad of Krosigk, bishop of Halberstadt in Saxony (r. 1202–8), was both the source of information for, and the main protagonist of, the *Gesta episcoporum Halberstadensium*.[52] The *Gesta episcoporum*'s treatment of the Fourth Crusade has been dated to 1209 and attributed to a single author (probably a cleric associated with the cathedral of Halberstadt), who is believed to have been under the supervision of the retired Conrad himself.[53] A second German (as inferred by Andrea) source for the Fourth Crusade is the *Devastatio Constantinopolitana*, a text that is striking both for its accusations that the crusade leadership was exploitative of the poorer participants, and for the almost total absence of miraculous themes.[54] The third German source for the Fourth Crusade discussed in this book is the *Hystoria Constantinopolitana* of Gunther of Pairis (c. 1150– c. 1210), a Cistercian monk of the abbey of Pairis.[55] Gunther is believed to have completed the *Hystoria* (all apart from the twenty-fifth chapter, which he appended later) before the end of 1205.[56] As we have seen, the work focuses on

---

[48] Loud, *The Crusade of Frederick Barbarossa*, pp. 7–8.

[49] Andrea, *Contemporary Sources*, p. 223. For a combined Latin edition and English translation of the relevant sections, see Anonymous of Soissons, 'De terra Iherosolimitana'.

[50] Andrea, *Contemporary Sources*, p. 224.

[51] Ibid., p. 239.

[52] Ibid., p. 239; '*Gesta episcoporum Halberstadensium*'.

[53] For the author of this particular section of *Gesta episcoporum Halberstadensium*, the Fourth Crusade represented a backdrop to his *apologia* for Bishop Conrad, whose tumultuous seven-year pontificate was followed by his retirement to the Cistercian monastery of Sittichenbach, despite it being forbidden by papal legates on two occasions. See Andrea, *Contemporary Sources*, p. 240.

[54] Andrea, 'The *Devastatio Constantinopolitana*'.

[55] GP. For a useful introduction to Gunther and his *Hystoria*, see Hodgson, 'Leading the People', pp. 201–3.

[56] GP, p. 3.

the crusade participation of Abbot Martin of Pairis, with an eye to his acquisition of Constantinopolitan relics during the crusader sack of the city in 1204.

Another account, attributed to an anonymous priest of Langres, is also concerned with relic theft. It is contained in the *Historia translationum reliquiarum S. Mamantis*, a text containing the translation accounts of several relics of St Mammes of Caesarea to Langres. It is the final relic discussed in the text, the head of the saint, which was supposedly taken from Constantinople in the wake of the crusader conquest, and thus a brief account of these events is included in the narrative.[57]

Chronicle evidence represents a substantial proportion of the available Latin Christian source material for the Fourth Crusade. Ralph of Coggeshall, author of the *Chronicon Anglicanum*, was abbot of the Cistercian abbey of Coggeshall in Essex, England, from 1206 until his retirement due to ill health in 1218.[58] Another chronicle was written between 1227 and 1251 by Alberic of Trois-Fontaines, a brother at the Cistercian monastery of Trois-Fontaines at Châlons-sur-Marne in Champagne.[59] Neither of these monasteries is known to have benefited from the influx of Constantinopolitan relics into western Europe post-1204. Consequently, Andrea had concluded that their detailed discussions of the Fourth Crusade are indicative of the broader Cistercian investment in the crusade shared by, among others, Gunther of Pairis and the Anonymous of Halberstadt.[60]

Finally, this book makes reference to two important Old French prose histories of the Fourth Crusade: namely Geoffrey of Villehardouin's *De la Conquête de Constantinople*, and Robert of Clari's *La Conquête de Constantinople*.[61] Both of these authors are believed to have been crusade participants. Geoffrey of Villehardouin, who was marshal of Champagne, one of the six envoys sent to negotiate with Venice on behalf of the counts of Flanders, Champagne and Blois in 1201, and an influential player during the crusade itself, likely wrote his

---

[57] Anonymous of Langres, 'Historia translationum', p. 34. In its most recent edition by Riant, originally published in 1877, it is noted that the editor was forced to rely on the version of the text as preserved in the *Bibliotheca Floriacensis* of Jean du Bois, as the manuscript which du Bois used, allegedly from the monastery of Celestine de Ternes, is no longer extant. See Riant, *Exuviae sacrae Constantinopolitanae*, vol. 1, p. lxiii. Riant notes that he relied on du Bois' version despite the existence of the then more recent edition in the *Acta Sanctorum*, J.B. Sollerio, J. Pinio, G. Cupero and P. Boschio, eds., 'De Sancto Mamante vel Mammete, martyre, Caesareae in Cappadocia' (Acta Sanctorum, 37; Paris, 1867), pp. 440–6.

[58] Andrea, *Contemporary Sources*, p. 265.

[59] Ibid. For Latin editions, see Alberic of Trois-Fontaines, 'Chronica Albrici'; and Ralph of Coggeshall, 'Chronicon Anglicanum'.

[60] Andrea, *Contemporary Sources*, p. 265.

[61] The most recent recent Old French edition of Villehardouin's Fourth Crusade history is Geoffrey of Villehardouin, *La Conquête de Constantinople*; Robert of Clari, *La Conquête de Constantinople*.

account from 1208.[62] By contrast, Robert of Clari is believed to have been a poor knight in possession of a small fief in Picardy, who participated in the crusade in the retinue of his overlord Peter of Amiens.[63] It is thought that his account was written in stages, with most of it being completed within a few years of 1205.[64]

[62] P. Noble, 'The Importance of Old French Chronicles as Historical Sources of the Fourth Crusade and the Early Latin Empire of Constantinople', *Journal of Medieval History*, 27 (2001), 403 and n. 27. On Geoffrey of Villehardoin and his text, see especially C. Morris, 'Geoffroy de Villehardouin and the Conquest of Constantinople', *History*, 53.177 (1968), 24–34; and Bull, *Eyewitness and Crusade Narrative*, pp. 260–92.

[63] Noble, *La Conquête de Constantinople*, p. xxiii. Understood to have been a member of the crusade's rank and file, Robert, and therefore his work, has received unflattering reviews from modern scholars, from the more generous 'naïve curiosity' attributed to him by Peter Noble, to his work's damning dismissal by Archambault as '…wrapped in a shroud of insuperable ignorance'. See Noble, 'The Importance of Old French chronicles', 410; and P. Archambault, *Seven French Chroniclers: Witnesses to History* (Syracuse, NY, 1974), p. 27. On the work's status as a sophisticated exercise in the writing of history, see S. Kinoshita, *Medieval Boundaries: Rethinking Difference in Old French Literature* (Philadelphia, PA, 2006), pp. 139–75; and Bull, *Eyewitness and Crusade Narrative*, pp. 292–336.

[64] Bull, *Eyewitness and Crusade Narrative*, p. 293.

Bibliography

Primary Sources

Alberic of Trois-Fontaines, 'Chronica Albrici monachi trium fontium', ed. P. Scheffer-Boichorst, *MGH SS*, 23, pp. 631–950.

Albert of Aachen, *Historia Ierosolimitana*, ed. and trans. S.B. Edgington (Oxford, 2007).

Albertus Magnus, *Summa theologiae, vol. II*, ed. A. Borgnet (Opera Omnia, 32; Paris, 1895).

Aldhelm of Malmesbury, *Prosa de Virginitate cum Glosa Latina atque Anglosaxonica*, ed. S. Gwara (CCSL, 124A; Turnhout, 2001).

Ambroise, *The History of the Holy War: Ambroise's Estoire de la Guerre Sainte*, ed. and trans. M. Ailes and M. Barber, 2 vols (Woodbridge, 2003).

'Annales Brunwilarenses', ed. G.H. Pertz, *MGH SS*, 16, pp. 724–8.

'Annales Magdeburgenses', ed. G.H. Pertz, *MGH SS*, 16, pp. 105–96.

Annales Marbacenses qui dicuntur, ed. H. Bloch (MGH SSRG, 9; Hanover, 1907).

'Annales Palidenses', ed. G.H. Pertz, *MGH SS*, 16, pp. 48–98.

'Annales Sancti Disibodi', ed. G.H. Pertz, *MGH SS*, 17, pp. 4–30.

'Annales Sancti Iacobi Leodiensis', ed. G.H. Pertz, *MGH SS*, 16, pp. 632–83.

Anonymous of Langres, 'Historia translationum reliquiarum S. Mamantis', in *Exuviae sacrae Constantinopolitanae*, 1, ed. P. Riant (Geneva, 1877–88, reprinted Paris, 2004), pp. 22–34; also in 'De Sancto Mamante vel Mammete, Martyre, Caesareae in Cappadocia', ed. J.B. Sollerio, J. Pinio, G. Cupero and P. Boschio (Acta Sanctorum, 37; Paris, 1867), pp. 440–6.

Anonymous of Soissons, 'De terra Iherosolimitana et quomodo ab urbe Constantinopolitana ad hanc ecclesiam allate sunt reliquie', in *Contemporary Sources for the Fourth Crusade: Revised Edition*, ed. and trans. A.J. Andrea (Leiden, 2008), pp. 223–38, 338–43.

Arnold of Lübeck, *Chronica Slavorum*, ed. J.M. Lappenberg and G.H. Pertz (MGH SSRG, 14; Hanover, 1868); trans. G. Loud, *The Chronicle of the Slavs by Arnold of Lübeck* (Crusade Texts in Translation; Abingdon, 2019).

Artemidorus Daldianus, *Artemidori Daldiani Onirocriticon Libri V*, ed. R.A. Pack (Leipzig, 1963); trans. R.J. White, *The Interpretation of Dreams: Oneirocritica*, 2nd edn (Park Ridge, NJ, 1990).

Augustine of Hippo, 'Contra Faustum Manichaeum Libri XXXIII', *PL*, 42, cols. 207–518; trans. P. Schaff, *Nicene and Post-Nicene Fathers of the Christian*

Church, Volume IV – St Augustine: The Writings Against the Manichaeans and Against the Donatists (Grand Rapids, MI, 1979).

—— 'De cura pro mortuis gerenda ad Paulinum', *PL*, 40, cols. 591–610.

—— *De Genesi ad Litteram, Libri Duodecim*, ed. and trans. P. Agaësse and A. Solignac, 7th series (Oeuvres de Saint Augustin, 49; Brussels, 1972); trans. J.H. Taylor, *The Literal Meaning of Genesis, Volume II, Books 7–12* (New York, NY, 1982).

—— 'De utilitate credendi ad Honoratum Liber Unus', *PL*, 42, cols. 63–92.

Baldric of Bourgueil, *The Historia Ierosolimitana of Baldric of Bourgueil*, ed. S. Biddlecombe (Woodbridge, 2014).

Bartolf of Nangis, 'Gesta Francorum Iherusalem Expugnantium', *RHC Oc.*, 3, pp. 491–543.

Bernard of Clairvaux, 'De consideratione libri quinque', *PL*, 182, cols. 727–808.

Caesarius of Heisterbach, *Caesarii Heisterbacensis monachi ordinis Cisterciensis Dialogus miraculorum*, ed. J. Strange, 2 vols (Cologne and Bonn, 1851).

La Chanson d'Antioche: chanson de geste du dernier quart du XIIe siècle, ed. and trans. B. Guidot (Champion classiques moyen âge, 33; Paris, 2011); trans. S.B. Edgington and C. Sweetenham, *The Chanson d'Antioche: An Old French Account of the First Crusade* (Crusade Texts in Translation, 22; Farnham, 2011).

La Chanson de Jérusalem, ed. N. Thorp, *The Old French Crusade Cycle*, 6 (Tuscaloosa, AL, 1992); trans. C. Sweetenham, *The Chanson des Chétifs and Chanson de Jérusalem: Completing the Central Trilogy of the Old French Crusade Cycle* (Crusade Texts in Translation, 29; Farnham, 2016), pp. 173–353.

Les Chétifs, ed. G.M. Myers, *The Old French Crusade Cycle*, 5 (Tuscaloosa, AL, 1981); trans. C. Sweetenham, *The Chanson des Chétifs and Chanson de Jérusalem: Completing the Central Trilogy of the Old French Crusade Cycle* (Crusade Texts in Translation, 29; Farnham, 2016), pp. 67–172.

Chronicles of the Investiture Contest: Frutolf of Michelsberg and his Continuators, trans. T.J.H. McCarthy (Manchester, 2014)

The Conquest of the Holy Land by Salah al-Din: A Critical Edition of the Libellus de expugnatione Terrae Sanctae per Saladinum, ed. and trans. K. Brewer and J.H. Kane (Crusade Texts in Translation; Abingdon, 2019).

Contemporary Sources for the Fourth Crusade: Revised Edition, ed. and trans. A.J. Andrea (Leiden, 2008).

The Crusades: A Documentary Survey, ed. J. Brundage (Milwaukee, WI, 1962).

Ekkehard of Aura, 'Hierosolymita', *RHC Oc.*, 5, pp. 1–40.

Eugenius III, 'Quantum praedecessores', in *Gesta Friderici imperatoris*, ed. R. Wilmans, *MGH SS*, 20, pp. 371–2.

Eusebius, *Life of Constantine*, trans. A. Cameron and S.G. Hall (Oxford, 1999).

De expugnatione Lyxbonensi: The Conquest of Lisbon, ed. and trans. C.W. David, rev. J.P. Phillips (New York, NY, 2001).

Frutolfi Chronici Continuationes anonymae ad annum 1101 et ad annum 1106, ed. B. Marxreiter (Digitale Vorabedition, 2018), http://www. mgh.de/fileadmin/Downloads/pdf/Bamberger_Weltchronistik/ Continuatio_I_und_II/Satzlauf_2018-08-09T0918/Frutolf-Fortsetzungen_ bis_1101_und_1106_Satzlauf_2018-08-09T0918.pdf (accessed August 28, 2019).

Fulcher of Chartres, *Historia Hierosolymitana, 1095–1127*, ed. H. Hagenmeyer (Heidelberg, 1913); trans. F.R. Ryan, *A History of the Expedition to Jerusalem* (Knoxville, TN, 1969).

Garnier of Rochefort, 'Sermo XL. De Arca Spirituali', *PL*, 205, cols. 824–8.

Geoffrey of Malaterra, *De Rebus Gestis Rogerii Calabriae et Siciliae Comitis et Roberti Guisgardi Ducis Fratris Eius*, ed. E. Pontieri (Rerum Italicarum Scriptores, 5.1; Bologna, 1928).

Geoffrey of Villehardouin, *La conquête de Constantinople*, ed. E. Faral, 2 vols (Paris, 1938).

Gerald of Wales, *Concerning the Instruction of Princes*, trans. J. Stevenson (Felinfach, 1991).

—— *Giraldi Cambrensis Opera*, ed. J.S. Brewer, J.F. Dimock and G.F. Warner, 8 vols (Rolls Series, 21; London, 1861–91).

—— *Expugnatio Hibernica: The Conquest of Ireland*, ed. and trans. A.B. Scott and F.X. Martin (Dublin, 1978).

Gervase of Tilbury, *Otia imperialia, Recreation for an Emperor*, ed. and trans. S.E. Banks and J.W. Binns (Oxford, 2002).

'Gesta episcoporum Halberstadensium', ed. L. Weiland, *MGH SS*, 23, pp. 73–123.

Gesta Francorum et aliorum Hierosolimitanorum, ed. and trans. R. Hill with R.A.B. Mynors (Edinburgh, 1962).

Gregory VIII, 'Audita tremendi', *PL*, 202, cols. 1539–42.

Guibert of Nogent, *Dei gesta per Francos*, ed. R.B.C. Huygens (CCCM, 127A; Turnhout, 2002); trans. R. Levine, *The Deeds of God through the Franks: a Translation of Guibert of Nogent's Gesta Dei per Francos* (Woodbridge, 1997).

—— *De pignoribus sanctorum*, ed. R.B.C. Huygens (CCCM, 127; Turnhout, 1993), pp. 79–175.

Gunther of Pairis, *Hystoria Constantinopolitana: Untersuchung und kritische Ausgabe*, ed. P. Orth (Hildesheim and Zürich, 1994); trans. A.J. Andrea, *The Capture of Constantinople, The Hystoria Constantinopolitana of Gunther of Pairis* (Philadelphia, PA, 1997).

Helmold of Bosau, *Slavenchronik*, ed. B. Schmeidler (MGH SSRG, 32; Hanover, 1937); trans. F.J. Tschan, *The Chronicle of the Slavs* (New York, NY, 1966).

Henry of Huntingdon, *Historia Anglorum: The History of the English People*, ed. and trans. D. Greenway (Oxford, 1996).

Henry of Livonia, *Chronicon Livoniae*, ed. L. Arbusow and A. Bauer (MGH SSRG, 31; Hanover, 1955).

'Historia de expeditione Friderici Imperatoris', in *Quellen zur Geschichte des Kreuzzuges Kaiser Friedrichs I.*, ed. A. Chroust (MGH SSRG Nova Series, 5; Berlin, 1928), pp. 1–115; trans. G. A. Loud, *The Crusade of Frederick Barbarossa: The History of the Expedition of the Emperor Frederick and Related Texts* (Crusade Texts in Translation, 19; Farnham, 2010), pp. 33–134.

'Historia Peregrinorum', in *Quellen zur Geschichte des Kreuzzuges Kaiser Friedrichs I.*, ed. A. Chroust (MGH SSRG Nova Series, 5; Berlin, 1928), pp. 116–72; trans. G.A. Loud, *The Crusade of Frederick Barbarossa: The History of the Expedition of the Emperor Frederick and Related Texts* (Crusade Texts in Translation, 19; Farnham, 2010), pp. 135–47.

Homer, *The Iliad*, trans. M. Hammond (London, 1987).

Hystoria de via et recuperatione Antiochiae atque Ierusolymarum (olim Tudebodus imitatus et continuatus): Normanni d'Italia alla prima Crociata in una cronaca cassinese, ed. E. D'Angelo (Florence, 2009).

Isidore of Seville, *Isidori Hispalensis Episcopi Etymologiarum sive Originum Libri XX*, ed. W.M. Lindsay (Oxford, 1911); trans. S.A. Barney, W.J. Lewis, J.A. Beach and O. Berghof, *The Etymologies of Isidore of Seville* (Cambridge, 2006).

'Itinerarium Peregrinorum', in *Das Itinerarium Peregrinorum: Eine Zeitgenössische Englische Chronik zum Dritten Kreuzzug in Ursprünglicher Gestatt*, ed. H.E. Mayer (Stuttgart, 1962).

Itinerarium Peregrinorum et Gesta Regis Ricardi, ed. W. Stubbs, *Chronicles and Memorials of the Reign of Richard I* (Rolls Series, 38.1; London, 1864); trans. H.J. Nicholson, *The Chronicle of the Third Crusade: A Translation of the Itinerarium Peregrinorum et Gesta Regis Ricardi* (Crusade Texts in Translation, 3; Farnham, 1997).

John Kinnamos, *The Deeds of John and Manuel Comnenus*, trans. C.M. Brand (New York, NY, 1976).

John of Salisbury, *Policraticus I–IV*, ed. K.S.B. Keats-Rohan (CCCM, 118; Turnhout, 1993); trans. J.P. Pike, *Frivolities of Courtiers and Footprint of Philosophers, Being a Translation of the First, Second, and Third Books and Selections from the Seventh and Eighth Books of the Policraticus of John of Salisbury* (London, 1938); and C.J. Nederman, ed. and trans., *John of Salisbury: Policraticus, Of the Frivolities of Courtiers and the Footprints of Philosophers* (Cambridge, 1990).

Macrobius Ambrosius Theodosius, *Macrobius, Vol. II. Commentarii in Somnium Scipionis*, ed. J. Willis (Leipzig, 1970); trans. W.H. Stahl, *Commentary on the Dreams of Scipio* (New York, NY, 1990).

Niketas Choniates, *O City of Byzantium*, trans. H.J. Magoulias (Detroit, MI, 1984).

Odo of Cluny, 'De Vita Sancti Geraldi Auriliacensis Comitis', *PL*, 133, cols. 639–710; trans. G. Sitwell, *St. Odo of Cluny: Being the Life of St. Odo of Cluny by John of Salerno and the Life of St. Gerald of Aurillac by St. Odo* (London, 1958).

Odo of Deuil, *De profectione Ludovici VII in Orientem*, ed. and trans. V.G. Berry (New York, NY, 1948).

Orderic Vitalis, *The Ecclesiastical History of Orderic Vitalis,* ed. and trans. M. Chibnall, 6 vols (Oxford, 1969–80).

Otto of Freising, *Gesta Frederici I. imperatoris*, ed. G. Waitz (MGH SSRG, 46; Hannover, 1912); trans. C.C. Mierow, *The Deeds of Frederick Barbarossa* (Toronto, ON, 1994).

—— *Chronica sive historia duabus civitatibus*, ed. W. Lammers and trans. A. Schmidt (Berlin, 1960); trans. C.C. Mierow, *The Two Cities* (New York, NY, 1928).

Paulus Orosius, 'Historiarum Libri Septem', *PL*, 31, cols. 663–1174.

Peter Tudebode, *Historia de Hierosolymitano itinere*, ed. J.H. Hill and L.L. Hill (Paris, 1977); trans. J.H. Hill and L.L. Hill, *Historia de Hierosolymitano itinere* (Philadelphia, PA, 1974).

Ralph of Caen, *Radulphi Cadomensis Tancredus*, ed. and trans. Edoardo D'Angelo (CCCM, 231; Turnhout, 2011); and in 'Gesta Tancredi in expeditione Hierosolymitana', *RHC Oc.*, 3, pp. 587–716; trans. B.S. Bachrach and D.S. Bachrach, *The Gesta Tancredi of Ralph of Caen, A History of the Normans on the First Crusade* (Aldershot, 2005).

Ralph of Coggeshall, 'Chronicon Anglicanum', ed. J. Stephenson, *Rerum Britannicarum Medii Ævi Scriptores*, 66 (London, 1875), pp. 1–208.

Raymond of Aguilers, *Le 'Liber' de Raymond d'Aguilers*, ed. J.H Hill and L.L. Hill (Paris, 1969); trans. J.H. Hill and L.L. Hill, *Historia Francorum Qui Ceperunt Iherusalem* (Philadelphia, 1968).

Die Register Innocenz' III, ed. O. Hageneder, A. Sommerlechner, H. Weigl, C. Egger and R. Murauer (Graz, 1964–).

Richard of Devizes, *The Chronicle of Richard of Devizes of the Time of King Richard the First*, ed. and trans. J.T. Appleby (London, 1963).

Robert of Clari, *La Conquête de Constantinople*, ed. and trans. P. Noble (Edinburgh, 2005).

Robert the Monk, *The Historia Iherosolimitana of Robert the Monk*, ed. M.G. Bull and D. Kempf (Woodbridge, 2013); trans. C. Sweetenham, *Robert the Monk's History of the First Crusade, Historia Iherosolimitana* (Crusade Texts in Translation, 11; Aldershot, 2005).

Roger of Howden, *Gesta Regis Henrici Secundi Benedicti Abbatis, The Chronicle of the Reigns of Henry II, and Richard I, A.D. 1169–1192; known commonly under the name of Benedict of Peterborough*, ed. W. Stubbs, 2 vols (Rolls Series, 49.1–2; London, 1867).

—— *Chronica: Magistri Rogeri de Houedene*, ed. W. Stubbs, 4 vols (Rolls Series, 51.1–4; London, 1868–71); trans. H.T. Riley, *The Annals of Roger de Hoveden: Comprising the History of England and of Other Countries of Europe from A.D. 732 to A.D. 1201*, 2 vols (London, 1853).

Roger of Wendover, *Rogeri de Wendover Liber qui dicitur flores historiarum*, ed. H.G. Hewlett (Rolls Series, 84.2; London, 1887).

Saxo Grammaticus, 'Ex Saxonis Gestis Danorum', ed. G. Waitz, *MGH SS*, 29, pp. 37–161.

Thomas Aquinas, 'De potentia', in *Quaestiones disputatae*, 2, ed. P. Bazzi, M. Calcaterra, T.S. Centi, E. Odetto and P.M. Pession (Turin and Rome, 1965).

—— *Summa theologiae* (Sancti Thomae de Aquino Opera Omnia iussu Leonis XIII P.M. edita, 4–12; Rome, 1888–1906).

'De Ulixbona Saracensis erepta', ed. M.M-.M-.J. Brial, *Recueil des Historiens des Gaules et de la France*, 14 (Paris, 1877), pp. 325–7.

Virgil, *Bucolics, Aeneid, and Georgics Of Vergil*, ed. J.B. Greenough (Boston, MA, 1900), Perseus Digital Library, http://data.perseus.org/texts/urn:cts:latin-Lit:phi0690.phi003 (accessed March 28, 2019).

Walter the Chancellor, *Galterii Cancellarii, Bella Antiochena*, ed. H. Hagenmeyer (Innsbruck, 1896).

William of Malmesbury, *Gesta Regum Anglorum, The History of the English Kings*, ed. and trans. R.A.B. Mynors, R.M. Thomson and M. Winterbottom, 2 vols (Oxford, 1998–9).

William of Poitiers, *The Gesta Guillelmi of William of Poitiers*, ed. and trans. R.H.C. Davis and M. Chibnall (Oxford, 1998).

William of St Thierry, *De erroribus Guillelmi de Conchis*, *PL*, 180, cols. 333–40.

William of Tyre, *Chronicon*, ed. R.B.C. Huygens (CCCM, 63 and 63a; Turnhout, 1986); trans. E.A. Babcock and A.C. Krey, *A History of Deeds Done Beyond the Sea*, 2 vols (New York, NY, 1943).

Secondary Works

Abbott, H.P., *The Cambridge Introduction to Narrative*, 2nd edn (Cambridge, 2008).

Adams, G.W., *Visions in Late Medieval England: Lay Spirituality and Sacred Glimpses of the Hidden Worlds of Faith* (Leiden, 2007).

Ailes, M.J., 'The Admirable Enemy? Saladin and Saphadin in Ambroise's *Estoire de la Guerre Sainte*', in *Knighthoods of Christ: Essays on the History of the Crusades and the Knights Templar, Presented to Malcolm Barber*, ed. N. Housley (Aldershot, 2007), pp. 51–64.

Akbari, S.C., *Idols in the East: European Representations of Islam and the Orient, 1100–1450* (Ithaca, NY, 2009).

Albu, E., *The Normans in their Histories: Propaganda, Myth and Subversion* (Woodbridge, 2001).

Andrea, A.J., 'The *Devastatio Constantinopolitana*, a Special Perspective on the Fourth Crusade: An Analysis, New Edition, and Translation', *Historical Reflections*, 19.1 (1993), 107–49.

Andrea, A.J., and P.I. Rachlin, 'Holy War, Holy Relics, Holy Theft: The Anonymous of Soisson's *De terra Iherosolimitana*: An Analysis, Edition, and Translation', *Historical Reflections*, 18.1 (1992), 147–56.

Archambault, P., *Seven French Chroniclers: Witnesses to History* (Syracuse, NY, 1974).

Arnold, J., *Belief and Unbelief in Medieval Europe* (London, 2005).

—— 'The Materiality of Unbelief in Late Medieval England', in *The Unorthodox Imagination in Late Medieval Britain*, ed. S. Page (Manchester, 2010), pp. 65–95.

Asbridge, T., *The Creation of the Principality of Antioch, 1098–1130* (Woodbridge, 2000).

—— 'The Holy Lance of Antioch: Power, Devotion and Memory on the First Crusade', *Reading Medieval Studies*, 33 (2007), 3–36.

—— *The Crusades: The War for the Holy Land* (London, 2012).

Baer, F., 'Eine jüdische Messiasprophetie auf das Jahr 1186 und der dritte Kreuzzug', *Monatsschrift für Geschichte und Wissenschaft des Judentums*, 3 (1926), 155–65.

Bagge, S., 'Ideas and Narrative in Otto of Freising's *Gesta Frederici*', *Journal of Medieval History*, 22.4 (1996), 345–77.

Barber, M., 'The Impact of the Fourth Crusade in the West: The Distribution of Relics after 1204', in *Urbs Capta: The Fourth Crusade and its Consequences*, ed. A.E. Laiou (Paris, 2005), pp. 325–34.

Barnes, T., *Constantine: Dynasty, Religion and Power in the Later Roman Empire* (Chichester, 2014).

Bartlett, R., *Gerald of Wales: A Voice of the Middle Ages* (Stroud, 2006).

—— *The Natural and the Supernatural in the Middle Ages* (Cambridge, 2008).

—— *Why Can the Dead Do Such Great Things? Saints and Worshippers from the Martyrs to the Reformation* (Woodstock, 2013).

Bennett, M., 'Virile Latins, Effeminate Greeks, and Strong Women: Gender Definitions of Crusade?', in *Gendering the Crusades*, ed. S.B. Edgington and S. Lambert (Cardiff, 2001), pp. 16–30.

Biddlecombe, S., 'Baldric of Bourgueil and the *Familia Christi*', in *Writing the Early Crusades: Text, Transmission and Memory*, ed. M.G. Bull and D. Kempf (Woodbridge, 2014), pp. 9–23.

Blake, E.O., and Morris, C., 'A Hermit Goes to War: Peter and the Origins of the

First Crusade', in *Monks, Hermits, and the Ascetic Tradition*, ed. W.J. Sheils (Studies in Church History, 22; Oxford, 1985), pp. 440–53.

Bolton, B., 'Signs, Wonders, Miracles: Supporting the Faith in Medieval Rome', in *Signs, Wonders, Miracles: Representations of Divine Power in the Life of the Church*, ed. K. Cooper and J. Gregory (Studies in Church History, 41; Woodbridge, 2005), pp. 157–78.

Booth, W.C., *The Rhetoric of Fiction,* 2nd edn (Chicago, 1983).

Bouet, P., 'De l'origine troyenne des Normands', in *Mélanges René Lepelley: Recueil d'études en homage au Professeur René Lepelley*, ed. C. Bougy, P. Boissel and B. Garnier (Caen, 1995), pp. 401–13.

Brewer, K., *Wonder and Scepticism in the Middle Ages* (Abingdon, 2016).

Bron, B., *Das Wunder: Das theologische Wunderverständnis im Horizont des neuzeitlichen Natur- und Geschichtsbegriffs* (Göttingen, 1975).

Browe, P., *Die eucharistischen Wunder des Mittelalters* (Breslau, 1938).

Brown, E.A.R., 'The Cistercians in the Latin Empire of Constantinople and Greece, 1204–1276', *Traditio*, 14 (1958), 63–120.

Brown, P., 'The Rise and Function of the Holy Man in Late Antiquity', *The Journal of Roman Studies*, 61 (1971), 80–101.

Brundage, J., 'Prostitution, Miscegenation and Sexual Purity in the First Crusade', in *Crusade and Settlement: Papers Read at the First Conference of the Society for the Study of the Crusades and the Latin East and Presented to R.C. Smail*, ed. P.W. Edbury (Cardiff, 1985), pp. 57–65.

Buc, P., *Holy War, Martyrdom, and Terror: Christianity, Violence and the West, ca. 70 C.E. to the Iraq War* (Philadelphia, PA, 2015).

Buck, A.D., *The Principality of Antioch and its Frontiers in the Twelfth Century* (Woodbridge, 2017).

Bull, M.G., *Knightly Piety and the Lay Response to the First Crusade. The Limousin and Gascony, c.970–c.1130* (Oxford, 1993).

—— trans., *The Miracles of Our Lady of Rocamadour: Analysis and Translation* (Woodbridge, 1999).

—— 'The Western Narratives of the First Crusade', in *Christian-Muslim Relations: A Bibliographical History. Volume 3 (1050–1200)*, ed. D. Thomas, A. Mallett et al. (Leiden, 2011), pp. 15–25.

—— 'The Relationship between the *Gesta Francorum* and Peter Tudebode's *Historia de Hierosolymitano Itinere*: The Evidence of a Hitherto Unexamined Manuscript (St. Catharine's College, Cambridge, 3)', *Crusades*, 11 (2012), 1–17.

—— 'Robert the Monk and his Source(s)', in *Writing the Early Crusades: Text, Transmission and Memory*, ed. M.G. Bull and D. Kempf (Woodbridge, 2014), pp. 127–39.

—— 'Narratological Readings of Crusade Texts', in *The Crusader World*, ed. A.J. Boas (Abingdon, 2016), pp. 646–60.

—— *Eyewitness and Crusade Narrative: Perception and Narration in Accounts of the Second, Third and Fourth Crusades* (Woodbridge, 2018).

Bull, M.G., and Kempf, D., eds., *Writing the Early Crusades: Text, Transmission and Memory* (Woodbridge, 2014).

Burnett, C., 'Adelard, Ergaphalau and the Science of the Stars', in *Adelard of Bath: An English Scientist and Arabist of the Early Twelfth Century* (London, 1987), pp. 133–45.

—— 'The Coherence of the Arabic-Latin Translation Program in Toledo in the Twelfth Century', *Science in Context*, 14.1–2 (2001), 249–88.

—— 'Adelard of Bath', in *Medieval Science, Technology and Medicine: An Encyclopedia*, ed. T.F. Glick, S.J. Livesey and F. Wallis (London, 2005), pp. 5–6.

Busby, K., 'Narrative Genres', in *The Cambridge Companion to Medieval French Literature*, ed. S. Gaunt and S. Kay (Cambridge, 2008), pp. 139–52.

Bynum, C.W., 'Wonder', *The American Historical Review*, 102.1 (1997), 1–26.

—— *Wonderful Blood: Theology and Practice in Late Medieval Germany and Beyond* (Philadelphia, 2007).

—— *Christian Materiality: An Essay on Religion in Late Medieval Europe* (New York, NY, 2011).

Bysted, A.L., Jensen, C.S., Jensen, K.V., and Lind, J.H., *Jerusalem in the North: Denmark and the Baltic Crusades, 1100–1552* (Turnhout, 2012).

Cameron, A., 'The Date and Identity of Macrobius', *The Journal of Roman Studies*, 56.1–2 (1966), 25–38.

Campion, N., *The Great Year: Astrology, Millenarianism and History in the Western Tradition* (London, 1994).

Carty, C.M., 'The Role of Medieval Dream Images in Authenticating Ecclesiastical Construction', *Zeitschrift für Kunstheschichte*, 62 (1999), 45–90.

Chenu, M.-D., *Nature, Man and Society in the Twelfth Century: Essays on New Theological Perspectives in the Latin Medieval West*, ed. and trans. J. Taylor and L.K. Little (London, 1997).

Chibnall, M., *The World of Orderic Vitalis: Norman Monks and Norman Knights* (Woodbridge, 1984).

Christiansen, E., *The Northern Crusades*, revised edn (London, 1997).

Cole, P., *The Preaching of the Crusades to the Holy Land, 1095–1270* (Cambridge, MA, 1991).

Constable, G., 'The Second Crusade as Seen by Contemporaries', *Traditio*, 9 (1953), 213–79; and revised in G. Constable, 'The Second Crusade as Seen by Contemporaries', in *Crusaders and Crusading in the Twelfth Century: Collected Studies* (Aldershot, 2008), pp. 229–300.

—— 'The Cross of the Crusaders', in *Crusaders and Crusading in the Twelfth Century: Collected Studies*, ed. G. Constable (Aldershot, 2008), pp. 45–92.

Cormack, R., and Mihalarias, S., 'A Crusader Painting of St. George: "Maniera greca" or "lingua franca"?', *Burlington Magazine*, 126 (1984), 132–41.

Cowdrey, H.E.J., 'Martyrdom and the First Crusade', in *Crusade and Settlement: Papers Read at the First Conference of the Society for the Study of the Crusades and the Latin East and Presented to R.C. Smail*, ed. P.W. Edbury (Cardiff, 1985), pp. 46–56.

D'Alverny, M.-T., 'Translations and Translators', in *Renaissance and Renewal in the Twelfth Century*, ed. R.L. Benson, G. Constable and C.D. Lanham (London, 1991), pp. 421–62.

Daniel, E.R., 'Apocalyptic Conversion: The Joachite Alternative to the Crusades', *Traditio*, 25 (1969), 127–54; reprinted in E.R. Daniel, *Abbot Joachim of Fiore and Joachinism* (Farnham, 2011), 11.

—— 'Joachim of Fiore: Patterns of History in the Apocalypse', in *The Apocalypse in the Middle Ages*, ed. R.K. Emmerson and B. McGinn (London, 1992), pp. 72–88; reprinted in E.R. Daniel, *Abbot Joachim of Fiore and Joachinism* (Farnham, 2011), 4.

—— 'A New Understanding of Joachim: The Concords, the Exile, and the Exodus', in *Gioacchino da Fiore tra Bernardo di Clairvaux e Innocenzo III: Atti del V Congresso Internationale di Studi Gioachimiti (San Giovanni in Fiore, 16–21 September 1999)*, ed. R. Rusconi (Rome, 2001), pp. 209–22; reprinted in E.R. Daniel, *Abbot Joachim of Fiore and Joachinism* (Farnham, 2011), 5.

—— *Abbot Joachim of Fiore and Joachinism* (Farnham, 2011).

Daston, L., and Park, K., *Wonders and the Order of Nature, 1150–1750* (New York, NY, 1998).

David, C.W., 'The Authorship of the *De Expugnatione Lyxbonensi*', *Speculum*, 7.1 (1932), 50–7.

de Weever, J., *Sheba's Daughters: Whitening and Demonizing the Saracen Woman in Medieval French Epic* (London, 1998).

Draelants, L., 'Le Temps dans les Textes Historiographiques du Moyen Âge', in *Le temps qu'il fait au Moyen Âge: phénomènes atmosphériques dans la littérature, la pensée scientifique et religieuse*, ed. J. Ducos and C. Thomasset (Paris, 1998), pp. 91–138.

Dronke, P., ed., *A History of Twelfth-Century Western Philosophy* (Cambridge, 1988).

Edbury, P.W., 'Preaching the Crusade in Wales', in *England and Germany in the High Middle Ages*, ed. A. Haverkamp and H. Volrath (Oxford, 1996), pp. 221–33.

—— 'Celestine III, the Crusade and the Latin East', in *Pope Celestine III (1192–1198): Diplomat and Pastor*, ed. J. Doran and D.J. Smith (Farnham, 2008), pp. 129–43.

Edbury, P.W., and Rowe, J.G., *William of Tyre: Historian of the Latin East* (Cambridge, 1988).

Edgington, S.B., 'The Lisbon Letter of the Second Crusade', *Historical Research*, 69 (1996), 336–9.

—— 'The First Crusade: Reviewing the Evidence', in *The First Crusade: Origins and Impact*, ed., J.P. Phillips (Manchester, 1997), pp. 207–27.

—— 'Albert of Aachen and the *Chansons de Geste*', in *The Crusades and their Sources, Essays Presented to Bernard Hamilton*, ed. J. France and W.G. Zajac (Farnham, 1998), pp. 23–37.

—— 'Albert of Aachen, St Bernard and the Second Crusade', in *The Second Crusade: Scope and Consequences*, ed. J.P. Phillips and M. Hoch (Manchester, 2001), pp. 54–70.

—— 'The *Gesta Francorum Iherusalem expugnantium* of "Bartolf of Nangis"', *Crusades*, 13 (2014), 21–35.

Fletcher, R.A., *The Barbarian Conversion: From Paganism to Christianity* (New York, NY, 1997).

Flint, V.I.L., 'The Transmission of Astrology in the Early Middle Ages', *Viator*, 21 (1990), 1–27.

Flori, J., 'Mort et martyre des guerriers vers 1100. L'exemple de la première croisade', *Cahiers de civilisation médievale*, 34 (1991), 121–39.

—— 'La caricature de l'Islam dans l'Occident médiéval. Origine et signification de quelques stéréotypes concernant l'Islam', *Aevum*, 66 (1992), 245–56.

Folda, J., 'Mounted Warrior Saints in Crusader Icons: Images of the Knighthoods of Christ', in *Knighthoods of Christ: Essays on the History of the Crusades and the Knights Templar*, ed. N. Housley (Aldershot, 2007), pp. 87–107.

Fonnesberg-Schmidt, I., *The Popes and the Baltic Crusades, 1147–1254* (Leiden, 2007).

Forey, A., 'The Siege of Lisbon and the Second Crusade', *Portuguese Studies*, 20 (2004), 1–13.

France, J., 'The Anonymous *Gesta Francorum* and the *Historia Francorum qui ceperunt Iherusalem* of Raymond of Aguilers and the *Historia de Hierosolymitana itinere* of Peter Tudebode: An Analysis of the Textual Relationship between Primary Sources for the First Crusade', in *The Crusades and Their Sources: Essays Presented to Bernard Hamilton*, ed. J. France and W.G. Zajac (Aldershot, 1998), pp. 39–69.

—— 'Logistics and the Second Crusade', in *Logistics of Warfare in the Age of the Crusades: Proceedings of a Workshop held at the Centre for Medieval Studies, University of Sydney, 30 September to 4 October 2002*, ed. J. Pryor (Aldershot, 2006), pp. 87–93.

—— 'Two Types of Vision on the First Crusade: Stephen of Valence and Peter Bartholomew', *Crusades*, 5 (2006), 1–20.

Galloway, A., 'Visions and Visionaries', in *The Oxford Handbook of Medieval*

Literature in English, ed. G. Walker and E. Treharne (Oxford, 2010), pp. 257–60.

Gaposchkin, C., *The Making of Saint Louis: Kingship, Sanctity, and Crusading in the Later Middle Ages* (London, 2008).

Gaster, M., 'The Letter of Toledo', *Folklore*, 13.2 (1902), 115–34.

Geary, P., *Furta Sacra: Thefts of Relics in the Central Middle Ages*, revised edn (Princeton, NJ, 1990).

Gibson, M., 'Adelard of Bath', in *Adelard of Bath: An English Scientist and Arabist of the Early Twelfth Century*, ed. C. Burnett (London, 1987), pp. 7–16.

Gillingham, J., 'Roger of Howden on Crusade', in *Richard Cœur de Lion: Kingship, Chivalry and War in the Twelfth Century* (London, 1994), pp. 141–53.

—— 'Preaching the Crusade in Wales', in *England and Germany in the High Middle Ages*, ed. A. Haverkamp and H. Volrath (Oxford, 1996), pp. 221–33.

Goodich, M., *Miracles and Wonders: The Development of the Concept of Miracle, 1150–1350* (Aldershot, 2007).

Grauert, H., 'Meister Johann von Toledo', *Sitzungsberichte der königlich bayerischen Akademie der Wissenschaften*, 2 (1901), 111–325.

Grotowski, P.Ł., *Arms and Armour of the Warrior Saints: Tradition and Innovation in Byzantine Iconography (843–1261)*, trans. R. Brzezinski (Leiden, 2010).

Hamilton, B., *The Latin Church in the Crusader States* (London, 1980).

—— '"God Wills It": Signs of Divine Approval in the Crusade Movement', in *Signs, Wonders, Miracles: Representations of Divine Power in the Life of the Church*, ed. K. Cooper and J. Gregory (Studies in Church History, 41; Woodbridge, 2005), pp. 88–98.

Harari, Y.N., 'Eyewitnessing in Accounts of the First Crusade', *Crusades*, 3 (2004), 77–99.

Haring, N.M., 'The Liberal Arts in the Sermons of Garnier of Rochefort', *Mediaeval Studies*, 30 (1968), 47–77.

Harris, J., *Byzantium and the Crusades*, 2nd edn (London, 2014).

Haverkamp, E., 'What Did the Christians Know? Latin Reports on the Persecutions of the Jews in 1096', *Crusades*, 7 (2008), 59–86.

Hodgson, N., 'The Role of Kerbogha's Mother in the *Gesta Francorum* and Selected Chronicles of the First Crusade', in *Gendering the Crusades*, ed. S.B. Edgington and S. Lambert (Cardiff, 2001), pp. 163–76.

—— *Women, Crusading and the Holy Land in Historical Narrative* (Woodbridge, 2007).

—— 'Reinventing Normans as Crusaders? Ralph of Caen's *Gesta Tancredi*', *Anglo-Norman Studies*, XXX (2008), 117–32.

—— 'Reputation, Authority and Masculine Identities in the Political Culture of the First Crusaders: The Career of Arnulf of Chocques', *History*, 102.353 (2017), 889–913.

—— 'Leading the People "as Duke, Count, and Father": The Masculinities of Abbot Martin of Pairis in Gunther of Pairis, *Hystoria Constantinopolitana*', in *Crusading and Masculinities*, ed. N.R. Hodgson, K.J. Lewis and M.M. Mesley (Abingdon, 2019), pp. 199–221.

Holdenried, A., *The Sibyl and Her Scribes: Manuscripts and Interpretation of the Latin Sibylla Tiburtina c. 1050–1500* (Aldershot, 2006).

Holt, A., 'Between Warrior and Priest: The Creation of a New Masculine Identity during the Crusades', in *Negotiating Clerical Identities: Priests, Monks and Masculinity in the Middle Ages*, ed. J.D. Thibodeaux (Basingstoke, 2010), pp. 185–203.

—— 'Crusading Against Barbarians: Muslims as Barbarians in Crusades Era Sources', in *East Meets West in the Middle Ages and Early Modern Times, Transcultural Experiences in the Premodern World*, ed. A. Classen (Berlin, 2013), pp. 443–56.

Hooker, M., 'The Use of Sibyls and Sibylline Oracles in Early Christian Writers', PhD diss., University of Cincinnati, 2007.

Housley, N., *Contesting the Crusades* (Oxford, 2006).

Hudson, B., 'Time Is Short: The Eschatology of the Early Gaelic Church', in *Last Things: Death and the Apocalypse in the Middle Ages*, ed. C.W. Bynum and P. Freedman (Philadelphia, PA, 2000), pp. 101–23.

Jenkins, R.J.H., 'The Bronze Athena at Byzantium', *The Journal of Hellenic Studies*, 67 (1947), 31–3.

John, S., 'Historical Truth and the Miraculous Past: The Use of Oral Evidence in Twelfth-Century Latin Historical Writing on the First Crusade', *The English Historical Review*, 130.543 (2015), 263–301.

Joranson, E., 'The Palestine Pilgrimage of Henry the Lion', in *Medieval and Historiographical Essays in Honor of James Westfall Thompson*, ed. J.L. Cate and E.N. Anderson (Chicago, IL, 1938), pp. 146–225.

Justice, S., 'Did the Middle Ages Believe in Their Miracles?', *Representations*, 103.1 (2008), 1–29.

Kempf, D., 'Towards a Textual Archaeology of the First Crusade', in *Writing the Early Crusades: Text, Transmission and Memory*, ed. M.G. Bull and D. Kempf (Woodbridge, 2014), pp. 116–26.

Keskiaho, J., *Dreams and Visions in the Early Middle Ages: The Reception and Use of Patristic Ideas, 400–900* (Cambridge, 2015).

Kieckhefer, R., *Magic in the Middle Ages*, 2nd edn (Cambridge, 2014).

Kinoshita, S., *Medieval Boundaries: Rethinking Difference in Old French Literature* (Philadelphia, PA, 2006).

Koopmans, R., *Wonderful to Relate: Miracle Stories and Miracle Collecting in High Medieval England* (Philadelphia, PA, 2011).

Kostick, C., 'A Further Discussion on the Authorship of the *Gesta Francorum*', *Reading Medieval Studies*, 35 (2009), 1–14.

—— 'The Afterlife of Adhémar of Le Puy', in *The Church, the Afterlife and the Fate of the Soul*, ed. P. Clarke and T. Claydon (Studies in Church History, 45; Woodbridge, 2009), pp. 120–9.

Kruger, S.F., *Dreaming in the Middle Ages* (Cambridge, 1992).

Laiou, A.E., 'Byzantium and the Crusades in the Twelfth Century: Why Was the Fourth Crusade Late in Coming?', in *Urbs Capta: The Fourth Crusade and its Consequences*, ed. A.E. Laiou (Paris, 2005), pp. 17–40.

Landes, R., 'The Birth of Heresy: A Millennial Phenomenon', *Journal of Religious History*, 24.1 (2000), 26–43.

Lapina, E., 'Demetrius of Thessaloniki: Patron Saint of Crusaders,' *Viator*, 40.2 (2009), 93–112.

—— 'The Maccabees and the Battle of Antioch', in *Dying for the Faith, Killing for the Faith: Old-Testament Faith-Warriors (1 and 2 Maccabees) in Historical Perspectives*, ed. G. Signori (Leiden, 2012), pp. 147–59.

—— *Warfare and the Miraculous in the Chronicles of the First Crusade* (University Park, PA, 2015).

Lapina, E., and Morton, N., eds., *The Uses of the Bible in Crusader Sources* (Leiden, 2017).

Lay, S., 'Miracles, Martyrs and the Cult of Henry the Crusader in Lisbon', *Portuguese Studies*, 24.1 (2008), 7–31.

—— *The Reconquest Kings of Portugal: Political and Cultural Reorientation on the Medieval Frontier* (Basingstoke, 2009).

Le Goff, J., *The Medieval Imagination*, trans. A. Goldhammer (London, 1988).

Lehtonen, T.M.S., 'By the Help of God, Because of Our Sins, and by Chance. William of Tyre Explains the Crusades', in *Medieval History Writing and Crusading Ideology*, ed. T.M.S. Lehtonen and K.V. Jensen (Helsinki, 2005), pp. 71–84.

Lester, A.E., 'Translation and Appropriation: Greek Relics in the Latin West in the Aftermath of the Fourth Crusade', *Studies in Church History*, 53 (2017), 88–117.

Livermore, H., 'The "Conquest of Lisbon" and its Author', *Portuguese Studies*, 6 (1991), 8–12.

Lock, P., *The Routledge Companion to The Crusades* (London, 2006).

MacGregor, J.B., 'The Ministry of Gerold d'Avranches: Warrior-Saints and Knightly Piety on the Eve of the First Crusade,' *Journal of Medieval History*, 29.3 (2003), 219–37.

—— 'Negotiating Knightly Piety: The Cult of the Warrior-Saints in the West, ca. 1070–ca. 1200,' *Church History*, 73.2 (2004), 317–45.

Macrides, R., 'Constantinople: The Crusaders' Gaze', in *Travel in the Byzantine World. Papers from the Thirty-fourth Spring Symposium of Byzantine Studies, Birmingham, April 2000*, ed. R. Macrides (Aldershot, 2002), pp. 193–212.

Maier, C., 'Crisis, Liturgy and the Crusade in the Twelfth and Thirteenth Centuries', *The Journal of Ecclesiastical History*, 48 (1997), 628–57.

Markowski, M., 'Richard Lionheart: Bad King, Bad Crusader?', *Journal of Medieval History*, 23.4 (1997), 351–65.

Mayer, H.E., *The Crusades*, trans. J. Gillingham, 2nd edn (Oxford, 1988).

Mayr-Harting, H., 'Odo of Deuil, the Second Crusade, and the Monastery of Saint-Denis', in *The Culture of Christendom: Essays in Medieval History in Memory of Denis L.T. Bethell*, ed. M.A. Meyer (London, 1993), pp. 225–41.

McCarthy, T.J.H., trans., *The Continuations of Frutolf of Michelsberg's Chronicle* (Monumenta Germaniae Historica Schriften, 74; Wiesbaden, 2018).

McGinn, B., 'Iter Sancti Sepulchri: The Piety of the First Crusaders', in *Essays on Medieval Civilization*, ed. B.K. Lackner and K.R. Philip (Austin, TX, 1978), pp. 33–72.

McMullen, A.J., and Henley, G., eds., *Gerald of Wales: New Perspectives on a Medieval Writer and Critic* (Cardiff, 2018).

Mentgen, G., *Astrologie und offentlichkeit im Mittelalter* (Stuttgart, 2005).

Mesley, M.M., and Wilson, L.E., eds., *Contextualising Miracles in the Christian West, 1100–1500* (Oxford, 2014).

Metlitzki, D., *The Matter of Araby in Medieval England* (London, 1977).

Morris, C., 'Geoffroy de Villehardouin and the Conquest of Constantinople', *History*, 53.177 (1968), 24–34.

—— 'A Critique of Popular Religion: Guibert of Nogent on *The Relics of the Saints*', in *Popular Belief and Practice*, ed. G.J. Cuming and D. Baker (Studies in Church History, 8; Cambridge, 1972), pp. 55–60.

—— 'Policy and Visions: The Case of the Holy Lance at Antioch', in *War and Government in the Middle Ages. Essays in honour of J.O. Prestwich*, ed. J. Gillingham and J.C. Holt (Woodbridge, 1984), pp. 33–45.

—— 'Martyrs on the Field of Battle Before and During the First Crusade', in *Martyrs and Martyrologies*, ed. D. Wood (Studies in Church History, 30; Oxford, 1993), pp. 93–105.

—— 'The *Gesta Francorum* as Narrative History', *Reading Medieval Studies*, 19 (1993), 55–71.

Morton, N., 'The Defence of the Holy Land and the Memory of the Maccabees', *Journal of Medieval History*, 36 (2010), 275–93.

—— *Encountering Islam on the First Crusade* (Cambridge, 2016).

Murray, A.V., 'The Enemy Within: Bohemond, Byzantium and the Subversion of the First Crusade', in *Crusading and Pilgrimage in the Norman World*, ed. K. Hurlock and P. Oldfield (Woodbridge, 2015), pp. 31–47.

Ní Cléirigh, L., 'Gesta Normannorum? Normans in the Latin Chronicles of the First Crusade', in *Norman Expansion. Connections, Continuities and Contrasts*, ed. K.J. Stringer and A. Jotischky (Farnham, 2013), pp. 207–26.

Nicholson, H.J., '"Martyrum collegio sociandus haberet": Depictions of the

Military Orders' Martyrs in the Holy Land, 1187–1291', in *Crusading and Warfare in the Middle Ages: Realities and Representations. Essays in Honour of John France*, ed. S. John and N. Morton (Farnham, 2014), pp. 101–18.

Niskanen, S., 'The Origins of the *Gesta Francorum* and Two Related Texts: Their Textual and Literary Character', *Sacris Erudiri*, 51 (2012), 287–316.

Noble, P., 'The Importance of Old French Chronicles as Historical Sources of the Fourth Crusade and the Early Latin Empire of Constantinople', *Journal of Medieval History*, 27 (2001), 399–416.

O'Banion, P.J., 'What has Iberia to do with Jerusalem? Crusade and the Spanish Route to the Holy Land in the Twelfth Century', *Journal of Medieval History*, 34 (2008), 383–95.

O'Callaghan, J.F., *Reconquest and Crusade in Medieval* Spain (Philadelphia, PA, 2003).

Otter, M., *Inventiones: Fiction and Referentiality in Twelfth-Century English Historical Writing* (Chapel Hill, NC, 1996).

Page, S., *Astrology in Medieval Manuscripts* (London, 2002).

Pages, M., 'Medieval Roots of the Modern Image of Islam: Fact and Fiction', in *Bridging the Medieval-Modern Divide: Medieval Themes in the World of the Reformation*, ed. J. Muldoon (London, 2013), pp. 23–44.

Parsons, S.T., 'The Valiant Man and the *Villain* in the Tradition of the *Gesta Francorum*', in *Crusading and Masculinities*, ed. N.R. Hodgson, K.J. Lewis and M.M. Mesley (Abingdon, 2019), pp. 36–52.

Partner, N., *Serious Entertainments: The Writing of History in Twelfth-Century England* (London, 1977).

—— 'Richard of Devizes: The Monk Who Forgot to be Medieval', in *The Middle Ages in Text and Texture: Reflections on Medieval Sources*, ed. J. Glenn (Toronto, ON, 2011), pp. 231–44.

Paul, N., *To Follow in Their Footsteps: The Crusades and Family Memory in the High Middle Ages* (Ithaca, NY, 2012).

Peden, A.M., 'Macrobius and Medieval Dream Literature', *Medium Aevum*, 54 (1985), 59–73.

Perry, D., *Sacred Plunder: Venice and the Aftermath of the Fourth Crusade* (University Park, PA, 2015).

Phillips, J.P., 'St Bernard of Clairvaux, the Low Countries, and the Lisbon Letter of the Second Crusade', *The Journal of Ecclesiastical History*, 48.3 (1997), 485–97.

—— 'Ideas of Crusade and Holy War in *De expugnatione Lyxbonensi* (*The Conquest of Lisbon*)', in *The Holy Land, Holy Lands and Christian History*, ed. R.N. Swanson (Studies in Church History, 36; Woodbridge, 2000), pp. 123–41.

—— 'Odo of Deuil's *De profectione Ludovici VII in Orientem* as a Source for the

Second Crusade', in *The Experience of Crusading, 1: Western Approaches*, ed. M. Bull and N. Housley (Cambridge, 2003), pp. 80–95.

—— *The Fourth Crusade and the Sack of Constantinople* (London, 2004).

—— *The Second Crusade: Extending the Frontiers of Christendom* (London, 2007).

—— *The Crusades, 1095–1204*, 2nd edn (London, 2014).

Pinner, R., *The Cult of St Edmund in Medieval East Anglia* (Woodbridge, 2015).

Pringle, D., 'The Spring of Cresson in Crusading History', in *Dei gesta per Francos: Études sur la croisades dédiées à Jean Richard: Crusade Studies in Honour of Jean Richard*, ed. M. Balard, B.Z. Kedar and J. Riley-Smith (Aldershot, 2001), pp. 231–40.

Purkis, W.J., 'Stigmata on the First Crusade', in *Signs, Wonders, Miracles: Representations of Divine Power in the Life of the Church*, ed. K. Cooper and J. Gregory (Studies in Church History, 41; Woodbridge, 2005), pp. 99–108.

—— *Crusading Spirituality in the Holy Land and Iberia, c. 1095–c. 1187* (Woodbridge, 2008).

——'Crusading and Crusade Memory in Caesarius of Heisterbach's *Dialogus miraculorum*', *Journal of Medieval History*, 39 (2013), 100–27.

—— 'Memories of the Preaching for the Fifth Crusade in Caesarius of Heisterbach's *Dialogus miraculorum*', *Journal of Medieval History*, 40.3 (2014), 329–45.

Queller, D., and Madden, T., *The Fourth Crusade: The Conquest of Constantinople*, 2nd edn (Philadelphia, PA, 1997).

Queller, D., and Stratton, S.J., 'A Century of Controversy on the Fourth Crusade', *Studies in Medieval and Renaissance History*, 6 (1969), 233–77.

Reeves, M., *Joachim of Fiore and the Prophetic Future* (London, 1976).

Reynolds, S., 'Social Mentalities and the Case of Medieval Scepticism', *Transactions of the Royal Historical Society, Sixth Series*, 1 (1991), 21–41.

Riley-Smith, J., 'Death on the First Crusade', in *The End of Strife*, ed. D.W. Loades (Edinburgh, 1984), pp. 14–31.

—— *The First Crusaders, 1095–1131* (Cambridge, 1997).

—— *The First Crusade and the Idea of Crusading*, 2nd edn (London, 2009).

—— 'An Army on Pilgrimage', in *Jerusalem the Golden: The Origins and Impact of the First Crusade*, ed. S.B. Edgington and L. García-Guijarro (Turnhout, 2014), pp. 103–16.

—— *The Crusades: A History*, 3rd edn (London, 2014).

Roach, D., 'Orderic Vitalis and the First Crusade', *Journal of Medieval History*, 42.2 (2016), 177–201.

Roche, J.T., 'The Second Crusade: Main Debates and New Horizons', in *The Second Crusade: Holy War on the Periphery of Latin Christentom*, ed. J.T. Roche and J. Møller Jensen (Turnhout, 2015), pp. 1–32.

Rossignol, S., 'Bilingualism in Medieval Europe: Germans and Slavs in Helmold of Bosau's *Chronicle*', *Central European History*, 47 (2014), 523–43.

Rozier, C.C., Roach, D., Gasper, G.E.M., and van Houts, E., eds., *Orderic Vitalis: Life, Works and Interpretations* (Woodbridge, 2016).

Rubenstein, J., *Guibert of Nogent: Portrait of a Medieval Mind* (New York, NY, 2002).

—— 'How, or How Much, to Reevaluate Peter the Hermit', in *The Medieval Crusade*, ed. S.J. Ridyard (Woodbridge, 2004), pp. 53–69.

—— 'Putting History to Use: Three Crusade Chronicles in Context', *Viator*, 35 (2004), 131–68.

—— 'What is the *Gesta Francorum*, and Who was Peter Tudebode?', *Revue Mabillon*, 16 (2005), 179–204.

—— *Armies of Heaven: The First Crusade and the Quest for Apocalypse* (New York, NY, 2011).

—— 'Miracles and the Crusading Mind: Monastic Meditations on Jerusalem's Conquest', in *Prayer and Thought in Monastic Tradition, Essays in Honour of Benedicta Ward*, ed. S. Bhattacharji, R. Williams and D. Mattos (London, 2014), pp. 197–210.

—— *Nebuchadnezzar's Dream: The Crusades, Apocalyptic Prophecy, and the End of History* (Oxford, 2019).

Rubin, M., *Mother of God: A History of the Virgin Mary* (London, 2009).

Runciman, S., 'The Holy Lance Found at Antioch', *Analecta Bollandiana*, 68 (1950), 197–209.

Russo, L., 'The Monte Cassino Tradition of the First Crusade: From the *Chronica Monasterii Casinensis* to the *Hystoria de Via et Recuperatione Antiochiae atque Ierusolymarum*', in *Writing the Early Crusades: Text, Transmission and Memory*, ed. M.G. Bull and D. Kempf (Woodbridge, 2014), pp. 53–62.

Schmitt, J.-C., *Ghosts in the Middle Ages: The Living and the Dead in Medieval Society*, trans. T.L. Fagan (London, 1998).

Schuste, B., 'The Strange Pilgrimage of Odo of Deuil', in *Medieval Concepts of the Past: Ritual, Memory and Historiography*, ed. G. Althoff, J. Fried and P.J. Geary (Cambridge, 2002), pp. 253–78.

Scior, V., 'Zwischen *terra nostra* und *terra sancta*. Arnold von Lübeck als Geschusshreiber', in *Die Chronik Arnolds von Lübeck: Neue Wege su ihrem Verständnis*, eds. S. Freund and B. Schutte (Oxford, 2008), pp. 149–74.

Shepkaru, S., 'To Die for God: Martyrs' Heaven in Hebrew and Latin Crusade Narratives', *Speculum*, 77 (2002), 311–41.

Sigal, P.-A., 'Un aspect du culte des saints: le chatiment divin aux XIe–XIIIe siècles d'après la littérature hagiographique du Midi de la France', in *La religion populaire en Languedoc du XIIIe siècle à la moitié du XIVe siècle*, ed. E. Privat (Cahiers de Fanjeaux, 11; Toulouse, 1976), pp. 39–59.

—— *L'homme et le miracle dans la France médiévale: XIe–XIIe siècles* (Paris, 1985).

Smirnova, V., Polo de Beaulieu, M.A., and Berlioz, J., eds., *The Art of Cistercian Persuasion in the Middle Ages and Beyond: Caesarius of Heisterbach's Dialogue on Miracles and Its Reception* (Leiden, 2015).

Smith, C., 'Martyrdom and Crusading in the Thirteenth Century: Remembering the Dead of Louis IX's Crusades', *Al-Masaq*, 15.2 (2003), 189–96.

—— *Crusading in the Age of Joinville* (Aldershot, 2006).

Snoek, G.J.C., *Medieval Piety from Relics to the Eucharist: A Process of Mutual Interaction* (Leiden, 1995).

Spacey, B.C., 'The Celestial Knight: Evoking the First Crusade in Odo of Deuil's *De Profectione Ludovici VII in Orientem* and in the Anonymous *Historia de Expeditione Friderici Imperatoris*', *Essays in Medieval Studies*, 31 (2015), 65–82.

—— 'Martyrdom as Masculinity in the *Itinerarium Peregrinorum et Gesta Regis Ricardi*', in *Crusading and Masculinities*, ed. N.R. Hodgson, K.J. Lewis and M.M. Mesley (Abingdon, 2019), pp. 222–36.

—— 'Refocusing the First Crusade: Authorial Self-Fashioning and the Miraculous in William of Tyre's *Historia Ierosolymitana*', *Journal of Religious History, Literature and Culture*, 5.2 (2019), 51–66.

Spear, D.S., 'The School of Caen Revisited', *The Haskins Society Journal*, 4 (1992), 55–66.

Spencer, S.J., 'The Emotional Rhetoric of Crusader Spirituality in the Narratives of the First Crusade', *Nottingham Medieval Studies*, 58 (2014), 57–86.

—— 'Piety, Brotherhood and Power: The Role and Significance of Emotions in Albert of Aachen's *Historia Ierosolimitana*', *Literature Compass*, 13.6 (2016), 423–43.

—— '"Like a Raging Lion": Richard the Lionheart's Anger during the Third Crusade in Medieval and Modern Historiography', *The English Historical Review*, 132.556 (2017), 495–532.

Spiegel, G., 'History, Historicism, and the Social Logic of the Text', in *The Past as Text* (Baltimore, 1997), pp. 3–28.

Staunton, M., *The Historians of Angevin England* (Oxford, 2017).

Stephenson, F.R., *Historical Eclipses and Earth's Rotation* (Cambridge, 2008).

Stevenson, J., 'Constantine, St Aldhelm and the Loathly Lady', in *Constantine: History, Historiography and Legend*, ed. S.N.C. Lieu and D. Montserrat (London, 2002), pp. 189–206.

Sweetenham, C., '"*Hoc enim non fuit humanum opus, sed divinum*": Robert the Monk's Use of the Bible in the *Historia Iherosolimitana*', in *The Uses of the Bible in Crusader Sources*, ed. E. Lapina and N. Morton (Leiden, 2017), pp. 133–51.

—— 'When the Saints Go Marching In: The Memory of the Miraculous in the Sources for the First Crusade' (forthcoming in *Crusades Subsidia*).

Swietek, F.R., 'Gunther of Pairis and the *Hystoria Constantinopolitana*', *Speculum*, 53.1 (1978), 62–78.

Tamm, M., 'How to Justify a Crusade? The Conquest of Livonia and New Crusade Rhetoric in the Early Thirteenth Century', *Journal of Medieval History*, 39.4, (2013), 431–55.

Tamminen, M., 'Who Deserves the Crown of Martyrdom? Martyrs in the Crusade Ideology of Jacques de Vitry (1160/70–1240)', in *On Old Age: Approaching Death in Antiquity and the Middle Ages*, ed. C. Krötzl and K. Mustakallio (Turnhout, 2011), pp. 293–313.

Throop, S., 'Christian Community and the Crusades: Religious and Social Practices in the *De expugnatione Lyxbonensi*', *The Haskins Society Journal*, 24 (2012), 95–126.

Tolan, J.V., 'Muslims as Pagan Idolaters in Chronicles of the First Crusade', in *Western Views of Islam in Medieval and Early Modern Europe*, ed. D.R. Blanks and M. Frassetto (Basingstoke, 1999), pp. 97–117.

—— *Saracens: Islam in the Medieval European Imagination* (New York, NY, 2002).

—— *Sons of Ishmael: Muslims through European Eyes in the Middle Ages* (Gainesville, FL, 2008).

Tyerman, C., *England and the Crusades, 1095–1588* (London, 1996).

van der Lugt, M., 'The *Incubus* in Scholastic Debate: Medicine, Theology and Popular Belief', in *Religion and Medicine in the Middle Ages*, ed. P. Biller and J. Ziegler (York, 2001), pp. 175–200.

van Engen, J., 'The Christian Middle Ages as an Historiographical Problem', *The American Historical Review*, 91.3 (1986), 519–52.

van Houts, E., 'The Norman Conquest through European Eyes', *The English Historical Review*, 110.438 (1995), 832–53.

von Stuckrad, K., 'Interreligious Transfers in the Middle Ages: The Case of Astrology', *Journal of Religion in Europe*, 1 (2008), 34–59.

—— *Locations of Knowledge in Medieval and Early Modern Europe: Esoteric Discourse and Western Identities* (Leiden, 2010).

Vielliard, F., 'Richard Coeur de Lion et son Entourage Normand: Le Témoignage de l'Estoire de la Guerre Sainte', *Bibliothèque de l'École des Chartes*, 160.1 (2002), 5–52.

Ward, B., *Miracles and the Medieval Mind: Theory, Record and Event, 1000–1215* (London, 1987).

Watkins, C., *History and the Supernatural in Medieval England* (Cambridge, 2007).

Webber, N., *The Evolution of Norman Identity, 911–1154* (Woodbridge, 2005).

Weltecke, D., 'Die Konjunktion der Planeten im September 1186: Zum

Ursprung einer globalen Katastrophenangst', *Saeculum Jahrbuch für Universalgeschichte*, 54 (2003), 179–212.

Wetherbee, W., *Platonism and Poetry in the Twelfth Century: The Literary Influence of the School of Chartres* (Princeton, NJ, 1972).

Whalen, B., 'Joachim of Fiore, Apocalyptic Conversion, and the "Persecuting Society"', *History Compass*, 8.7 (2010), 682–91.

White, H., 'The Value of Narrativity in the Representation of Reality', *Critical Inquiry*, 7.1 (1980), 5–27.

Wilson, J., 'Enigma of the *De Expugnatione Lyxbonensi*', *Journal of Medieval Iberian Studies*, 9.1 (2017), 99–129.

Wolf, K.B., *Making History: The Normans and Their Historians in Eleventh-Century Italy* (Philadelphia, 1995).

Wormald, F., 'The Rood of Bromholm', *Journal of the Warburg Institute*, 1.1 (1937), 31–45.

Yarrow, S., *Saints and their Communities: Miracle Stories in Twelfth-Century England* (Oxford, 2006).

—— 'Miracles, Belief and Christian Materiality: Relic'ing in Twelfth-Century Miracle Narratives', in *Contextualising Miracles in the Christian West, 1100–1500*, ed. M.M. Mesley and L.E. Wilson (Oxford, 2014), pp. 41–62.

Index